GROVER S. KRANTZ

BIG FOOT- PRINTS

A SCIENTIFIC INQUIRY INTO THE REALITY OF SASQUATCH

Johnson Books • Boulder

Cover design: Robert Schram
Cover photograph: TIB/West/David DeLossy ©1992
Text photographs by author unless otherwise noted.

Library of Congress Cataloging-in-Publication Data
Krantz, Gover S.
    Big footprints: a scientific inquiry into the reality of sasquatch/
Grover S. Krantz.
    p.   cm.
    Includes bibliographical references (p. 293) and index.
    ISBN 1-55566-099-1 (pbk.)
    1. Sasquatch.   I. Title.   II. Title: Big footprints.
QL89.2.S2K73 1992
001.9' 44--dc20   92-25265
                                                        CIP

Printed in the United States of America by
Johnson Printing Company
1180 South 57th Court
Boulder, Colorado 80301

CONTENTS

1

INTRODUCTION

When I began looking into the sasquatch/bigfoot problem in the mid-1960s there was a great deal of information on the subject, but the vast majority of this was in the hands of private individuals and had little circulation. Like most American investigators of my generation, the first compilation of information I ran across was Ivan Sanderson's *Abominable Snowman: Legend Come to Life*, which was published in 1961. We all knew about the Himalayan yeti from numerous press reports, but similar stories from other parts of the world came mostly as a surprise. Sanderson wrote in what might best be called an "enthusiastic" manner, reporting data from a variety of sources with what seemed to be little concern for consistency or verification. His conclusion that there were at least four different species of unverified, hairy, bipedal hominoids around the world certainly lowered his credibility in the eyes of the few scientists who read his work.

Bernard Heuvelmans had long been collecting the same kind of data on hairy bipeds, as well as on a host of other unverified animals that have been reported around the world. His basic work was published in French in 1955. An abridged English edition of *On the Track of Unknown Animals* appeared in 1958; I eagerly read it a few years later. Heuvelmans was the first trained zoologist to devote his career to this subject, for which he coined the term "cryptozoology," the study of hidden animals. (In French this is *cryptozoologie*.) His compilation of reports is about as carefully done as possible without personal field work in all areas, and this would be an impossible task even for a large team of scientists. Heuvelmans favors distinguishing as many species as the evidence indicates, but he does not support the number of clear-cut types that Sanderson advocated.

A Canadian newspaperman, John Green, began collecting data on hairy bipeds from the Pacific Northwest in 1958. He published *On the Track of the Sasquatch* in 1968 and other books subsequently. He has concentrated on his immediate area and attempted to directly verify as many reports as possible. This involved personal interviews with many people who claimed to have made sightings and direct observation of footprints, making plaster casts of them on many occasions. Green worked closely with Robert Titmus and Rene Dahinden who also made direct field investigations of reports throughout their area from northern California to central British Columbia. The limited geographical scope of this ongoing investigation is, in my opinion, outweighed by their direct contact with the data. Anecdotal information within this area is thereby kept to a minimum.

The U.S. evidence for hairy bipeds drawn from these three published sources is concentrated in the Pacific Northwest coastal strip and extends inland through the Rocky Mountains. As of 1965 John Green's first book had yet to appear, but since he was actively accumulating information, I can use his works to help fill in the evidence for that time and earlier. My personal contacts with Green, Titmus, Dahinden, and Heuvelmans in recent years have helped me to round out the picture for the mid-1960s.

Hundreds of eyewitness accounts of the creatures were already on record at that time, some of which included footprint observations as well. The typical description was an upright-walking, hair-covered, huge animal with an apelike face. Estimated statures were typically six-and-a-half to eight feet (2 to 2.4 m), though larger and smaller individuals were occasionally reported. Weight estimates are notoriously unreliable, as most people have little concept of how rapidly weight increases with height. An appropriately heavy-set body 6.5 feet tall would weigh about 500 pounds (227 kg), and standing close to 8 feet tall it would weigh more like 800 pounds (365 kg). Bob Titmus, who has seen and tracked sasquatches closely, accepts these as minimum estimates but would extend the range to include substantially larger sizes.

Virtually all sasquatch sightings were (and still are) in or near forests. Mostly these have been in the hilly and mountainous regions of northern California, Oregon, Washington, southeastern Alaska, and most of British Columbia. Typical encounters indicated that the sasquatches were rather shy and preferred to avoid human contact; it was widely assumed that they were retreating from human developments. By 1965, observations of their behavior had already indicated that we were dealing with a fairly intelligent animal species, but an animal nonetheless.

Track reports also numbered in the hundreds, sometimes accompanied by sightings, more often not. Individual footprints had a roughly human design, being a good deal longer than wide, rather flat, with five toes across the wider front end, and without any claw marks. It was their size that aroused so much attention—typically they were twice as wide as a logger's boot and half-again longer. (This direct method of measurement led to their rapid obliteration in most instances.) Even with three times the surface area of a man's shod foot, they were impressed much more deeply into the ground. This evidence supported the estimates of great size and weight. Often the ball of the foot appeared to be divided into two impressions, one in front of the other. Plaster casts were sometimes made of the clearest of these footprints.

Hair samples were occasionally reported, as well as fecal deposits, neither of which could be ascribed to any known animal. As of 1965 no truly dependable scientific analyses of any of this evidence had been made available. (During the period from 1959 to 1962, the Texas oilman Tom Slick financed expeditions in the Pacific Northwest with experienced hunters and trackers who collected vast amounts of information. He also hired specialized scientists to study and analyze this data. Unfortunately, all of the material and reports were closely guarded secrets, and since Slick's death they have remained hidden.) From the outset, most scientists regarded the whole subject as foolishness. To them it seemed most unlikely that they could have missed such a large animal right here in North America; that it appeared to be an upright-walking primate made it even harder for them to accept. It should be noted that the scientists who made such pronouncements had almost no information on the subject, and they would be the first to acknowledge that fact.

Proof

Science requires solid evidence for the existence of a new species—footprints and sightings by local people are never enough. A "type specimen" must be obtained, which is then described in a scientific journal and continues to be available for other experts to examine. For modern mammals this normally consists of a skin and skull that show distinctions from all similar specimens. For fossils it consists of some skeletal material that is clearly distinct from what appear to be its closest relatives. Nothing of the kind has been recovered for the sasquatch; therefore it does not exist in the eyes of science.

Actually the rules of evidence vary somewhat, depending on the nature of the animal whose existence is proposed. The more unusual and/or unexpected it is, the more proof is required to establish its existence. A new subspecies of chipmunk or sparrow might be provisionally accepted on the basis of clear observations by one or two competent biologists. For a higher taxonomic level, that of a new species, a specimen is normally required no matter who saw it.

Even a good specimen is not always sufficient. The first skin of a colobus monkey to reach Europe was called a fake; clearly, in the opinion of experts, the many long white hairs had been artificially inserted into a solid coat of shorter black hairs. The first skin of a platypus was greeted with even more derision; the bill and tail were obviously attached to some mammal's skin. Yet these soon proved to be perfectly real animals, just as their skins had first indicated.

Just try to imagine what it would be like if we had no clear evidence of the giraffe—none of them in our zoos, no mounted skins nor skeletons in our museums, just some unsubstantiated native stories. You go to Africa and see some giraffes for yourself, then come back and try to convince the zoologists that they are real. You describe the animal as being 16 feet tall (5 m), half of which is just its neck; the reaction is predictable. So you add that it has two short, skin-covered horns on its head with round balls on their ends, and you lose what little credibility you might have had. Now imagine yourself trying to describe an elephant to someone who has no knowledge of them.

Clearly the sasquatch does not constitute a new order of mammals like the elephant. Almost certainly it is not even a distinct family like the giraffe. Its physical distinctions from known primates would most likely rate a new genus, nothing higher. And that genus is quite possibly one that is already known in the fossil record; it might even be a known fossil species. Things could have been much worse.

All government agencies take the same skeptical view as does the Scientific Establishment. There are no laws regulating or prohibiting the hunting of sasquatch any more than there are for hunting unicorns, gremlins, or trolls. Sasquatches have no more civil rights than angels, fairies, or leprechauns. Any political official who proposed legal protection for the sasquatch at this time, such as a game preserve, would probably be removed from office without the formality of a recall election.

In the state of Washington, for example, the Game Department does not recognize the sasquatch as an existing species. The head of their legal division told me that officially they would take no notice even if a hunter brought one in. They would formulate a policy only if and when the scientists decided that it was real. Similarly, the U.S. Forest Service assures me that their only responsibility is to maintain the environment within their jurisdiction. They would not be concerned with identifying or caring for a specimen of a new animal species. On the other hand, private contacts have indicated to me that the Federal Game Department would immediately declare sasquatch to be an endangered species if and when the first specimen is produced for scientific confirmation. The views of the state game officials and the Forest Service are evidently of long standing; the attitude in the Federal Game Department stems from the early 1980s.

Alternative Explanations

If there is no such animal as the sasquatch, then there must be some other explanation(s) for all the evidence that was available, still using 1965 as my base line. It is a fact that people say they have seen sasquatches; whether their reports are true is another matter. Apparent footprints do occur in the ground, but it can be argued as to exactly what it was that made these impressions. We must always distinguish clearly between factual data and how that data is interpreted.

A standing bear could be mistaken for a sasquatch, provided the observer did not see the bear's protruding muzzle, narrow shoulders, or short legs. (It is similarly possible that an observed sasquatch was assumed to be a standing bear.) An oddly shaped tree stump or rock formation could be mistaken for a sasquatch if they were only briefly glimpsed. The observation may indeed be of a bipedal primate—a man dressed in furs and viewed under circumstances that did not permit a clear estimate of size. This could be just a coincidence, or else the man in furs was deliberately costumed to get the desired effect. (Anyone attempting this is risking his life.)

In any of the above scenarios, a certain amount of imagination is probably involved, even when the sighting is reported as clear and unequivocal. With enough imagination almost any object of about the right size and shape can be seen as a sasquatch. Likewise, with enough imagination the clearest sighting of a sasquatch can be interpreted as something else. To a large degree we see what we want to see; people who believe in sasquatches sometimes manage to see them even when they are not there, while people who believe they don't exist might not see the obvious. There may be some accuracy in modifying the old saying into "I'll see it when I believe it." (My thanks to Dural Horton for this observation.)

A final source of erroneous sighting reports is outright fabrication. Any embellishment on an actual observation is a lie, at least to some degree, but some claimed sightings may be completely made up. People do this kind of thing for various reasons, but mostly to draw some attention to themselves. It has also been said that, in a sense, sasquatches often come out of whisky bottles.

It should be mentioned that there is a special category of what might be termed "inadequate" reports; these are not necessarily erroneous, nor are they effectively real either. This is when a person may well have seen a sasquatch, but his or her observation was too unclear or fleeting for any conclusions to be drawn. Reports like this would be insufficient for us to base an animal's description on, but in certain circumstances they can be perfectly true. My wife once had a sighting of this type but said nothing at the time, even though I was in the car with her. Only after several miles of travel, while carefully eliminating in her mind all other possible explanations, did she tell me what she had seen.

Explaining away footprints is somewhat more difficult, especially when photographs and plaster casts of them are available for later examination. One of the options discussed above, that the observer simply lied about it, can apply only to those footprints that were not recorded in any manner. A sasquatch might be photographed only if you are well prepared, calm, fast, and lucky; but you can take pictures of footprints later and many times over if you wish. A footprint can be cast in plaster or even dug up intact; the equivalent recording of a sasquatch sighting itself is a great deal more problematical.

Some of the giant footprints that were reported up to the year 1958 might have been no more than chance irregularities in the ground, but such cases probably were few. It is hard to imagine why anyone would have paid much attention to such things at that time, well before sasquatch mania got underway. Since then, by contrast, anything that even remotely resembles a giant human footprint has a good chance of being reported as sasquatch evidence. At my own introduction to the subject in 1965, sasquatch mania had been underway for only seven years.

It has been pointed out that human and other animals' footprints in snow can melt out to larger sizes, but this won't create toe marks. Likewise, a series of tracks would not melt uniformly, and the length of stride certainly cannot be changed. The same objections can be directed against the explanation that they result from a long line of people stepping in each other's tracks. Before 1958 I think that almost all errors of interpretation consisted of incorrect rejections; since 1958 the pendulum has swung somewhat the other way and a lot of incorrect tracks are being accepted as real by naive investigators as well as by much of the public. And this has been the continuing situation throughout the entire time of my own investigation.

Other animal tracks can be described as being of sasquatch only if they are very poorly recorded. Bears have elongated, flat hind feet with five toes, but there the similarity ends. Bears leave claw marks, their first toe is the smallest of the five, their heels are narrow, and their feet are nowhere near as large as the supposed sasquatch imprints.

The overall view of the skeptics is that if *some* of this evidence can be explained away by errors of observation and hoaxing, then *all* of the evidence can be ascribed to those sources. The other side of the same coin is that if any *one* item of evidence is true, then the purported species *must* in fact exist. Unfortunately for the proponents, this apparent stand-off is resolved in favor of the skeptics. The truth of that required one item of evidence must be demonstrated to the satisfaction of the skeptics. If they are not convinced, the issue cannot be resolved favorably. The skeptics are under no obligation to disprove all or, for that matter, any of the evidence. The burden of proof rests with those who think that the animals are real. The skeptics are not obligated even to look at the evidence. If that seems unfair, consider what happens when someone insists that you pay attention to the arguments for his/her religion. Are you under any obligation to defend your position, or even to listen to them?

Normal Sequence

Many animals that are now known to exist were reported but unproven for some time. One of the most notable of these is the gorilla, which was known to European scholars by rumor and vague descriptions since about the year 1600, but was first proven with a skin and skull in 1849. During those two-and-a-half centuries it was a known phenomenon to some of the local people, and was occasionally seen by outsiders, but the scientific authorities of the day doubted that any such creatures existed. More recently, native stories about a short-necked relative of the giraffe were long discounted until 1912, when a specimen of the okapi was obtained. Many other animals have had a similar history, being cryptic (hidden) for many years from science, yet known to the people where they lived.

In all these cases, and with most other animals, there has been a series of steps that we have gone through in recognizing and dealing with them:

Stage 1. Local residents describe the animal, occasionally outsiders do so too; sometimes other evidence is found, like footprints, feces, or nests. At this stage it may be described as "cryptozoological."

Stage 2. Skeletal material is brought to the attention of scientists, usually a skull and sometimes more; other material like a skin might also be recovered. At this point the animal is studied, classified, and becomes a scientific reality.

Stage 3. A complete body is recovered, maybe several, for more detailed anatomical studies and comparisons.

Stage 4. The first live specimen is captured.

Stage 5. The species is studied in its native habitat to learn (among other things) if it is endangered and, if so, what might be done to assist its survival.

The famous coelacanth moved from Stage 1 to Stage 3 in 1938 when South African scientists saw their first complete specimen. It could be argued that Stage 2 had occurred in its proper sequence in the form of fossils that are eighty million and more years old, even if they weren't the same species. But the existence of fossils does not constitute evidence for a living form.

Sasquatch is presently at Stage 1 of this sequence, thus it is cryptozoological and not a scientific reality. It is possible that its Stage 2 already exists in the fossil record as *Gigantopithecus* (see Chapter 7), but this speculation requires confirmation with a specimen from the living species. More complete remains of the fossil form, if they confirmed the appropriate size along with erect bipedalism, would greatly strengthen the case for the reported living species, but this would still fall far short of proof in the eyes of most authorities.

The normal sequence of events would be that some body parts will be the next discovery (Stage 2), though it is possible that a full body might be recovered (Stage 3). Like most scientists, I think any and all serious efforts should be directed toward one or the other of these goals.

Some investigators say that they are actively working at effecting a live capture (Stage 4). A few of them might be serious about this, but most of them are using such claims only as a publicity gimmick to cover their real intention—that of obtaining a dead specimen at Stage 3. Those who actually plan on attempting a live capture are generally quite unaware of the problems involved.

Other people are actively pursuing Stage 5, the study of sasquatch ecology, or are openly advocating that this be done. In the first place, no scientific organization will support any investigation of the habits of an unknown animal. In the second place, no scientists or government agencies will believe any ecological data on an animal that does not officially exist, no matter who brings it in or how accurate that data may appear to be. In the third place, even if the sasquatch is someday proven to exist, any data collected before that time will be suspect—it was gathered by someone who presumably was acting on faith rather than on knowledge. It will be presumed that his/her data may be correspondingly colored by a lack of objectivity.

The skeptics rightly demand that a specimen be produced (Stage 2) before it can be taken seriously. Only then will the Scientific Establishment willingly devote its considerable resources to moving on through the other steps.

Why No Bones?

The most common question asked by skeptics is, "If the sasquatch exists, why don't we find its bones?" If it is a viable species consisting of thousands of individuals, then dozens of them are certainly dying every year. Most people think this means that someone should stumble across one of their skeletons every now and then. Our museums are full of the skeletons of other animals, why not this one? No wildlife biologists ask this question because they all know the answer: in the normal course of events we would never expect to find bones of an animal of this description. For the nonbiologists this requires some explanation.

Most animal deaths may be divided into two categories, abrupt and delayed, with only a few cases in between. An abrupt death is when the animal is killed by a predator or by another natural event; in this case the victim has no choice as to how, when, or where it meets its end. A delayed death is when the animal succumbs to old age, starvation, or illness; in this case the individual can and will carefully choose the place where its death occurs. The few intermediate cases are usually where the animal is badly injured by an attack or accident and survives, but perishes too soon for it to reach the most suitable hiding place that it may be seeking.

In nature, most species can be characterized as predominantly abrupt or predominantly delayed in terms of how their individuals usually die. Cattle, deer, and most rodents are killed by other animals; their bones are sometimes found where the carnivore leaves them. Larger bones last longer and are more visible, so the remains of deer will occasionally be seen, but almost never do you find those of a squirrel. Pumas, coyotes, and mink generally die from body failure of some kind; they carefully hide themselves as though to recover from a temporary ailment, and one of these ailments someday proves to be fatal. They are then quickly reduced to skeletons by carrion eaters of all sizes, from mammals to microbes. Carnivores' bones will end up hidden under a cover of vegetation and usually in damp ground that soon envelops them; they are almost never seen in nature. I have yet to meet anyone who has found the remains of a bear that was not killed by human activity. (A self-proclaimed naturalist once told me that he finds puma skeletons frequently; if this is true, he has a skill that no field biologist even remotely approaches.)

Bones also deteriorate, with most of them being completely reincorporated into the soil in several years, and only a few ever becoming fossils. Someone once calculated that if all bison skeletons from the last 40,000 years were still here, the Great Plains would be thirty feet deep in stacked bone. One cannot find a trace of them on the surface today. Long-term preservation requires burial; mineral replacement from ground water then has at least a possibility of fossilizing the bones.

The sasquatch would be at the top of the food chain in the sense that no other animal normally kills or eats them. Barring human intervention, we should expect to find a dead sasquatch about as easily as we find a dead bear (assuming they occurred in the same numbers and had similar life spans). Frequencies of footprints suggest that there are now at least a hundred bears for every one sasquatch, and dead bears are almost never found. Being primates, sasquatches probably live much longer than bears, thus correspondingly reducing the number of deaths per year, per thousand population. Desirable as it may be, the discovery of the remains of a naturally dead sasquatch is about the least likely possibility of demonstrating their existence. If someone could devise a method to locate the remains of large numbers of dead bears, then perhaps some sasquatch remains will eventually be found as well. (This approach is discussed at length in Chapter 11.)

Strong Opinions

When asked for their thoughts on a subject where they have little or no information, most people will not express any firm opinion. The average person does not know whether a steam engine is more or less efficient than an internal combustion engine and will usually say so; most biologists are equally ignorant of this subject and will also freely admit it. But if you ask these same people whether bigfoot exists, a subject on which they are in most cases equally uninformed, a surprising number will state definitely "yes" or "no." There must be some good reason for this irrational behavior; there appears to be something in this subject that strikes deep emotional roots. In fact there must be two such factors, with one or the other being important to each person who has a strong opinion.

There are two philosophical views about what might be called the human condition: either we are simply an ordinary animal, one kind among many, or else we are a very unique form of life. While both observations are true to some degree, in many people's minds one view or the other is paramount. This same contrast of attitudes is also evident among the scientists who study human evolution. Those who lean toward the "ordinary" point of view think that humans are the result of some rapid evolutionary changes from a rather recent animal ancestor. Those who lean toward the "unique" point of view think that human evolution was a very long and slow process from animal ancestors that were much farther back in time. These two views affect whether the scientist thinks a particular fossil is a direct ancestor or an extinct side line, and whether a known fossil ancestor was more animal or more human in its behavior.

Adherents of the "ordinary" school of thought are receptive to the idea of a creature that is intermediate between the animal and human condition. Such an intermediate would tend to reinforce our presumed kinship with the natural world. People who lean toward this view seem to eagerly accept the sasquatch as providing us with that link to the rest of the animal kingdom. They find it emotionally satisfying to believe in the existence of a species that seems to constitute this "missing link."

Adherents of the "unique" school of thought are repelled by the idea that there might be a living intermediate between animals and humans. The existence of such a creature would tend to blur their otherwise sharp line between us and the animal world. People who lean toward this view firmly reject the sasquatch because it might threaten our special position. They find it emotionally satisfying to believe that there is a vast, unoccupied gulf separating us from the rest of the animal kingdom.

The fact of the matter is that both of these opinions are wrong, or at least irrelevant to the subject at hand, because the sasquatch is not an intermediate form at all. All available evidence points clearly to an animal status for this species in terms of its behavior and mental abilities. It walks bipedally, but so do chickens. It is highly intelligent, but dolphins are more so. It may be our closest living relative, but the chimpanzee occupies that status now and this fact has not elevated them to semi-humans.

It might be argued that we don't really know enough about sasquatch behavior to be absolutely certain about this judgment as to its animal status. But if we are in error, isn't it imperative that we find out as soon as possible?

Special Cases

The evidence for giant hairy bipeds in North America and elsewhere was not limited to sightings and footprints when I first joined in the investigation. There were also lurid accounts of property destruction, some people claimed to have been captured by them, some accounts had them captured by people, and a few photographs existed that seemed to show something. Much of this can be discounted as inaccurate descriptions, overinterpretation, or simple hoaxes. But a few are impressive enough to be mentioned here.

There is good documentation of many footprints appearing around road-making equipment near Bluff Creek in northern California in 1958. The big San Francisco newspapers covered this story—on a subject that previously had been relegated to small-town news media. Footprints and casts were photographed, and many road workers were interviewed. The activity went on for many nights (never by day), and most published reports indicate that it included the moving and throwing of objects far beyond the physical abilities of humans.

In 1957 a Canadian man, Albert Ostman, recounted a story of being captured by a sasquatch some thirty-three years previously. He told of being held with a family of four of them for six days before he managed to escape and return to civilization. His description of them agrees with that of other observers, but some points of behavior, particularly the capture itself, seem incongruous.

Historical sources describe the capture of a wild woman in southern Russia sometime in the middle of the last century. She was called Zana and was described as being large, hairy, and inarticulate. She eventually bore children by one of her captors. Another Russian capture occurred in late 1941 in the northern Caucasus region. The pressing needs of the war precluded any serious study, so the creature was released when the authorities were satisfied that it was not an enemy soldier.

In 1884 a Victoria, B.C., newspaper described the capture of what sounds very much like a young sasquatch. It was reported to be hair-covered and strong; at 4 feet, 7 inches and 127 pounds, it had a very heavyset body. Jacko, as the captors called him, was to be taken to England, but there is no further record of his fate.

The above accounts are only a sample of the extraordinary events that were reported up to 1965. (More details on these and other accounts are available, especially in Green's books.) These few are mentioned here partly because they have been taken seriously by most investigators, and also because I have some follow-up information that may be of interest on each of them.

At that date there was no photographic evidence available that could be taken seriously. This would soon change in 1967 when Roger Patterson filmed a one-minute sequence of what most investigators think is the only legitimate film available. It is the subject of another entire chapter.

This Book

The remainder of this book picks up the story in the mid-1960s, when I began my serious study of the sasquatch phenomenon, and carries it up to the time of this writing. In these twenty-seven years some of the most impressive evidence has come to light, as well as a continuing stream of the usual sightings and footprint reports. During this same time period public awareness has greatly increased (a mixed blessing), and a much more tolerant attitude has emerged in at least part of the academic community. More than ever before, a measure of scientific objectivity is now being directed to the sasquatch and similarly reported, but unverified, animals.

The emphasis here is on the more tangible evidence discovered in the last quarter century—mostly regarding those items that can be observed and studied at length. I have had some degree of personal involvement with almost all of the material in question. I am acquainted with many of the principal people involved in this activity, both in the discovery of the evidence and in its analysis. This degree of firsthand familiarity helps me to avoid the many distortions that inevitably creep into the data as it passes from one person to another. Having much of the tangible evidence in my own possession allows me to re-examine it repeatedly as new interpretations are suggested.

Sightings and footprint observation events are not emphasized here. I mention only a handful of these, mostly where the events were described directly to me, and not through intermediaries or published works. The interested reader should consult John Green's book, *Sasquatch: The Apes Among Us* (1978) for a detailed coverage of this kind of information. This is by far the largest and most accurate compilation of the pertinent information from North America. Some other sources for the same kind of information since the mid-1960s include John Napier's *Bigfoot: The Yeti and Sasquatch in Myth and Reality* (1972), Hunter and Dahinden's *Sasquatch* (1973), and Peter Byrne's *The Search for Bigfoot: Monster, Myth or Man* (1975).

Many other books on this subject have been published, almost all of them since 1967, and generally by people who investigated the subject only for a few years at most. Some of them contain a lot of original reports of uncertain reliability, but they also largely copy from the above sources and from the earlier, classic works that I mentioned before. They often include advocacy of one or another paranormal interpretation, and this substantially reduces their credibility in my mind. Rather than list the books of dubious value, I can mention two that stand out from the rest as having no notable faults: *The Bigfoot Casebook* by Janet and Colin Bord, and *Bigfoot: The Mysterious Monster* by Robert and Frances Guenette.

Since all of the above books take a favorable stand on the question of the creature's existence, I should mention the one and only significant work that takes the opposite stance. This is Kenneth Wylie's *Bigfoot: A Personal Inquiry into a Phenomenon* (1980), which is must to read for anyone who wants to keep a level head on this subject. Wylie convincingly exposes the weakness of some of the evidence in his area (Michigan) and the failings of some of the investigators there. When he tries to cope with the better evidence from the west he loses much of his objectivity and invents problems that simply are not there.

Mention should be made at this point of the more scientific literature that has recently begun to appear. The scientific journal *Northwest Anthropological Research Notes* has published many responsible articles on the subject since 1971. Its editor, Roderick Sprague, put many of these together in a book titled *The Scientist Looks at the Sasquatch*, published by the University of Idaho Press in 1977, with an expanded second edition appearing in 1979. We also have *Manlike Monsters on Trial: Early Records and Modern Evidence*, edited by Marjorie Halpin and Michael Ames, which was published in 1980. This book includes many of the papers that were presented at a conference on this topic at the University of British Columbia in 1978. Other papers from that conference, as well as some original ones, were compiled by Vladimir Markotic for *Sasquatch and Other Unknown Hominoids,* which appeared in 1984. Since 1982, a new journal, *Cryptozoology,* has published articles dealing with all types of unproven animals, including sasquatch, from a strictly scientific point of view.

The next two chapters of this book deal with the circumstances and the anatomy of some of the most important footprints. This is followed by a chapter on Patterson's film, then a chapter dealing with some of what might be called lesser evidence. After this I offer my own interpretation of what the species is like, then a chapter on the relevant fossil evidence, and another summarizing the data from other times and places. A major chapter is devoted to those who hunt the sasquatch, in every sense of the word, and this is followed by a chapter describing the scientists who work on it. The next chapter deals with prospects—what is underway and what might happen. Finally there is a summary in which I try to wrap up the impact and importance of the whole subject.

2

BIG FOOTPRINTS

The most tangible evidence of the sasquatch that is currently available consists of footprints. This evidence may be preserved in the form of photographs and/or plaster casts, and I have seen one that was excavated and brought back in its entirety. Personal accounts of people having seen such footprints, but without any of the above-mentioned physical evidence, must remain in the realm of testimony—just as with claimed sightings of the animal itself.

Footprints are commonly found in loose dirt, mud, wet sand, and snow. These surfaces usually make up only a small fraction of the area where these creatures are reported to exist. Most of the ground is covered, for most of the time, with vegetation and/or forest litter that records only the vaguest impressions at best. Other places consist of rock outcrops or hard-packed roads that cannot be indented by the feet even of a creature of this size. A good animal tracker can follow a trail over most of these types of terrain, but the signs he/she follows would rarely be seen in photographs or show in plaster casts. Dirt roads and stream banks are the primary places from which our best footprint evidence is retrieved for later examination.

The fact that the sasquatch walks on a large, flat foot means that it will distribute its weight over a much larger surface than will an elk or moose of equal size, thus making shallower indentations. Added to this is the usually rounded edge of the foot that does not leave sharp edge-marked imprints. It is also possible that a sasquatch might, at certain times, deliberately choose to walk where its footprints are less likely to be recorded. This last aspect is returned to in Chapter 6.

Footprints have been found near homesteads and small communities, in plowed farmland, and also in some of the most inaccessible places where human observers are able to travel. Since it requires both an imprinter and an observer for a track to be reported, such reports obviously do not reflect the actual distribution of those making the tracks. Almost any clear track close to human habitation is likely to be seen; in remoter areas, where observers are few and far between, a correspondingly smaller fraction of the existing tracks will be discovered. Any place that is never visited by humans will obviously have no reports, regardless of how many tracks may actually occur there. (Some years ago I saw a movie about a fictional bigfoot hunt where the target area was described as being totally uninhabited and unexplored, yet somehow had the highest known frequency of footprints.)

Another factor in footprint reporting is whether the human is inclined to report the footprints at all. On a few occasions I have been told by witnesses, quite frankly, that if we hadn't struck up an acquaintance or been introduced by a friend, they probably would have denied ever having seen the evidence that they described. There also appears to be a geographical pattern to this attitude, at least in my part of the country. Rural people in northern Idaho are not inclined to tell outsiders what they see; there are only a few sasquatch reports (sightings or tracks) from that area. Residents of western Washington, on the other hand, seem much more inclined to report unusual phenomena. There are many sasquatch sightings and footprints from there. I suspect that the evidence is actually about equally distributed between these two areas. I have no good theory to offer about this difference in the human attitude toward reporting it, and it may well be a common variable elsewhere.

The Data

Sasquatch footprints are roughly human in design. They progress over the ground in the same bipedal fashion as with ourselves, alternately placed up against either side of the line of travel. The footprints are in a nearly straight line when the subject was running. Initially it was their great size and often the depth of the impression that set them apart from human footprints, while their general design ruled out all other animal sources. Further observations include nearly equal-sized toes that lined up almost straight across, disproportionate width, flat foot, and often a double-ball. Smaller footprints that might be within the human size range could then be attributed to young sasquatches if they showed some or all of these other traits. See Figure 1 for photographs of some examples of these footprints.

Figure 1. Some typical sasquatch footprints.

At present my collection includes eighty-one plaster casts that fit this description, as well as a few more that are handprints. Most of these were borrowed from the finder, molds were made in latex or silastic, and the originals were returned along with at least one good copy. These casts appear to represent twenty-two different individuals, all but two of which are from the Pacific Northwest. John Green and Bob Titmus have casts of maybe twenty additional individuals. My total is greater than theirs only because I copied most of their more interesting casts. I have seen many more casts that appear to be real in other people's collections, and clear photographs of at least another fifty casts or actual imprints.

Thus far I have had the opportunity to examine, in some detail, the footprint evidence of well over one hundred different sasquatches, some of them from many separate impressions. Given the small proportion of prints that are likely to be discovered, the small fraction of these discoveries that are recorded in any manner, and the fact that few of these ever reach my hands, the original total of actual footprints must be very considerable.

John Green has reports of almost one thousand footprint events in his files from North America. I cannot believe that a significant proportion of all such cases has come to his attention; his reports depend mainly on people contacting him with the evidence that they encounter and choose to share. Other investigators are making their own data collections, often guarding them jealously. Most reports don't find their way into anybody's data files. There are likely a hundred locally known footprint events for every one in Green's files, thus maybe 100,000 of them probably exist. One could multiply this by another ten times for the discoveries that never get reported beyond the discoverer or a few close friends. Given the many prints that are found in distant and obscure places where their discovery was a very unlikely event (less than one chance in a hundred) we must multiply the total by yet another hundred times. This all multiplies out to something like 100 million potentially visible track events that have occurred within the last 40 years in areas where people coexist with sasquatches.

The discoverers commonly search a line of tracks with some care to select the clearest right and left footprints for casting. Their intent is to provide the best possible information on the feet that made the tracks. They are then often criticized because these casts are the least convincing to an experienced tracker. Only rarely does a planti-grade animal (human or bear) place its foot flat on the ground and then lift it up without kicking back some dirt. A good tracker looks for just this kind of disturbance, while the typical cast maker inno-cently goes to a great deal of trouble to avoid casting prints of this kind. At his famous movie site (see Chapter 4) Roger Patterson made two casts—the flattest, clearest, right and left imprints he could find (Fig. 2). Nine days later Bob Titmus located the filming site and cast ten imprints in a row, regardless of their quality (Fig. 3). This series of tracks is probably the most informative and convincing evidence that an experienced tracker could ask for. If one can only make two casts, both should be of the same foot if one wants to convince an good animal tracker that they are real.

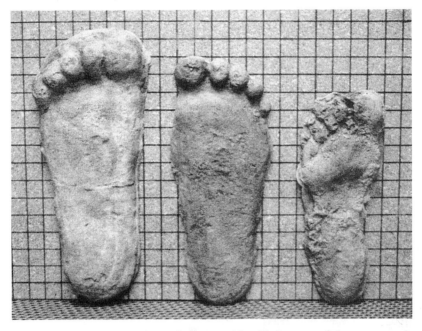

Figure 2. Casts made by Roger Patterson. After filming one of the creatures in 1967, Patterson located the clearest and flattest, left and right tracks, and made plaster casts of them. These copies, left and center in the picture, were made from molds of the originals. Both represent feet 14.5 inches long; they appear unequal in size mainly because they were not impressed to the same depth. On the right is a cast of a human foot 12 inches long for comparison, made by Russell Gebhart. The source of this print was a normal man, whom Gebhart estimated to have stood about seven feet tall. (The background of this photograph, and many following it, is a board marked with lines one inch apart.)

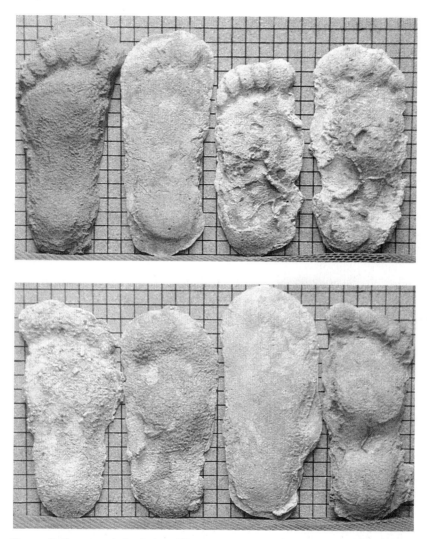

Figure 3. Casts made by Robert Titmus. Here are 8 of the 10 consecutive tracks cast at the site by Titmus just nine days after Patterson made his movie. These are especially instructive in showing the high degree of variation in a short series of natural footprints.

Walking

The best known and most often reported walking feature of these tracks is the length of its steps. Commonly these are in excess of three feet (one meter) from the heel of one footprint to the heel of the next one. (Steps are sometimes measured as the space *between* two adjacent footprints, which effectively subtracts one foot length from each step length.) The comfortable walking step for humans is about half of the individual's standing height, or a trace more. Sasquatch step measurements correspond, in general, with stature estimates that are reported from sightings. These steps also would be expected to vary with some terrain differences, and generally they do. I have personally seen both longer and shorter steps than the presumed stature would call for. Interestingly, step lengths often do not appreciably shorten when they are progressing up shallow inclines—just where a human hoaxer with fake feet would be sure to take smaller steps.

A "step" is the measured distance from the back edge of one heel print to the corresponding mark made by the next footprint, whether left to right, or right to left. There will normally be a slight diagonal or zigzag pattern in a series of such measurements because the footprints alternate on each side of the line of travel. This in turn slightly exaggerates the real length of the steps. The regular measuring point could instead be the front edge of the big toe, which would serve to lessen this discrepancy in most cases. It is preferable to measure the "stride" or "pace," which is the distance from a left heel edge to the next left heel edge, skipping over the intervening right footprint. (Or going from right to next right, skipping a left one.) Thus a stride is the length of two steps, measured directly along the line of travel.

Footprint trails are sometimes observed to cross unusual obstacles, these are often far beyond the ability of the largest and most athletic human. The most impressive of these that I have seen is where tracks passed easily over a tightly strung barbed-wire fence 44 inches high (1.1 m) off the ground. Stride lengths and obstacle crossings are abundantly recounted in the books by John Green and the other writers whom I have already mentioned.

If there actually are erect bipedal giants walking around in our forests, their tracks would be expected to show certain detailed characteristics. One of the most obvious of these is that repeated impressions of the same foot should not be identical to each other. This is well illustrated in the several cases where we do have multiple track casts of the same individual foot.

It must be remembered that a footprint is not just a negative copy of the foot that made it. Rather, the print should be thought of as the damage that foot made to the substratum that it walked on. Each footfall will be at least slightly different; speed and posture vary from moment to moment, and these affect the pressure of impact, hence the overall size of the footprint. Plantigrade walkers, including humans and apes, have thick fat pads on their soles that serve to cushion impacts. In the sasquatch, this pad should be at least 1.6 inches thick (4 cm) and maybe more. When this fat pad is vertically compressed it necessarily expands laterally, which leads to variations in the size and often in the shape of the imprint. The pad is thickest under the heel and is here capable of showing the greatest lateral variations.

Turns that are made in walking direction will impress one part of the foot more deeply than another, and just which part depends much on where in the stride the turn is being made, as well as how abrupt the turn is. Even movements of the upper body, such as turning to look at something, can be reflected in footprint variations. These motions may be seen in pressure ridges where the foot, or some part of it, pushed slightly to one side or the other.

A major form of pressure ridge occurs normally inside most footprints. This is where the forepart of the foot is pushed to the back just before lifting off—an action that imparts forward movement to the whole body. Because the living foot is flexible, almost half of it is in contact with the ground when this push-off is made. Typically this act pushes up a mound of dirt just behind the midpoint of the footprint. This appears much like an arch in that footprint and/or its cast. The top of this mound will consist of loose dirt that was shoved upward by the straight-back pressure of the forefoot's motion, and it will normally open up with several surface cracks. When such a footprint is cast, plaster will fill these cracks and later appear as raised, irregular ridges in the artificial "arch" of the print (Fig. 4). I have copies of eight out of the ten casts that Titmus made at the Patterson movie site; five of these show clear push-off ridges. Neither of the casts that Patterson made show any indication of these ridges because he deliberately avoided casting the footprints which showed them.

Toe positions can and do vary from one imprint to another of the same foot. We have several clear examples of this. It is my impression that sasquatch toes are more mobile than those on civilized human feet; other investigators have come to the same conclusion. Careful observation of bare human footprints on sandy beaches shows little toe movement in people who normally wear shoes, but sometimes it can be seen. People who do not wear shoes show much more variation in toe positions.

Figure 4. Push-off mound in a track cast. Just before a humanlike foot leaves the ground, its forepart shoves backward and usually pushes up a mound of dirt at or behind midfoot. Of all the tracks cast by Titmus at the Patterson movie site, this one (upper cast) shows the most extreme example of this action. It is compared with the flat track (lower cast) made by Patterson. The mound of dirt is recorded as a deep indentation near the middle of the cast in its natural position, thus giving a side view of what the foot impression looked like.

Sasquatch footprints sometimes show marked differences in how deeply the toes were dug into the ground. I have two casts of a particular foot, one of which was made on level ground with its toes impressed about as deeply as its sole. The other cast (just of the forefoot) occurred on an uphill slope with the toes tightly flexed and impressing almost an inch deeper than the plane of the foot parts immediately behind them.

Normal walking would include some sliding motions as the foot comes to rest, especially while walking downhill. In this case one would not expect the heel to strike with great pressure and expand laterally until it stops; this is just what often happens (Fig. 5, left). On other occasions the foot might not be fully lifted, and drag marks of the toes will extend out from the front of the footprint; these sometimes occur (Fig. 5, right). I have also seen the marks where a giant foot slid laterally downslope, then the ankle twisted to dig in with the uphill edge of the foot in an action that served to stop the slide.

All of these walking variations result in very different contours on the flat parts of the footprints from one step to another. Various anatomical parts of the foot, bones in particular, may be expected to

Figure 5. Footprint slide-in and drag-out. Left: on many occasions prints show that the heel contacted the ground with a forward movement before the full body weight pressed down and stopped that motion. Right: on rare occasions prints show that the foot was not entirely lifted off the ground immediately, and the toes extended their impressions after the major weight was lifted.

press differentially against the ground. Some observations of this kind are covered in the next chapter. Suffice it to say here that such variations do occur.

In addition to all of the variations that are caused by the anatomy and behavior of the makers of the footprints, further variation is caused by differences in the substratum itself. The ground may be hard or soft, moist or dry, and made up of coarse or fine particles. The surface may be covered with various amounts of loose material like leaves, pine needles, or stones. All of these variations can occur differentially, even within the area covered by a single footprint. And one footprint might be superimposed on another print, one made by a sasquatch or by a different animal. There is nothing unique to sasquatch footprints in all these ground variations, except that differential conditions can occur more easily within the area of a single impression simply because of its great size.

A special condition of the substratum is where there is a layer of soft, moist dirt underlain by a harder surface. This can easily occur on road surfaces where there may be a thick superficial layer of fine material that was stirred up by vehicle traffic, which is then rained on. In just this circumstance a series of tracks were found in western Washington in 1982, and I have casts of four of them (Fig. 6). In all cases the sole of the footprint was suspiciously flat, but the sides were often vertical, sometimes even overhanging, to a depth of just over an inch (about 3 cm). This implied a sole pad under the foot that expanded laterally when it pressed hard against an unyielding substratum. This lateral pressure left clearly recorded skin detail on the side walls of the imprint. When the pressure was relieved, the sole pad would have drawn back from the sidewalls just before it was lifted out.

On most ground surfaces there should be a differential depth of imprinting where more or less weight is pressed down, on a smaller or larger part of the foot's surface. The first action of a footfall is

Figure 6. Flat-bottomed tracks. These two tracks from Grays Harbor County, Washington, are an inch deep and unusually flat across their bottoms. At first glance this suggests they were made with rigid, fake feet made of wood. More likely, as on-site investigation indicated, these were real feet that passed through a thick mud cover and flattened out on the hard-packed road surface underneath. The track below is one of those shown in Fig. 1; the track above is another one from the same event.

most often when the entire weight presses down on the heel of a single foot, thus impressing that part deeply. Then the entire foot is applied to the ground with the same weight spread over more than twice as much surface area. Finally, the heel is lifted and the entire body weight presses only the forefoot into the ground. The amount of weight that is applied to the ground, per unit of surface area, is

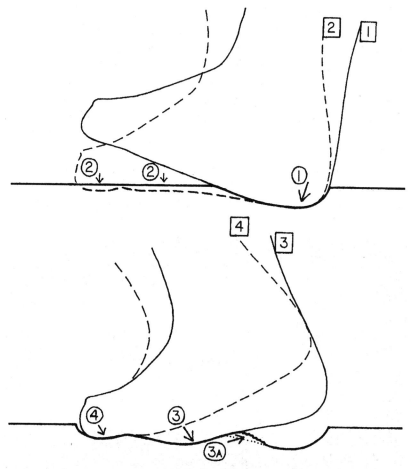

Figure 7. Four stages of track making. In the upper picture, solid outline 1 shows the deep indentation where the heel makes first contact under full body weight. Dashed outline 2 shows the shallower indentation of the rest of the foot with the body weight located directly above, and distributed over the entire foot. In the lower picture, solid outline 3 shows the heel lifting clear, and the forefoot pressing down and shoving slightly back with the full body weight. This common action pushes up the ridge of dirt indicated just behind midfoot. The dashed line 4 shows the final act of lifting the foot with only the toes still on the ground.

thus much greater at the heel and toes than it is in midfoot. This automatically results in many footprints that are longitudinally arched, and having what appears to be a raised instep. That these "arches" are artifacts of walking motions also can be seen in their great variability, which is generally in direct proportion to their stride length (walking speed). It is also notable that such arching is sometimes not present at all; in contrast, a truly arched foot cannot leave a flat imprint under any circumstance. Whatever is making these footprints is a flat structure with considerable internal flexibility. The raised, internal pressure ridge from the push-off adds to this apparent arching effect, but with a very different mechanical origin. (See Fig. 7 that gives four foot positions which are involved in making a footprint.)

Another dirt-shifting effect may be seen in footprints that occur in loose material. As the foot presses down, some of the dirt moves laterally and rises in a slight mound, often around the entire edge of the imprint. Experiments show that a human shoe imprint leaves the same kind of mound when pressed into the same soil. But with a rapid impact, as with stamping the foot, the dirt moves much faster and is spread farther away without leaving a mound. (See Fig. 16.)

One of the most interesting track casts I have seen is where a substantial stone (about a two-inch cube) apparently was driven into soft ground by the heel of the foot. The stone remained standing almost an inch (2 cm) up into the rear part of an otherwise clear footprint. The stone was pushed into the ground in a diagonally forward direction, not straight down, just as would be expected from the normal direction in which that heel should have been moving as it struck the ground. This movement left an inclined empty space behind the stone as it was driven forward as well as down. This space then filled with plaster when the cast was made.

When the cast was removed from the ground, the impressed stone came out attached to it. I first made a mold of the entire footprint with the stone included. Then I got permission to dig into the top of the original cast to remove the stone for examination. Its upper surface exhibited no sign of percussion that should have shown if it had been artificially driven into the ground. I then made another mold of the footprint just as it had appeared with the stone still embedded in the ground. Two cast versions of this footprint, with and without the stone, are shown in Fig. 8.

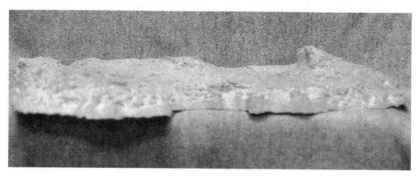

Figure 8. Stone in the heel of an imprint. The imprinting of an 18-inch foot drove a 2-inch stone into the ground with its heel impact. The stone was pressed downward leaving an open space behind because it was also pressed forward. Plaster filled this open space and the stone came out with the cast (top). The stone was removed from the original cast and this cast was copied again (bottom), showing what the imprint looked like with the stone still in the ground.

Animals

It is asserted by skeptics that at least some sasquatch tracks were actually made by other animals, bears being mentioned most often. No one who has seen clear footprints of each, especially side by side, would ever make that statement. The longest hind foot of a bear that I can find record of is 12 inches (30 cm); and 14 inches (35 cm) is the highest estimated for the biggest Kodiak bear. This is the general size range of only the smallest sasquatch tracks.

The heel of a bear's foot is somewhat pointed, in contrast to the widely rounded heel of the sasquatch. At a given distance forward from its most posterior point (about 2 inches, or 5 cm) the sasquatch heel imprint is easily twice as wide as the bear's. Bear footprints are often rather poorly impressed in midfoot along the inside edge, giving them the superficial appearance of a human instep. Sasquatch footprints might show an overall arching, but the inside edge is usually just as well marked as the outside edge.

Bear feet will show five clear toe pads in a good print, as does a sasquatch. Those of the bear arch across the front of the foot rather symmetrically, with digit III being the largest and most anterior, digits II and IV are a bit smaller, and digits I and V are the smallest and farthest back. They are not quite symmetrical because digit I is the smallest of all, being not quite as big as digit V. Sasquatch toes are much more human in that digit I is the largest, and usually the most anteriorly located, while the others are a little bit smaller and taper down in size and anterior projection toward the outside of the foot. An occasional variation in sasquatch feet is an almost bearlike arching of the toe projections, but in this case they are all about the same size and with no emphasis on the middle digit.

Probably the most marked contrast, other than size, is the regular appearance of claw marks in bear prints. These are ahead of, and well separated from, the ends of each of the toe pads. Black bears show claws if the imprint is as much as half an inch into the substratum. Grizzly bears show claw marks in even the shallowest possible footprints.

A bear will walk with its hind foot striking just behind, and often overlapping with, the spot where the front foot had been placed. This can result in a series of alternating footprint pairs that look as though they had been made by a bipedal creature. If they overlap only slightly, the front foot can easily add four inches (10 cm) to the length of the hind foot's print to reach well into the sasquatches' range of sizes. In this case it would still show claw marks at the front, and the heel is still narrow and rather pointed. It would then appear to have something like an instep, but this would be only in the far back part of the foot. Most conspicuous would be the toe marks (and claws) of the hind foot that would be superimposed on the rear part of the front foot's impression. Such a track could be mistaken for a sasquatch only if the track was very poorly marked and/or partly obscured. It could also fool someone if the tracks were in snow, especially if some new snow had lightly filled in the toe marks of the hind foot.

The bear's hind foot can also imprint ahead of the front foot that was just lifted, particularly if it is moving fast. In this case the wider front foot provides the apparent heel, and the hind foot makes five good toe imprints. The supposed instep in this case is rather farther forward and more convincing looking. The hind foot, being placed second, might obscure some of the toe marks of the front foot. This

Figure 9. Overlapping grizzly bear track casts. At left, the hind foot is pressed behind and overlapping the front foot, making what looks like a 15-inch-long track. It shows the narrow heel of a bear, two sets of claw marks, and very small first digits on the left edge of the picture. At right, the hind foot is pressed ahead of and overlapping the front foot, making a similarly compound track that is 12 inches long. This position allows the front foot to make a better-looking heel, but claw marks and toe sizes still are unmistakably those of a bear.

kind of double track would still have claw marks at its front end, and the claw marks of the front foot should still be visible in the middle of the print. Figure 9 illustrates casts of overlapping bear prints.

As mentioned earlier, a melted-out bear track or other imprint in snow can assume almost any appearance, but not a long line with all of the tracks changed in the same manner. Melt-out will obscure toe imprints, not create them, and it obviously cannot move the tracks to increase the stride length. And no natural agency can significantly increase the size or alter the shape of bear tracks in dirt.

No other animal leaves footprints even remotely resembling those of the sasquatch, even with overlapping and/or melt-out. The tracks of a gorilla are not nearly large enough to be so confused, and their divergent first toes are unmistakable. They also leave accompanying knuckle imprints at almost all times. Gorillas would not likely survive wild in sasquatch climates, and they would be seen and recognized easily if they were there.

Track Faking

It would appear that there is only one other possible source of sasquatch footprints, other than the reported animal itself, and that is fake tracks made by humans. Most of the reasons for ruling out this source have been alluded to already, but they are worth recounting in some detail here in order to dismiss this possibility more completely. (In the next chapter on more detailed foot anatomy the reader will find additional reasons to rule out hoaxing.)

Fake footprints resembling those of the sasquatch have been made; I have casts of three of these and have seen a few others. The shape of a footprint can be dug into the ground with the fingers and/or a hand tool, the interior pressed flat, and it can then be photographed or cast in plaster. My first footprint cast was made by a student in just this manner (Fig. 10). Roger Patterson told me he did this once in order to get a movie of himself pouring a plaster cast for the documentary he was making. (A few days later he filmed the actual sasquatch; see Chapter 4.) Another pair of rather obviously faked track casts were given to me some years ago by a man from western Washington (Fig. 11). These are mirror images that are too perfect, and their toe lines are too straight, among other things.

The more usual method of faking tracks is to make a pair of false feet, with shoes attached, with which a hoaxer can make any number of walking tracks. The first and most obvious problem with this explanation is the sheer number of tracks that are known to have been found, and the number of them that can be estimated to have occurred. Earlier in this chapter, I outlined the reasoning that came up with a total of something like 100 million track events that have been made within the last 40 years or so, many of which involve long lines of tens or even hundreds of individual footprints. If the typical event includes ten visible impressions, there may have been a billion separate footprints. If the hoaxer works a five-day week, he (or they) has been planting 100,000 footprints every day, or 12,500 per hour. (These numbers are also broadly compatible with the number of tracks that should have been left by a population of a few thousand actual sasquatches.)

It takes about one second for a man to make each step wearing awkward fake feet and stretching out between each of them. (This of course ignores the problems of matching the known depths of imprints and obstacle crossings.) Given the obscure and widely sepa-

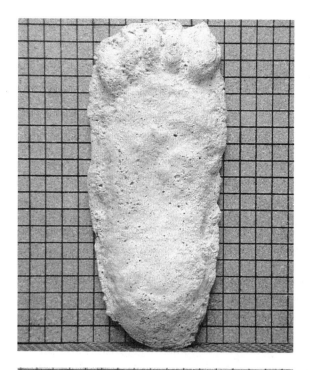

Figure 10. Fake sasquatch footprint cast. In 1969 Frank Weir, an artistic anthropology student, created this "footprint" by scraping and pressing into some dirt with his fingers, then making a plaster cast of the result. This illustrates how easy it can be to fake a single track cast. On the other hand, it has several anatomical errors that gave it away.

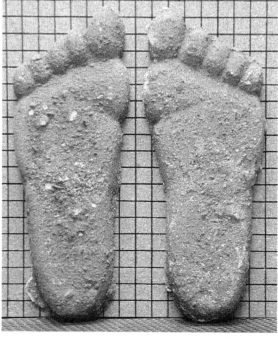

Figure 11. Pair of fake casts. Copies of these tracks were widely distributed in western Washington many years ago. They are anatomically too neat and mirror-imaged to be real. But the maker probably had some familiarity with actual tracks.

rated locations where tracks are found, the supposed fakers would certainly have to spend the vast majority of their time driving, riding, and hiking from one location to another. (This also ignores the difficulty of people putting tracks in many places without leaving evidence of their own presence.) Ten different sets of tracks, averaging ten footprints each is probably as much as any hoaxer could manage in a day. At this rate the skeptics must postulate a well-organized team of one thousand such people, working full-time, who are spread over all of North America with their greatest concentration in the Pacific Northwest.

The postulated hoaxers need to be equipped with a wide variety of fake feet, and they must have good methods of transportation and communication so as not to get into each other's way too much. We might presume that they draw a fair salary for this work—few would do it for under $25,000 a year (less in 1950 and more today). This then adds up to an operation that could cost twenty-five million dollars a year in salaries alone, plus much more for travel expenses and track-faking equipment for a thousand field workers. District organizers and local directors would add still more personnel to the cost. During the last forty years well over a billion dollars must have been expended on this project, and perhaps a similar amount was spent in all the time before that (allowing for inflation). In all this time, and with all these workers, no outsider has discovered the organization, and none of its members has exposed it. Sounds a little far-fetched, doesn't it?

Alternatively, the skeptics might try to explain the number of footprints by assuming that all or most of the fakers have been working independently, just copying each other's work over the years. Without any salary being paid for it, few people would put in more than one percent of their working time on a project like this. This idea requires something like 100,000 casual hoaxers who go out for a weekend of track making one or two times a year. I know of a few such people, but none of them worked at it for many years, and for most of them (4 out of 5) it was a one-time-only activity. To my mind, this amorphous horde of hoaxers is scarcely any more believable than the tightly knit organization of at least 1,000 paid professionals.

Whether the faking is being done by a large team of experts, or by a hundred times as many amateurs, there is still the problem of how they know just what kind of footprints to make. Not all sasquatch feet have exactly the same design. In fact, we recognize different individuals by such differences. But there are some underlying anatomical features that are rather constant, and some of these went quite unnoticed, or unappreciated, until my first publication on footprint anatomy back in 1972. Given all the sources of variation that can and do occur in sasquatch-type footprints, how have almost all of the 100,000 amateurs been able to know which of the irregularities to copy and which to ignore? Even the supposed professional organization must have gotten its start from someone who figured out the appropriate anatomical details many years ago.

It should be added that in my original study I left out two characteristics that often can help to recognize real sasquatch tracks. I have told these traits to no one and have never written them down. They continue to be a useful method for spotting fakes when someone tries to incorporate everything that appeared in my published description.

Costs and secrecy requirements are the major objections to the professional group as the source of these tracks. Continued anatomical accuracy of the prints is the main single reason why the amateurs could not have done it all. If both types of hoaxers were involved, then both types of objections apply, but to a correspondingly lesser degree. Yet one of these procedures for faking, or a combination of them, must be postulated by anyone who maintains that these tracks were not made by real sasquatches.

A totally different approach to the question of authenticity of footprints is to weigh the probability that particular known specimens are fake or real. These specimens, mostly represented by casts, can be theoretically arranged on a scale from most likely fake to most likely real. All investigators agree that at least some specimens occur on the fake end of this scale, but they often differ as to how far this designation progresses toward the more legitimate-looking end of the scale.

With the new approach we do not initially try to decide whether most of the casts are fake or real, but simply try to determine whether it is even possible that they could have been made by human hoaxers. Most skeptics look at no more than a few evident fakes, and a few more that could conceivably have been faked, then assume that this applies to all the rest of them. A more careful approach would be to temporarily set aside all of them that might have been made by any and all possible artificial means, and then to see if some remain unchallengeable. If none remain, then we can dismiss this line of evidence for the existence of sasquatch. But if any remain as valid, however few, the species may be presumed to exist.

Then we can go back down the line to reassess the legitimacy of those that previously had been set aside. There is no point in trying to weigh the pros and cons of the less-than-obvious specimens unless and until both ends of the scale, fake and real, are established beyond a reasonable doubt. If the decision goes in favor of legitimacy at the good end of the scale, then probably the vast majority of tracks in between are real, and the above numbers exercise is all the better founded. But we cannot logically begin this investigation by simply assuming that all or any of the tracks were really made by sasquatches. That must first be proven beyond any reasonable doubt for at least some of them.

Much of the evidence for authenticity is presented in the next chapter on footprint anatomy, but enough has been discussed up to this point that the question can be addressed in some detail. I have read and been told of the circumstances of many footprint events which, if true, cannot possibly have been faked. The trouble is that I am not certain these accounts are absolutely reliable—some error could have slipped in, a critical detail overlooked, or some deliberate lying might be involved. Accordingly, my judgment has to be based on my own personal observation of the evidence. Logically, the reader should make the same decision and reserve final judgment to be based on his/her own personal observations.

The push-off mound in midfootprint is one of the most impressive pieces of evidence to me. As has already been described (Figs. 4 and 7), this mound is shoved up by a horizontal push of the forefoot just before it leaves the ground. The location of this mound means that it was thrown up by a flexible foot, a large part of which was still in ground contact when the heel had already been lifted. Fake feet made from wood are rigid and will leave this kind of mound immediately behind the toes. Many years ago I made a pair of wooden feet to test this and other features that they might leave in their imprints. One also can observe that bare human feet will leave sasquatch-like push-off mounds in rapid walking. Most shoes will leave two such mounds, one in midfoot from the major push-off, and a minor one just at the toe tip where the rigid shoe sole dug in at the last moment.

Wooden fake feet also cannot leave any of the variations in size and shape that have been described. Neither can they leave changing sole contours and the toe impressions in various positions. To effect these variations the faker would have to carve a separate foot shape for each print; for a given line of tracks this might amount to ten or more, and they could rarely be used on other occasions in other places. Alternatively, a hoaxer could have two artificial feet of very complicated construction, the different parts of which can be rigidly set in many positions. I am sure some such devices could be made, but there are necessarily hundreds of them in use if the tracks are all fakes. Did so many people independently invent and build them, or are we back to the professional organization for yet another reason? Also, the use of adjustable fake feet greatly increases the amount of time needed to plant the tracks; it might multiply the total cost by ten times, from two billion to twenty billion dollars. It equally compounds the difficulties of the independent hoaxers, assuming that is the preferred explanation. How, for instance, were all of these 100,000 amateurs able to construct the same kind of devices, and how many different sizes did each of them build?

Fake feet often press down vertically into the ground and are drawn up vertically as well. The side walls of such imprints might have any degree of slope, depending on soil conditions, up to the limiting orientation of vertical. With such walls, the imprinting device necessarily slid along that surface in both directions, first down and then up. Yet we find clear imprinting of skin detail on vertical walls in perhaps ten of my casts (Fig. 12). This effect can be accomplished only by adding a thick pad to the sole of the fake foot that compresses on weight loading and expands laterally to press into the side walls of the imprint. This is especially necessary for those prints where the side walls actually overhang, as can be seen in some of my casts. In at least two cases, found by different people in far separated places, imprints of individual toes expand to both sides at the deepest level (Fig. 13). This sole pad is also necessary for the prints to vary in size with strength of impact.

Figure 12. Skin detail on side of cast. This photo shows lateral impressions made against a vertical wall in a footprint. A rigid fake foot could not have made an impression like this; it would have been obscured by the act of removing that "foot" from the impression.

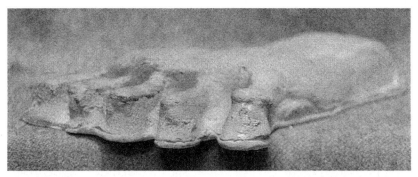

Figure 13. Expanding toe-pad imprints. These toes expanded laterally with the pressure of full weight, then withdrew medially about 20 percent before they were lifted out. No rigid object can make overhanging impressions like this. The imprinting structure necessarily had a flexible pad under its toes. Such a device could be built, but a new and different one had to be made for each of the several imprints that showed this overhang. This print is from the Blue Mountains of eastern Washington/Oregon.

Some indication of the thickness of any presumed artificial sole pad may be gained from the two instances where a stone was stepped on. In both cases the stone pressed almost an inch (2 cm) into the underside of the "foot," which was evenly pressed into the soil all around that object (Figs. 8 and 14). Thus the pad was well over an inch thick. How much more would depend on what it was made of and how well it compressed. It also had to have a tightly applied, flexible cover wrapped around it that somehow never got folded when the internal parts of the fake foot were repositioned. I think that all of the problems involved in such a construction are so great that no more than a handful, if any, of the known footprints can be accounted for in this manner.

Some of the more general considerations in footprint events include apparent weight of the subject, its length of stride, and abilities at obstacle crossing. My remarks on these phenomena are again confined to those instances where I have direct information. Since other investigators have reported many examples that are so similar, I am inclined to accept most of them as being real.

The depth of footprint impressions has been a continuing source of amazement and comment by those who find them. The usual measure is to place one's own shod foot firmly into the ground next to a few tracks and observe that it does not impress nearly as far. The typical sasquatch footprint has two or three times the surface area of

Figure 14. Footprint on a stone. Photo of one of the Blue Mt. tracks from 1982 with a stone located in the middle of the foot. Fingerprinter Edward Palma was able to follow dermal ridges across the entire width of this track, thus showing it was a single impression that spread down around all sides of the intruding object.

a fair-sized man's shoe. Thus it would appear that the track maker weighed in excess of 400 pounds (180 kg); how much more depends on how we interpret the greater depth of imprinting. This depth is almost always more than twice the discoverer's boot prints, often four or five times deeper. The implication is that we might be looking at weights of 1000 kg or more—well over an English ton.

Most sasquatch tracks appear at night and are discovered during the following day or later. Soil conditions will differ, usually being harder by day, thus limiting the imprinting of boot comparisons. This timing can account for at least part of the excessive weight indications in most instances.

Another factor that is commonly overlooked is that a striding foot imprints much more deeply than it does when slowly stepping or just standing. At heel impact there is an added forward component in the soil compacting; the forward movement continues into the full imprint, and then changes to a rearward shift while the foot is still flat; then upon stepping out there is a strong increase in the rearward component. These combine with the force of vertical impact and actual weight to "dig" the foot into the ground far deeper than might otherwise be expected.

This effect can be observed for yourself by striding "purposefully" over wet sand or moist dirt, then walking back casually to examine your own tracks. Now back off again to look at the tracks you just made while you were examining the first set. The difference can be startling. I have done this experiment many times with somewhat varying results, but my striding gait always leaves much deeper impressions than those left while I was looking at those first tracks (Fig. 15). In some cases I have stamped my feet hard, even jumped up and down, and could not match the depth of imprinting from my own striding gait.

One might conclude from this evidence that we are dealing with footprints that are functionally dug in and also impressed at least twice as deeply as those of a walking man. These factors may be combined as follows: A 200-pound standing man impresses one-eighth inch into the soil; he would impress more like one-half inch while walking in a striding gait; if his feet had twice the surface area he would impress only one-fourth inch. If the nearby sasquatch footprints are one inch deep, then it must have weighed about four times as much as that man. These are only very rough approximations, but they do indicate body weights similar to those arrived at by other lines of evidence—500 to 1,000 pounds (230 to 450 kg), and possibly more.

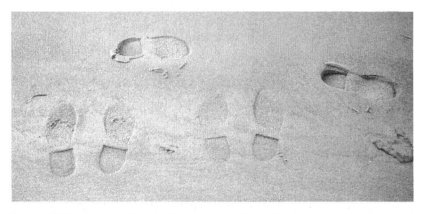

Figure 15. Footprints of the author, wearing shoes. My deep tracks in the moist sand pass from left to right across the picture, where I was striding in a "purposeful" manner. Walking more slowly in the right foreground and up to look at the first tracks, I left much fainter impressions. An additional pair of imprints, just to the left of the faintest steps, were made by backing off and jumping into that spot. Clearly, the manner of walking has a great influence on how deeply the tracks are impressed.

It should be mentioned that one investigator tried to estimate the body weight by means of a static test next to a sasquatch track. He placed on the ground a steel plate the size of the footprint, on top of which he jacked up the rear end of a U.S. Forest Service pickup truck, and the impression this produced was less than that of the track. From this information he announced that the creature must have weighed about 5,000 pounds (over 2,200 kg), and that it had to be made of titanium!

His first error was to assume that a full half of the truck's weight was on the rear axle. More important was the fact that his experimental "track" was not differentially impacted, and with no front-to-back movement as it was made. Finally, the test was conducted long after the track first appeared, and the ground had dried out somewhat in that time. Later, this same investigator was lavish in his praise for my study of the dermal ridges in the same tracks (see next chapter) that showed it was a species of higher primate. It is not likely that a living primate would be made of titanium, but this contradiction did not bother this self-proclaimed authority at all. This is a good illustration of the lunatic fringe from which I must distance myself.

Length of stride is often commented upon, both by sighters of the animals and by those who observe the tracks. It has already been mentioned that the typical step length is about half of the reported height of the creature, as might be expected. When this is combined with the evident weight with which the footprints are impressed we find a new difficulty for any supposed hoaxers to overcome.

We can easily imagine a man wearing big false feet and laying a trail of fake sasquatch footprints. It is much more difficult to picture a huge athlete, weighing almost 300 pounds (130 kg) carrying at least 440 pounds (200 kg) of extra weight on his back to make passable impressions in the ground. It is absolutely impossible for this heavily laden man to walk with strides well over a yard long, impacting with force; the best he could do is shuffle along clumsily.

Before we dismiss the above scenario too easily, it must be remembered that hoaxers can be very clever. I'll never forget one case of sasquatch-like footprints in thin snow that were spaced eight feet (2.4 m) from heel to opposite heel—obviously a running pace. The tracks went some distance along level ground, then they continued up a slope of maybe 20 degrees, maintaining the eight-foot steps all the way. I only saw photographs of the event and didn't like the footprint shape, but I had to admit that no person could have run up that slope with eight-foot steps, fake feet or not. It was later found out that a high school athlete had made the tracks; he wore fake feet that were put on *backwards*, and he ran *down* the slope. Whenever a new account is reported of incredible feats of footwork, I try to remember this case and wonder how the new one might have been faked.

Another method that might have been used to simulate excessive weight is to impress fake tracks by force of impact. The hoaxer could have a long pole with a heavy foot-shaped object at one end—right foot on one side and left foot inverted against it. He swings the pole overhead and down against the ground as fast as he can. Then he takes two steps forward, rotates the pole 180 degrees, and strikes again slightly to one side. After the appropriate number of "footprints" have been impacted, he brushes away his own tracks and departs.

While examining a set of tracks in southwestern Washington with Robert Morgan in 1975 the idea of impact faking occurred to me. In this particular instance most of the footprints were in loose dirt, and I had already noticed the pressure mound of dirt that surrounded many of them. A simple experiment showed that when I walked by, a similar pressure mound was pushed up around my own prints. But when I stamped my foot with some force, the dirt was shifted aside with much more speed and no mound developed (Fig. 16). My conclusion was that something there had placed those footprints with upwards of 800 pounds of weight coming down on them with no more impact than from a striding gait.

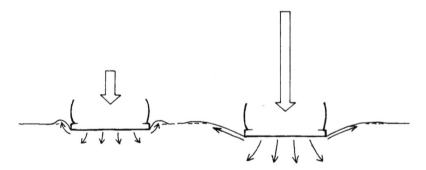

Figure 16. Pressure mounding. Soil compaction underneath a footprint is a product of impressed weight and speed of impact. These drawings are my interpretation of an experiment with shoes in loose dirt. At walking speed (left), soil is compacted directly under the sole, while some is pushed aside and rises in the direction of least resistance. With more forceful stamping (right), soil compaction is somewhat greater, and the side-shifted dirt is moved more rapidly. This rapid movement carries the dirt farther, leaving no mounding and a less distinct foot outline.

There are many reports of obstacles being crossed or stepped over that are quite beyond the ability of a human, with or without wearing fake feet. I have seen only one such case up to now, and this one was at my first good exposure to the evidence in early 1970 in the northeastern corner of Washington. My investigation was prompted by news reports; at that time I had no inside line of communication for any such information. This was the Bossburg incident of the notable Cripple Foot, as that particular sasquatch has come to be called. I was able to locate many people who saw some of the more than one thousand footprints from the main appearance, and others who saw footprints of the same individual from other incidents shortly before. It was at this time that I first met John Green, Rene Dahinden, and Ivan Marx, as well as many others who were temporarily interested in the subject. This is also where John Green uncovered for me the last of the many footprints that had been saved for situations like this. And here I obtained copies of the footprint casts that finally convinced me that the creatures were real.

All except the one covered footprint were gone when I examined the site. But with photographs to study, and good verbal directions to follow, I was able to locate a well-built fence that had been crossed by the line of footprints with scarcely a break in stride. The top barbed wire was 44 inches (1.1 m) above the ground and strung tightly. By pressing my thumbs firmly down I could push it maybe two inches lower, then lifted one leg over. I am a tall man—6 feet 3 inches, or 189 cm—but it was quite impossible to place my foot down on the other side; I could have managed that over a wire at only 33 inches (0.84 cm). By a well-considered hopping motion I crossed that fence, leaving scuffed foot marks turned sideways on each side of the crossing point. Photographs and testimony indicated that there were sasquatch tracks on both sides with no evidence of turning or other difficulty. The fence showed no sign of having been re-strung or tightened in recent weeks.

A skeptic might suggest that the tracks were made by a hoaxer with stilts, or some other kind of attachment adding 12 inches (30 cm) to his leg length. This would have made his walking very risky, as the tracks went over snow-covered ground with very uneven inclinations in some places. The trail also began and ended on a steep slope coming out of and going back into Lake Roosevelt behind the Grand Coulie Dam.

I was also impressed by the nature of the tracks themselves, including the one I saw directly. As a general rule they were quite free of loose snow. My own experiments show that snow tends to cake upon cold objects, like fake feet or plaster casts, with lumps being removed from some imprints and being deposited in others. A warm flexible foot that greatly compacts the snow under each step would leave just the kind of tracks that were found at this site.

An inventive mind can come up with many tricks to make footprints look real. Some of the cases on record no doubt were faked, possibly even some that I have examined first hand. But to suppose that they all were faked certainly strains the imagination for a number of reasons that have already been described.

Mention has already been made of a pair of big wooden feet that I carved back in about 1975. These were of 1.5-inch-thick wood (4 cm)

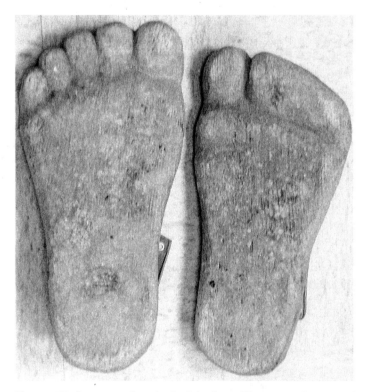

Figure 17. Bottoms of author's fake feet. These are the carved wooden "feet" with attached boots that I've used to experiment with track faking. They are 18 inches long by 8 inches wide. They graphically demonstrate what can and cannot be done with fakes of this kind. Note the four lesser toes on the left foot that were not separated, and which constitute something of a "signature" for any tracks made with them.

and measured 18 inches long by 8 inches wide at the front (46 by 20 cm). It took me three months of occasional free-time carving to make decent contours on parts of the soles, to evenly round off the edges, and to form the toes. I left the four lesser toes on one foot unseparated as a kind of "signature," just in case I ever made some tracks that got reported; this never happened. I nailed a pair of expendable boots to the tops of these wooden feet and proceeded to test them (Fig. 17).

The fake feet were very awkward to walk with. As the heel first touched ground the whole foot tended to immediately slap down flat. I soon learned it was easiest to progress in a rather flat-footed fashion. The width of these feet forced me to swing them past my standing leg somewhat out to the side so I wouldn't strike that leg. It also served to leave a series of tracks on either side of the line of travel, which is realistic, rather than overlapping that line. But the walking posture (sailor's gait) was quite uncomfortable, and I would not want to travel more than ten or twenty yards that way. (See Fig. 18 for some tracks recently made with these fake feet.)

Figure 18. Tracks made by author's fake feet. The wooden fakes progress from right to left in moist sand. My normal footprints, in every-day shoes, cross that trail moving away from the camera. Both sets of tracks and the photograph were made in the space of about five minutes. Note how much deeper my normal shoes pressed that did the oversized fakes. Note also the kick-back of material just behind the toes in the big fake footprint on the far left.

My fake feet tended to make flat imprints with every step. I could not twist my ankles to dig in deeply with one side, as I have seen in a sasquatch track. That would have required far more ankle strength than I had. With some exertion I could walk fast enough to kick up a ridge of dirt from the push-off, and this was only at the very front of the foot where logic says it should have occurred. In all, there were few surprises from this test, the most interesting being that the footprints were quite regularly one inch longer than the feet themselves. This follows from the slope of entry with the heel and slope of exit with the toes, and is illustrated in Fig. 19.

Moving rapidly on firm ground with my fake feet I found that the fifth toe sometimes made little or no impression. If the toes had been carved in an even arc across the front of the foot this effect should have been exaggerated. One or two such toes on the edge would dig in much less simply because of their less-projecting position. It is at least possible that some reports of four- and three-toed sasquatches resulted from faking attempts of this kind. I have not had the opportunity to study any such tracks to see if this might have been the case, but it should be easy to determine.

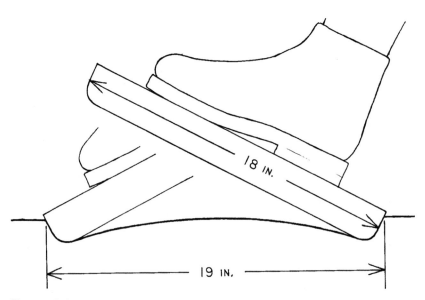

Figure 19. Imprinting with fake feet. This somewhat idealized diagram shows how my fake feet make imprints an inch longer than themselves. Half an inch is added at each end of a deep imprint by the slopes of entry and exit. The deeper impressions at the two ends of the track are also indicated.

It was in 1976 that I made the first major test of my fake feet on a sandy beach on the Oregon Coast at low tide. I left some long lines of footprints for the next tide to obscure, and wondered if anyone ever saw them. There were no such reports in the local media. At the end of 1991 I made further tests with these feet, again on the Oregon coast, in order to take some photographs of the results to illustrate this book.

Handprints

A quadruped will leave as many imprints of its front as of its hind feet. A biped normally walks on its hind feet alone, and one does not expect to find imprints of its anterior (now upper) limbs. Yet we human bipeds do touch our hands to the ground on many occasions. In the act of sitting and/or lying down and rising again we often put a hand on the ground; falling can be blocked with the hand(s); and activities engaged in while sitting can also leave imprints of the hands. The first two of these actions (sitting and falling) would be expected for sasquatch, the third (deliberate activities) is less certain. Human footprints should occur many hundreds of times more often than our handprints, so this kind of evidence might be equally rare for sasquatch. On the other hand (so to speak) only a small fraction of discovered footprints are cast in plaster by regular investigators, but virtually all handprints will be cast simply because of their novelty. I have copies of five such imprints, and a possible sixth, out of my total of eighty-six casts; a few rather vague prints might be of either hand or foot.

In 1972 Ivan Marx made casts of what appear to be imprints of two different left hands (Fig. 20). Both were placed flat on the ground with the fingers slightly spread. Marx indicated that in each case the sasquatch had been digging in the ground and had piled up some dirt. Presumably they then placed a hand flat on this dirt in the act of starting to stand up again—a typical human action. Marx was not forthcoming with much more information, and seemed to be even a bit vague on the above description of their origin. He told me nothing about where they were found, or even if they had occurred near to one another. This vagueness may be interpreted as trying to cover his faking or, more likely, that he didn't want to divulge too much information about what he considered to be a hot lead worthy of further investigation. I described these handprints in considerable detail in a 1971 publication, the essentials of which are recounted here and in the next chapter.

Both of Marx's handprints are about twice as wide as my own rather large hands, and half-again longer. In both of them the fingers are more nearly the same size than is the case with human hands; this applies to both the length and thickness of these fingers. Flexion creases show only faintly.

The two handprints differ slightly in size, the smaller one measures 10.4 inches long and 7.3 inches across the front of the palm (26.5 by 18.5 cm). It appears to be a double strike—that is, it contacted the ground one time, then lifted, moved a bit, and pressed down again more firmly. An outline of the outer edge of this hand is faintly indicated about half an inch inside of the clearer outline, and it follows the same contours. This first strike is not evident on any other parts of the print.

The smaller hand, shown in Figure 20, is best recognized by its fingers being quite flat; there is no appreciable indenting of their tips into the ground as with the other specimen. There is also very little relief over the palm—the entire imprint varies no more than about a quarter-inch in depth. Even its outline, around all the digits and palm, shows only a slight rounding. Quite understandably these facts raise the question of whether it might be a fake. There would be rather little carving required to make a fake hand of this shape with its sharp outline. Nevertheless, the slight relief that is there is mostly concaved into the surface; this would be very difficult to carve into a piece of wood without special tools. I looked carefully for traces of wood grain or carving lines showing in the print and found none.

The larger hand, also shown in Figure 20, measures 11.8 inches long by 6.9 inches across the palm (30.0 by 17.4 cm). Its finger and thumb tips are flexed and press an extra half-inch deeper than the palm and digit bases. The rest of the palm shows additional relief variations amounting to another quarter-inch or more. This hand is different in being well rounded along all of its edges, and around the digits as well as the palm. Its flexion creases are more evident than in the flatter specimen. This one would have required a great deal of work to fake—especially carving away the large mass of wood between all the digit tips.

There is no guarantee that either or both of these are genuine handprint casts, though they would have required much work and skill to fake. Their more detailed structure, which is discussed in the

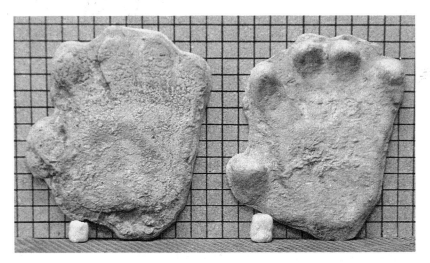

Figure 20. Two left hand prints. These casts were made in 1972 by Ivan Marx, who was then working on this research in northeastern Washington. They are clearly from different individuals, though both were impressed flat-handed into the ground in the same manner. The hands are disproportionately wide, the fingers are almost the same size as each other, and the thumbs are not opposed.

next chapter, also would appear to require a knowledge of primate anatomy that cannot easily be explained.

In the late 1980s Paul Freeman brought in some casts of hand imprints from the Blue Mountains on the Washington-Oregon border. The most impressive of these is a pair of almost flat prints that he told me were made on a stream bank when the sasquatch apparently stumbled onto one knee in midstream and slapped its hands down on the far bank as it fell. His description of the circumstances that he gave to Bob Titmus was rather different, which has raised some concern about their authenticity. The hands are complete except for a part of the "heel" of one where Freeman had built a cardboard dam to hold the plaster at the water's edge. Another specimen is the imprint of four knuckles and a thumb, evidently pressed into the ground as the sasquatch lost its footing and needed just a bit of additional support at that moment.

The pair of handprints from the stream bank are roughly similar to Marx's handprints from northeastern Washington in that they are very large and disproportionately wide (Fig. 21). They measure 8.5 and 9 inches across the widest parts of the palms, and the complete right hand is almost 13 inches long including the third digit; its wrist is also represented in the impression and the exact edge of the palm

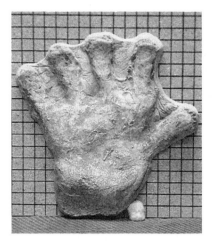 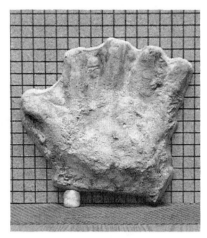

Figure 21. Pair of handprints. These casts were made in 1986 by Paul Freeman in the Blue Mountains. They are slightly larger than the Marx handprints, but of similar design. The left hand (right picture) was on the edge of a stream and the cast is cut off by a cardboard dam that held back the water during casting. The right hand (left picture) is complete.

itself is not clearly discernable. (In metric, these hands are 20.6 and 22.9 cm wide, and one of them is 33 cm long.) The fingers are also all similar to each other in lengths and widths, and the flexion creases are poorly indicated. Palm and finger edges are well rounded, and some of the finger tips turn into the substratum slightly.

The major part of each hand is again nearly flat, but with a relief this time of close to an inch (2 cm), while the heel of the hand is indented about twice as deeply, giving the handprints an arched appearance. I think this is easiest explained by the full weight of impact being borne on the heels of the hands in the first instant, then they slapped down in an arching movement with somewhat less pressure. There is an incongruity of the thumb location—it seems too far forward in relation to the transverse crease—that might also be explained by this rolling motion of the hand.

Freeman was unable to positively identify the only associated footprint that was in the stream bed, along with what he said was a knee impression. He was sure that the footprint was from one of the larger individuals reported in the area, and their footprints were all about 17 inches long (43 cm). I measured the ratio of my own hand and foot lengths, and that of a much shorter young man. Our ratios differed slightly, and the sasquatch hand-to-foot ratio was between ours.

The knuckle imprint was from a considerably smaller hand, only half-again wider than my own instead of twice as wide (Fig. 22). Freeman assured me that it was planted right in a trail of footprints made by a known individual of whom we have many casts. Its feet are just over 14 inches long (36 cm), and the indicated hand size is a good size match for it. The thumb is impressed with its edge into the ground and shows a clear mark of part of the thumbnail. That thumb tip is also excessively thick, about 1.7 inches (4 cm), which may be interpreted as a thick fat pad added to its palmar surface. The fact that no fingernails or toenails show on any other track casts, even when they are pressed in more than an inch deep, may be a consequence of a consistent feature of fat padding on the soles and palms. Again, some of its more detailed anatomy is saved for the next chapter.

Figure 22. Knuckle and thumb imprint. According to Paul Freeman, this print was found in a line of tracks of an individual known as "Dermals," from the best case of recorded dermal ridges (see Chapter 3). Note especially the edge of a thumbnail showing at the near end. Its position again indicates a nonopposed thumb. The apparent thickness of the thumb is also impressive, and implies a considerable pad on the palmar surface of the hand.

3

PRINT ANATOMY

It has long been noted that sasquatch footprints differ from enlarged versions of human prints in several particulars that have already been mentioned. They have no longitudinal arch and are disproportionately wide; their toes are more nearly equal in size than ours and they line up more nearly straight across the end of the foot; and a double depression often appears at the ball of the foot. That they are especially large in relation to stature is not properly a foot characteristic.

In his 1961 book, Ivan Sanderson suggested that these feet had very long toes that were webbed for much of their length. The rear bulge of the double ball would then correspond to ours, and the forward bulge would be an enlarged joint at the base of the big toe. This interpretation was made largely in response to the often reported aquatic behavior of sasquatch, thus the feet were seen as effective flippers. Sanderson was also inclined to accept Alistair Hardy's suggestion (1960) that our ancestors had passed through an aquatic stage shortly before becoming fully human, and this may have colored his thinking on the subject of foot anatomy. (The aquatic theory of human ancestry is so contradicted by the facts as not to be worthy of rebuttal here.)

Unfortunately for Sanderson's view, some simple biomechanics rule out the idea of long toes on the sasquatch feet. In order for the toes to leave deep imprints in hard soil, and in some cases to dig down into it in a gripping manner, they must be flexed with unusual power. Each toe segment functions as a lever, the fulcrum being near the center of the joint, the power is applied by muscles pulling back on tendons that attach to the lower edge of the bone at the near end, and the resistance is at the far end of that toe segment (Fig. 23). The longer the toe the less powerfully it can be flexed, all else being equal. The long, webbed toes that might serve as swim flippers could not be impressed into the ground with anywhere near the force necessary to make the many tracks that have been found.

When I had the opportunity to study the track casts of Cripple Foot in early 1970 it quickly became evident how the responsible feet were constructed—assuming, of course, that they actually were feet. Going into that study I gave sasquatch only a 10 percent chance of being real, however much I may have wanted it to be; a few weeks later I increased that estimate to 100 percent. Two publications resulted from this and other related data that appeared in 1972, and

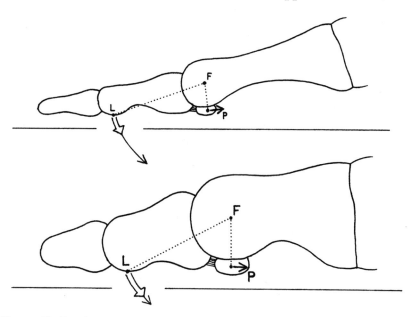

Figure 23. Toe flexion leverage. Shown here are the first digits of the foot—human above, and calculated sasquatch below, set to the same length. The large bone on the right in each picture is the metatarsal, which does not flex. The first toe segment is moved downward with the action of a simple lever. The fulcrum (F) is its center of rotation against the bone to the right, power (P) is applied to the lower edge by a muscle pulling straight back, and the load (L) is at the bottom of the far end of that toe bone. As power is applied (short, solid arrows) the bone rotates around its fulcrum point and its far end swings down (long, solid arrows). If the same force is applied, the thicker bone with its longer power arm (dotted line F—P), has a shorter action stroke, but that action will be proportionally stronger. The thinner bone has a longer action stroke, but it is much weaker. Relative power of movement is indicated by the lengths of the open arrows. The distal toe bone rotates against the proximal one in the same manner.

have been reprinted in Byrne's book (1975) and Sprague's collection of articles (1977 and 1979).

The pair of track casts I had to work with were copies of a pair made from some excellent tracks that appeared near Bossburg, Washington, in December 1969 (Fig. 24). This was some weeks before the famous long line of tracks of the same individual were found in snow, leading out of and back into a reservoir and crossing a substantial fence along the way. The original casts had been copied by pressing them into a prepared bed of fine dirt, the casts resulting from this action being the ones I borrowed. I made good latex molds of these, and thus lost no more detail of consequence. (The originals were rediscovered many years later by Rene Dahinden, and that is an interesting story in itself.)

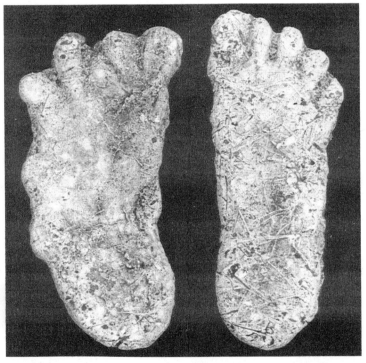

Figure 24. Best track casts of "Cripple Foot." These 17-inch-long tracks of one individual were cast in northeastern Washington in late 1969. The right foot (left, as seen from the bottom) is greatly distorted by some disease and/or injury; the left foot appears normal. The author's analysis of the apparent anatomy of these tracks proved to be the first convincing evidence to him that the animals were real.

These casts were put to another use many years later in an art exhibit at the international section of the San Francisco Airport in 1987. Some artist friends urged me to submit some of my material for the show titled "The Right Foot." I set these casts of Cripple Foot's tracks against a background of published articles on the subject (as shown in Fig. 25). Apparently it was a big hit, but nothing tangible resulted from this effort.

Cripple Foot's two track casts are far from being mirror images of each other. The left foot is normal, but the right foot is clearly bent along its long axis by some 25 degrees, concave along its inner edge. Its third digit is missing or permanently displaced upward, and the other four toes are spread out so that their tips are about evenly spaced. Two other casts of the same foot, as well as photographs of other tracks, show that this spacing was at least roughly maintained at all times. The distorted right foot also had two conspicuous bulges standing out from its outer edge. At first glance this "anatomy" made no sense at all.

It was immediately evident that the two heel segments were good mirror images of each other. The most posterior point on the heel of

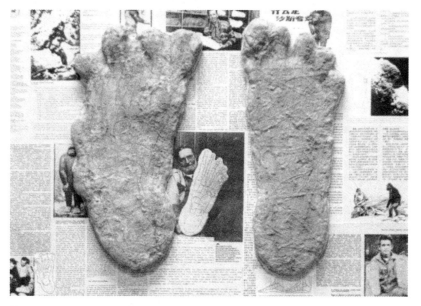

Figure 25. Airport art. Casts of Cripple Foot are mounted on a background of printed articles on the subject in English, German, French, Swedish, Russian, and Chinese. It was displayed as part of "The Right Foot" art exhibit at the San Francisco International Airport in 1987.

the left track thus could be morphologically pinpointed on the distorted right track. It was then a simple matter to measure the lengths along both edges of both tracks from heel center, around the contours, and up to the bases of the first and fifth toes. This distance along the inside edge of each foot was the same. Measured along the outside edge, and passing straight through the two bulges, the distorted right print was 1.5 inches (3.8 cm) longer than the left print.

If the two feet were made up of identical bones, then these bones must have fitted together on the inside edge of the distorted foot, but were somewhat spread apart on its outside edge. If the bones were not mirror images in each foot, then it would be an unlikely chance that the inside edges of the two should have matched so well. Some pathology might have expanded the cartilage between the bones on the outside edge of one foot, with the condition fading to nothing at its inside edge. At least this was a working hypothesis, and nothing has since contradicted it.

Excluding the toe, there are just three bones on the outside edge of a primate's foot, thus the postulated expansion had only two places in which to occur. Allowing for substantial flesh lateral to the bones, I estimated that these two spaces must have been forced apart by about half an inch each (1.3 cm), and adding a good inch to the foot

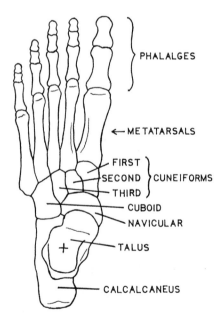

Figure 26. Human foot bones, top view. For the readers' reference, these bones are illustrated and named. The underside of the foot looks much the same, except that the calcaneus extends forward to obscure the talus almost entirely.

PHALALGES

←—METATARSALS

FIRST
SECOND } CUNEIFORMS
THIRD

CUBOID

NAVICULAR

TALUS

CALCALCANEUS

length along that interior line. If the cartilage had expanded out to the sides by the same amount as it had between the bones, then two substantial projections there could form the basis for further development of callousing. This would easily account for the two bulges on the outer edge of that foot. More importantly, it would also serve to locate the positions of the two interbone spaces. (See Fig. 26 for an illustration of the human foot with its bones named.)

From this information it was a fairly simple matter to draw the outlines of the bones of each foot; individually they should be mirrored pairs, but they would have to be spaced somewhat apart in much of the right foot. I drew some oversized copies of human bones, which were altered only as needed to put the two spaces adjacent to the outside bulges of the crippled foot. Figure 27 illustrates these casts, and an enlarged human foot, with the bones of all three drawn in.

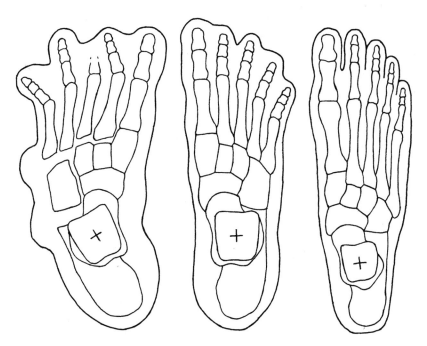

Figure 27. Cripple Foot's bone structure. An enlarged human foot (right) is compared with the author's reconstruction of the foot bones of this sasquatch, as deduced in 1970. The foot outlines are seen from below, while the bones are drawn as seen from above. This effectively mirror-images the feet—the picture on the left is based on the crippled right foot. It may be noted how the center of weight-bearing (+) is shifted relatively forward in the sasquatch.

A simple enlargement and twisting of a human foot would put these spaces (metacarpal-cuboid and cuboid-calcaneus) much closer to the heel than they are indicated to be in the cast. In order to achieve the desired positioning I had to increase the heel (calcaneus) length considerably and relatively shorten the forefoot (metatarsals). This had the effect of shifting the ankle joint somewhat forward along the length of the foot. This forward shift was reconstructed as carefully as possible, based strictly on trying to accommodate a giant human foot skeleton into the required outline and conforming to the locations of the two spaces. I then marked the center of the weight-bearing part of the talus—the surface that articulates with the bones of the lower leg—and set this reconstruction aside for a while.

All eyewitnesses agree that the sasquatch walks like a man, and this includes "stepping off" with each stride. This means that the heel of the supporting foot is lifted and the body thrust forward by backward pressure of the forefoot against the ground. In this action the walking biped lifts its entire body by extending the foot at the ankle (Fig. 28). The foot is a fairly rigid lever with its fulcrum at the center of rotation of the ankle. Power is applied by pulling up on the heel with the gastocnemius and soleus muscles that are located in the calf. This rotates the foot, pushing down its forward part and thus lifting the body. The major application of force against the ground is at the distal (forward) ends of the five metatarsals. For most of the action of walking, the freely moving toes are too weak to add significantly to this push.

Being much larger than a man, the presumed sasquatch is both heavier and stronger; but with increasing size, weight increases faster than strength. This follows from the changing geometric ratios between volume and surface area when an object is increased in size. Weight is in proportion to volume (obviously), while muscle strength increases only with the cross-sectional area of that muscle, and thus increases with surfaces in general. The increased length of an enlarged muscle adds to its weight, and to the length through which it pulls, but this adds nothing to the number of contained fibers (strength) that run through its entire body. The strength of a muscle's pull is directly proportional only to the number of fibers that pass through its cross-section, which is a surface measurement.

If an object's shape is held constant, and it is doubled in height, it will have four times the surface area and eight times the volume that it had before (Fig. 29). A one-inch cube contains one cubic inch and

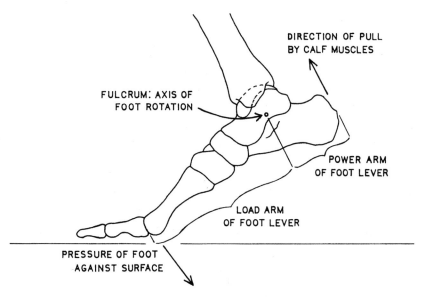

Figure 28. Human foot bones, side view. For the readers' reference, these bones are illustrated and named as seen from the medial (inside) edge. In the normal stepping-off action the foot functions as a simple lever—pulling up at the heel and pushing down at the forefoot, with a fulcrum in the ankle joint. (This can also be considered as a different type of lever, where the fulcrum is in contact with the ground, while the power and load arms begin at the heel and ankle, respectively; the resulting mechanics are the same with either interpretation.)

has a surface of six square inches, for a volume-to-surface ratio of 1:6. If this cube is doubled in length, width, and height it will contain eight cubic inches and have a surface area of twenty-four square inches, for a volume-to-surface ratio of 1:3. It now has twice as much volume, per unit surface area, as it had before. One may visualize the larger cube as being made of eight of the smaller cubes, each presenting three square inches to the outside, and three square inches against adjacent cubes, thus losing their surface areas within the larger unit.

Lesser and greater size increases can be calculated by noting the ratio of linear increase. This is squared (times itself) to get the new surface, and cubed (times itself once more) to get the volume. Thus a 50% increase in length is 1.5 times more for all linear dimensions, 2.25 (1.5 x 1.5) times more for all surfaces, and 3.375 (1.5 x 1.5 x 1.5) times more for all volume components. The volume thus gains 1.5 times as much as the surface area. Volume always gains over surface to the same degree by which the lineal measurement is increased.

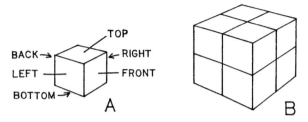

Figure 29. Volume vs. surface. A one-inch cube (A) contains one cubic inch and has a total surface of six square inches. If its linear dimensions are doubled (B) it contains 8 cubic inches and has a total surface of 24 square inches. The volume-to-surface ratio for the small cube is 1:6, for the larger cube it is 1:3. This illustrates how surface area fails to keep up with increasing volume as an object becomes larger. Muscle strength varies with surface, and weight varies with volume, thus larger animals have to be redesigned because their strength is not keeping up with their weight.

All geometric shapes follow this same rule of size increase, whether they be cubes, spheres, cones, blobs, or human bodies. In the case of humans, the difference between thin and heavyset bodies does not affect this relationship. As long as height is held constant, increasing girth adds equally to weight and to cross-sectional areas of muscles. Thus we may compare the weight and strength of the average man with that of the sasquatch as though they had the same body build.

A well-built athlete might be postulated as standing 5 feet 8 inches tall (173 cm) and weighing 160 pounds (73 kg). He can be compared with an adult male sasquatch approaching 8 feet tall. This would be the expected height of Cripple Foot, his 17-inch footprints most likely represent feet of just that length; being flexible, they need not be corrected according to my fake foot experiment (compare Figs. 7 and 18). In our one measurable case the sasquatch's visible walking height was just five times its foot length. (See my analysis of Patterson's film in the next chapter.) The walking height is less than the standing height because of its inclined torso, bent knees, and footprints indenting into the ground; these heights differ by the ratio of 12 to 13. Our cripple-footed subject should have an apparent walking height of 7 feet 1 inch (216 cm) according to my calculations, but he would stand 7 feet 8 inches (234 cm) when fully upright on a firm surface. This is the stature that we should use for most of our comparisons. The stature ratio here (between the human athlete and the male sasquatch) is 1 to 1.353, which is just a bit over a 3 to 4 ratio. This may not seem remarkable unless it is translated into actual measurements or marked on a wall.

At the same body build (which is not the case), this sasquatch would have 1.83 times the athlete's surface area and strength, but 2.48 times that man's volume and weight. The sasquatch thus has 1.353 times as much weight, per unit strength, as the man. If the sasquatch is assumed to be more heavyset than the man, both his surface and volume would be greater, but the contrast between their ratios of increase would remain the same 1.353 times. The discrepancy between a biped's weight, and his strength to move that weight, will always be the same as the ratio by which his height is increased.

In order for the sasquatch to walk and run as well as a healthy human, many small differences must exist throughout its anatomy for its strength to keep up with its weight. In terms of foot structure, this means that the ankle must be set somewhat forward—exactly how far forward may now be determined. (It should be noted that my bone reconstruction was made several weeks before any of these calculations, and thus could not have been influenced by them in any way.)

Foot leverage is commonly presented by expressing the power arm of the lever as a percentage of its load arm. The power arm is the distance from the tip of the calcaneus to the center of the talus where the tibia articulates; load arm is from the distal end of the third metacarpal to the same talar center (Fig. 30). In my reconstruction of Cripple Foot, these measure 121 mm and 223 mm, respectively. Thus its power arm was 54.3% of its load arm (Fig. 27). This means that for every unit of force by which its heel was lifted, the ball of the foot pressed down just over half as powerfully.

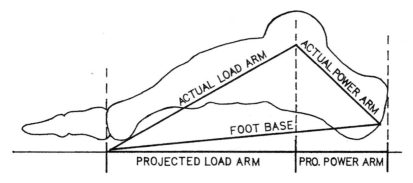

Figure 30. Lever arms of the foot. Actual levers are the two sloping lines that converge high at the center of rotation of the ankle joint. Projected lever arms, measured along the base of the foot, are the ones used here to compare living primate foot levers with sasquatch.

Aldolph Schultz (1968) published some diagrams of the feet of other higher primates. These have been measured to provide figures that may be of interest to compare with our present subject:

Orang utan	19.4%	Gorilla	45.2%
Chimpanzee	27.3%	Sasquatch	54.3%
Human	39.0%		

It may be noted that, with one exception, the relative length of the power arm increases regularly with increasing body size. The orang utan measures only 19.4%, though it is larger than the chimp, but it does not push-off with its foot as the others do when walking bipedally.

To change from the typical human size to that of the sasquatch requires a 1.353 times increase in relative foot strength for the push-off. This can be accomplished by making the load arm's percentage 1.353 times greater than the 39% of the human foot, and this comes to 52.8%. This comparison suggests that the sasquatch, with a foot lever at 54.3%, has slightly greater walking strength than is necessary for its size. The small discrepancy may also reflect some small error in my reconstruction of Cripple Foot's bones. One might use somewhat different stature estimates for the ideal human and sasquatch, and get slightly different figures than the 1.353 ratio used here, but the results will still be very close to what I found.

Following a slightly different line of reasoning, I compared the major apes' foot leverages with the actual human male average stature of 5 feet 6 inches. Since both males and females all have the same foot leverages within a given species, all of these may be taken as representing males for present purposes. (The orang is omitted for the reason given above.)

In the foot lever, the power arm as a percentage of the load arm is directly proportional to the weight-lifting ability of that foot. If all else is equal, these percentages should be directly proportional to the statures of the creatures. Starting with 66 inches for the human subject, they should follow this pattern:

Primate	Power Arm	Stature	Metric
Chimpanzee	27.3%	46.2 inches	117 cm
Man	39.0%	66.0 inches	168 cm
Gorilla	45.2%	76.5 inches	194 cm
Sasquatch	54.3%	91.9 inches	233 cm

It will be noted that the typical man's foot leverage accurately predicts the male sasquatch stature, which has been calculated by other means. This method also lines up the other two apes in the proper size sequence—one larger and the other smaller than the man. However, these apes are predicted rather far off their actual statures. Chimps are almost always taller than the predicted 3 feet 10 inches, and the gorilla is almost never as tall as 6 feet 4 inches. Differences in their locomotor designs are the source of these discrepancies, and are of no further consequence to this study.

In my judgment, no hoaxer could have figured out just how far forward to shift the ankle for a biped of the indicated size, then have left footprints with some subtle distortions that just *might* lead an anatomist to the reconstruction I made. I figured the whole thing out after studying the footprints; any hoaxer had to plan it all out from nothing. This requires an expert anatomist with a very inventive mind, more so than me, and I seriously doubt that any such person exists. And this does not take into account any of the other problems relating to how the tracks could have been planted, nor any of the other evidence that has been found.

This still does not tell us what the sasquatch weighs. With an average human body build the adult male sasquatch should weigh 2.48 times as much as our athlete, or about 400 pounds (180 kg). With the type of heavyset body that is regularly described, it would likely weigh twice as much or even more, and that would be consistent with the observations on depth of footprint impressions.

It should be mentioned that my original study of these footprints, 1972a, did not allow for the fact that different body builds do not affect foot leverages. I decided then that the sasquatch foot was designed to carry 814 pounds (370 kg) of body weight—with a heavyset build that would be true, but that idea was based on other evidence and should not have been presumed. That the stature itself is so closely predicted by this foot design is remarkable enough.

In a rather indirect manner the width of a heel imprint can be used as some indication of body weight (see my 1972b article). At each step the entire body weight is carried on one foot, and this weight is borne by the articulating surfaces at each joint of the leg, one of which is the ankle. Each such joint surface must provide enough area to distribute that weight safely; if the area is too little the cartilage on that surface might be damaged by the pressure.

Thus the area on the top of the articulating ankle bone (talus) is directly proportional to body weight. (Actually the ankle is designed for maximum stress, but this is a fairly constant multiple of body weight in most primates.)

The upper talar surface is similarly shaped in all higher primates, so if we square its width we get a good indication of its weight-bearing (and stress) capacity. Talar width is a fairly regular fraction of total heel width in humans, and it might be presumed to hold the same fraction in sasquatch as well. To have a disproportionately narrow heel base would mean a less stable support; to have a wider one would mean building a probably unnecessary structure. This all suggests that the square of the heel width should be directly proportional to body weight, at least approximately.

From a series of measurements I found that six-foot-tall men (173 cm) have heels that are 2.8 inches wide (7.1 cm). This may be compared with presumed male sasquatch heels that are 5.5 inches wide (14 cm). The sasquatch heel is two times as wide as that of a large man, and the square of this number means that they should weigh four times as much. If that man weighs 190 pounds (86 kg) then the sasquatch should weigh about 757 pounds (334 kg). Since my measurements of human heels were at the widest point, well above the floor level, their heel prints in the ground would only rarely be that wide. Accordingly, the ratio of heel widths may well be higher than two to one, and a five-times-greater weight is at least possible; this would be 946 pounds (430 kg). Some of the assumptions made here are less than certain, so the weights of 757 and 946 pounds are no more than rough indications.

There is considerable evidence for the existence of a thick pad of tightly compartmentalized fat under the soles of the feet. The first indication of this was in one of the U.S. Forest Service casts from the Blue Mountains in 1982. A foot (real or fake) was pressed into the ground directly on top of a stone that projected nearly an inch (2 cm) up into an otherwise nearly flat footprint (Fig. 14). According to police fingerprinter Edward Palma, skin detail can be seen evenly distributed over the rest of the print, thus indicating a single impression with no rocking of the object around the intruding stone. This single case suggests that there was a fat pad more than 1.5 inches thick (4 cm) in this midpart of the foot. (Cachel commented extensively on the subject in *Cryptozoology* in 1985; my reaction and her response appeared there in 1986.)

At about the same time two sheriff's deputies in western Washington (Grays Harbor County) made several casts of footprints that appeared on a dirt road. These indentations impressed about an inch into soft surface material and were stopped completely at a hard, underlying surface that left the tracks quite flat on their bottoms (Fig. 6). The side walls of these impressions were steep or vertical around much of the footprint, and even overhanging in some places. This requires that the feet had a compressible layer on the sole that bulged out to the sides under full pressure, and which immediately retracted when that pressure was relieved. There is no other way that clear skin detail could have been impressed against these vertical or overhanging side walls (Fig. 12). Some of the toe impressions spread out to one or both sides, leaving toe prints that are as much as 20 percent wider at the bottom of the imprint than they are nearer to the top. This also makes it difficult to pull cast copies of these tracks out of their molds.

A few years later a pair of track casts were made in the Blue Mountains that also showed the same steep and clearly impressed walls, as well as some toes that spread out measurably at the lowest level (Fig. 13).

Finally, another footprint was recently cast that again had a stone intruding into it, this time directly into the heel (Fig. 8). (I have already discussed the removal of this stone that came up with the cast.) Again, the impression went nearly an inch up into the heel—an action that would result in debilitating injury to a human foot with its relatively thin fat pad.

Given these four examples, and some hints from other footprints, we get a picture of a sole pad far in excess of that found in human feet. Our pads are 1 to 2 cm thick (about half an inch), with the emphasis at the heel. My best estimate is that the sasquatch sole pad is almost 2.5 inches thick at the heel (6 cm), and thinning gradually to less than half of that amount under the toes. A fat pad of almost an inch (2 cm) on the fingers, and presumably on the palms as well, was indicated by the knuckle imprint that included a side impression of the thumb and its nail (Fig. 22). This helps to explain the absence of fingernail impressions, with this one exception.

The presumed fat pads would somewhat restrict the flexing ability of fingers and toes. In the knuckle imprint, the fingers are not flexed to the 90° that we manage—they look more like about 60°–70°. The other handprints have very little finger flexion, and one of them shows none at all. The most flexed toes are impressive feats in themselves, but the degree of flexing at each joint is never more than 30°. As noted before, the near absence of flexion creases would seem to be an automatic consequence of these thick pads.

The gross anatomy of the handprints shows one feature of special interest because it was almost totally unexpected. The five available casts, representing four individuals from two locations, all show a nonopposed thumb (Figs. 20, 21, and 22). There is an eyewitness account from about 1970 of a sasquatch picking up large rocks and putting them aside, apparently in pursuit of hibernating rodents. It was noted that the thumb did not seem to be used, which could be interpreted as meaning that all five digits turned in the same direction around the rock. No one seemed to take any special notice of that seemingly minor point until Ivan Marx first announced his two handprints in 1972.

Marx's casts clearly show all digits, flattened to some degree, with the evident palmar surface of the thumb facing directly down into the dirt (Fig. 20). There is no trace of the 80° rotation that occurs in human thumbs when they are placed in that same position. In the flat handprint, with its sharply defined edges, the palmar surface of the thumb is unmistakable. This flat thumb surface is in the same plane as the palm. The larger handprint, with more rounded edges throughout, shows substantial indentations of the tips of all five digits. The direction of thumb flexion does not face across the palm as in human hands, but rather it is turned toward the wrist in almost exactly the same direction as the other digits. They are all turned as though converging on a point located on the forearm.

The muscles that flex all the joints of the digits, three for each finger and two for the thumb, are located well up in the forearm. They act by means of long tendons that pass through the wrist and insert on the undersides at the near end of each of the phalanges (finger or toe bones). The muscles that draw the human thumb across the palm act on the first metacarpal, not the phalanges. These muscles are located in the palm itself, creating a large bulge at the base of the thumb that is known as the thenar pad.

In Marx's handprints there are no thenar pads, the surface there being either flat or smoothly rounded just like the other side of the palm. The combination of a nonopposed thumb with the absence of a thenar pad is anatomically consistent. If this is a hoax, the perpetrator had to be very familiar with a variety of primate hands, most of which do have opposed thumbs and thenar pads, while some are lacking both. And this is above and beyond all the other physical problems of producing such fakes.

These two hands also show another peculiarity, the significance of which is unclear. When a human spreads his/her fingers, these four rays can be extrapolated back to meet at a point at the center of the palm-wrist juncture. In both of Marx's hand casts the fingers are fairly well spread, and these converge at a point near the wrist, but this occurs at the very outermost corner of the palm instead of at the center (Fig. 20).

Over the next two years I looked at many tens of hands to check the location of their finger-line converging point, and they all met at the middle of the wrist. Then I saw the hands of one person whose finger lines converged exactly on what might be called the sasquatch corner; this was a young woman of mixed European ancestry. Since then I have casually noted many more hands and have seen no further examples. After I first noted this trait in the hand casts it seemed like a good idea to check the finger-spread pattern of Ivan Marx himself, but I have not had the opportunity.

The knuckle imprint includes an equally nonopposed thumb (Fig. 22). When a human hand is placed in the same "knuckles-down" position, the volar pad of the thumb rests directly on the ground. In this specimen the thumb is rotated almost 90 degrees to put the edge of the thumbnail into the impression. This rotation is in the proper direction to place that nail in the same plane as the backs of the fingers.

The other pair of handprints, which were found by Paul Freeman on a stream bank in the Blue Mountains, were impressed into the ground with all digits clearly showing (Fig. 21). Fingers and thumbs were all slightly flexed, with their tips more deeply indented. The direction of thumb flexion is again clearly toward the wrist rather than across the palm. They likewise show no thenar pads. These casts also indicate unusually wide hands, with fingers of nearly uniform size, and showing little indication of flexion creases. In all these features they resemble the hand casts that Ivan Marx had obtained more than ten years earlier.

Freeman was familiar with the Marx hand casts—I had previously given him a copy of one of them. This fact might be used by skeptics to argue that he simply incorporated their major features into a new pair of fake hands, to which he added a few novelties so the that copying would not be too obvious. But if these were legitimate casts of a different individual of the same species, and from a different location, then a few variations on the basic theme is exactly what we might expect to find. In fact, the spread digit rays converge on a point on the wrist near to its inside edge, just the opposite of the peculiar location that can be seen in the Marx hand casts.

The most conspicuous variation in the Freeman hand casts is that the thumb appears to separate from the palm too far up the side of the hand. In the human hand there is a wide separation of almost an inch (2 cm) between the leading edge of the thumb and the major crease across the front of the palm. In the Freeman handprints this crease is also discernable, and the thumb's leading edge is right up against it. In contrast, the thumbs of both of the Marx handprints seem to arise very low from the side of the palm. Individual variation might be the explanation for this difference, but there are other possibilities to be considered.

The action of arching the hand in the act of imprinting might account for the odd relationship of thumb to palm. The thumb would have imprinted at the same instant as the heel of the hand. A split-second later the forward part of the hand and fingers would press down with a slight shift of location back in a wristward direction. This scenario would account for at least some of the discrepancy, but I'm dubious that it could explain all of it. Also there are no internal distortions thrown up in the imprints, as might be expected with this action. There is something unusual going on here, but I'm not sure exactly what. Among the least likely explanations would be that Freeman made an elaborate fake, with close attention to many fine anatomical details, yet failed to see this rather obvious discrepancy.

Skin Detail in the Prints

When I made a mold of the large handprint that Marx had loaned me, I first coated it with one layer of white latex and that supply was exhausted. By chance my next bottle of latex was colored red, and this was used for the remaining eight layers. When the mold was pulled off, a series of red and white parallel lines fairly "jumped" out along the edge of one finger tip. The white latex had filled some fine furrows and provided almost no cover on the ridges. The red latex showed clearly along the ridges in a pattern that was immediately recognizable.

The parallel ridges were oriented just like fingerprint lines along the edge of the last segment of the second digit, on its thumbward side. They rose only slightly, moving toward the volar surface, then faded out before the pattern type could be clearly read. My impression was that they best fit the pattern of a slowly rising arch design. If this interpretation is correct, this is the first-noticed example of dermal ridges being recorded in a sasquatch print of any kind.

There are other possible sources of parallel ridging in a cast like this, all of which should be examined before jumping to any conclusions. One possibility would be that the imprint was made with a piece of wood carved into this shape, and that the wood grain showed in just this location. The relief could result from weathering of the softer layers on this spot—why it occurs at all, and why there and nowhere else is not easily explainable. It might also result from the shaping process, like a rotary buffer that lined up with the grain in this place. Wood grain usually consists of narrow bands of hard substance alternating with wider bands of soft. The pattern here is just the reverse, with wider ridges and narrower furrows, thus making the wood-grain theory even less likely.

Another possibility that occurred to me is that these lines might represent a layering of sediments in the substratum that the hand was impressed into. This would contradict the story about its indicated origin by the act of pressing into the dirt that the hand had just dug up, but that is a secondary point. It may safely be presumed that any such depositional layering was horizontally disposed in the ground. This would mean that the hand would have to be tilted steeply for the layers to run across the finger as they do. At such a tilt one cannot easily pour a cast and keep the plaster in the impression. Yet the back of the original cast had the appearance of plaster that had freely set there in a horizontal orientation.

There is still another pertinent phenomenon of what might be called "pressure cracks" that appear in damp soil when a smooth object is pressed in and slid along its surface. These look more like a series of parallel cracks rather than fingerprint ridges, so this is not a reasonable possibility for explaining the observed lines. Since other people might be aware of this phenomenon it seemed to be at least worth mentioning.

The only thing that makes me less than sure about their identification as dermal ridges is that they are regularly spaced one millimeter apart. This is not normal for primate friction skin where in almost all species the ridges are spaced twice as closely, with two per millimeter, or fifty per inch. Spacing does vary somewhat with individuals, and especially on different parts of the hand (and foot), so I am inclined to think this actually is a small piece of a real fingerprint.

Dermal ridges appeared more dramatically in some tracks cast by U.S. Forest Service personnel in the Blue Mountains in June of 1982. I have the five casts they made at two sites in that month, and I made a mold of one cast made by a nearby Search and Rescue team that stumbled upon the first site. This is also where Paul Freeman had his first encounter with sasquatch evidence, an event that stimulated him to pursue it ever since.

The track casts in question are from two individuals, one was at the place where Freeman described seeing the animal clearly, and two sets of tracks were found six days later that included the original and a new individual. While a few traces of ridge detail showed in both casts of the first individual, these were vague enough that they alone would have stirred little more excitement than did the ridges on the earlier handprint (Fig. 31). All three casts of the unseen individual showed ridge detail on larger areas, in many more places, and much more clearly (Fig. 32). It was one of these footprints (Fig. 32, center) that had the stone protruding into its middle part. I described the overall anatomy and skin details of these casts in a lengthy article that appeared in *Cryptozoology* in 1983. The anatomical aspects are covered elsewhere in this book, and the essentials of the skin evidence are given at this point.

Clear dermal ridges can be seen on many parts of these track casts, especially around the toes, but also sporadically elsewhere over the foot. Figures 33, 34, and 35 illustrate ridge detail on various toes of the best footprint that is shown in Figure 32, right; while Figure 36 illustrates some ridge detail between two toes of the short footprint shown in Figure 32, left. This distribution is a normal occurrence because pieces of dirt tend to adhere to the more rigid parts of a living foot, being removed from one imprint and being irregularly deposited in another. The more flexible toes tend to move more cleanly from one imprint to the next. In addition, foot-pad compression often pressed skin detail into the sides of the footprints (Fig. 37), and this too was most clearly recorded in the toes.

These footprints casts have been examined in detail by police experts in the cities of Pullman, Stevenson, and Seattle in Washing-

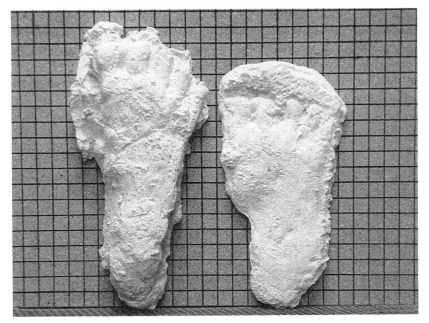

Figure 31. Tracks of 1982 sighting in the Blue Mountains The cast on the right was made where Paul Freeman reported seeing the animal on June 10. The cast on the left was made six days later and a few miles away at a place called Elk Wallow; it was impressed much more deeply into softer material. The two casts indicate the same general size and shape of foot, and in both cases the second digit shows some lateral flaring.

ton; Davis, Oakland, San Francisco, San Jose, and San Diego in California; Cheyenne, Wyoming; Denver, Colorado; Salem, Oregon; and Vancouver, British Columbia. They have been studied by the top state investigators in Wyoming, Washington, and Kansas (by Robert Olson, Sr.). The current and former heads of fingerprinting at the F.B.I. have examined them, as have several experts each at the Smithsonian Institution and Scotland Yard. Cast copies or lifts have been sent to experts in Toronto (Ontario), London (England), Moscow (old U.S.S.R.), and Beijing (China). I have omitted most of the names of these authorities because the few I did make note of would only clutter these pages, and most of these people are too busy to be pestered with numerous inquiries.

The opinions of almost all of the more than forty experts ranged from "very interesting" and "they sure look real" to "there is no doubt these are real." The only exception was the F.B.I. expert who said, approximately, "The implications of this are just too much; I can't believe it is real."

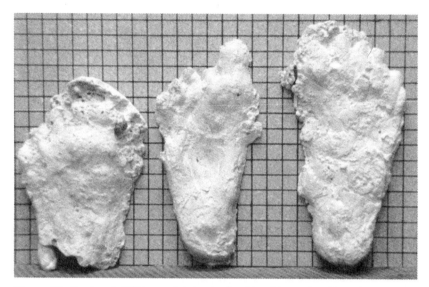

Figure 32. Tracks of 1982 non-sighting in the Blue Mountains. These casts were made at Elk Wallow on June 16 by two Forest Service workers. The individual is referred to as "Dermals" because of the clear dermal ridges that show in these imprints. Ridge details from these prints are enlarged in the next six figures.

A similar list of physical anthropologists and primatologists have seen these same casts at the Smithsonian and the universities of Washington, California, and Michigan, among others. The expressed opinions ranged from "very interesting" to "these are obvious fakes." The major exception was Tim White, at U.C. Berkeley, who studied the casts carefully and opted for a neutral stand, having found no good reason to reject them. It was interesting to note how most of these scientists looked briefly at the best cast, and then quickly handed it back to me as though it might be contagious. The only anthropologists who were satisfied that the casts represented real footprints were those few who had already decided that the creatures were real. This further illustrates the new adage, "I'll see it when I believe it."

The attitudes of most anthropologists contrasted sharply with those of most fingerprinters. Virtually all of the anthropologists were already on record as saying that the sasquatch did not exist. If they hadn't specifically said so, they did so indirectly by not including it in their list of living primates. To admit that their discipline might have missed such a large and important animal is too much to swallow. On the other hand, most of the fingerprinters are not on record as having

any opinion about the sasquatch. Its possible existence is of no particular significance to their profession. If anything, they might be concerned that someone has devised a method of making fake
fingerprints—thus their much greater interest in carefully studying
the casts.

What these fingerprinters see in the tracks are patterns of fine
parallel ridges that are oriented on various parts of the foot much as
they are on human feet. In some cases ridge detail can be seen over
entire toes, with consistent size and pattern changes from one toe to
another (Figs. 33, 34, and 36). In one case, the indented footprint
shown in Figure 32, center, ridges can be followed across the entire
forefoot without a break. Areas that should receive the most abrasion
in walking are in fact slightly worn down. What these observations
indicate is that this friction skin, as they call it, is distributed just as it
should be if these were actual footprints of a real sasquatch.

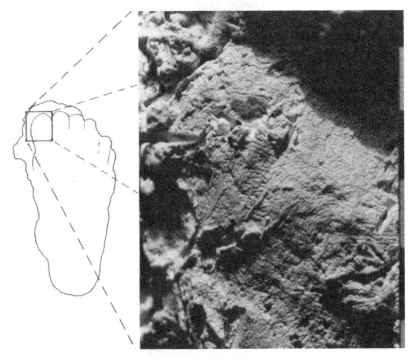

Figure 33. Ridge detail on digit I. Part of the complete left footprint of Dermals
(Fig. 32, right) is shown here with a skimming light source on one area. The general dermatoglyphics can be made out over most of the toe, and an evident scar
disrupts the pattern in the middle of this picture. (Photo by Frank Leonhardy.)

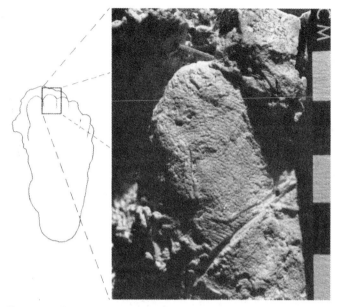

Figure 34. Ridge detail on digit II. An arching pattern can be seen over the entire toe. The center shows what appears to be abrasion from use. (Photo by Frank Leonhardy.)

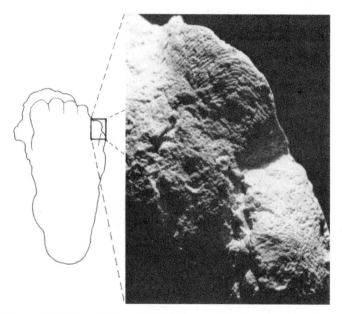

Figure 35. Ridge detail on digit V. This last digit shows perhaps the clearest ridges of the entire foot. They pass on to an additional bulge that might be an incipient sixth toe. (Photo by Frank Leonhardy.)

Figure 36. Ridge detail between digits II and III. On this incomplete cast (Fig. 32, left), two sets of dermal ridges can be seen meeting in a crease between the bases of the toes. (Photo by Frank Leonhardy.)

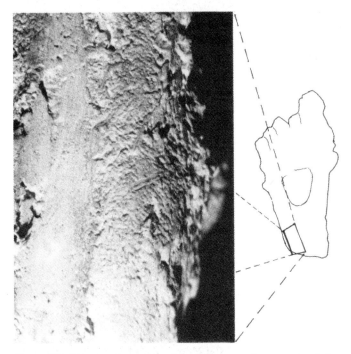

Figure 37. Skin detail on edge of foot. Dispersed segments of dermal ridges can be seen in the upper half of this photograph (Fig. 32, center). The lower part is an accidental gouge in the cast itself. This part of the cast is essentially vertical, including the area where the skin imprint occurs. (Photo by Frank Leonhardy.)

In terms of even finer detail, this friction skin passes all known tests of legitimacy. The spacing of the ridges varies somewhat, but tends to average about 20 lines per centimeter (50 per inch) just as in humans and other higher primates. In some places one can see many small indentations along the ridges, spaced about 0.5 mm apart, with these spots tending to line up in rows that run perpendicular to the ridges themselves. (See Fig. 38, which is an enlargement of part of Fig. 34.) This is just how sweat pores are distributed, so their identification seems secure.

In making cast copies of prints with friction skin, small air bubbles can be trapped along the ridges, which are actually fine furrows in the mold. Some people, including anthropologist Tim White, wondered whether the supposed sweat pores might instead be just numerous bubbles of this kind. Such bubbles do occur occasionally in the casts, but they usually can be distinguished by their greater size and their sharp, instead of rounded, edges. I tested this possibility further by making a cast of lines in a piece of clay, impressed by a fine-toothed comb. Some tiny air bubbles did occur, but they were few and easily recognized (Fig. 39). More important is the positioning of the pores in crosscutting lines running at right angles to the ridges. Air bubbles would not, and do not, orient themselves in that manner.

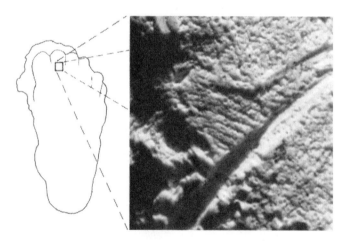

Figure 38. Magnified part of digit II. This is a small area of Fig. 34 from the center, near the bottom. What appear as small holes along the dermal ridges are interpreted by the fingerprint experts as active sweat pores. They are usually spaced about half a millimeter apart along each ridge, and tend to line up in rows running at right angles to the ridges themselves.

Figure 39. Cast of comb marks in mud. I tested the possibility that tiny air bubbles could explain the apparent sweat pores on the footprint casts, by making ridges that could not have any pores. Air bubbles did occur in this test a few times, especially along the wider lines, but more rarely on the closer-spaced ones. Actual dermal ridges are even more closely spaced. My conclusion is that a few of the larger, sharp-edged holes in the dermal ridges are air bubbles, but the majority must actually be sweat pores.

One police expert, Benny Kling, who was the first to examine these prints, commented that anyone who could engrave ridge detail of such quality and quantity should be making counterfeit money instead. When he realized how consistent the sweat pores were, he changed his mind somewhat, stating that no engraver could have produced that much consistent detail; and this doesn't even take into consideration that the faker must be an expert in dermatoglyphics as well. Further, there is the problem of how the tracks were planted, and so on.

Another characteristic that was seen by the experts is what is known as displaysia. This is a failure of the ridges to line up properly in development, so that there are patches of skin with randomly oriented short segments of ridges, often only two or three sweat pores in length. This condition occurs occasionally in human friction skin, often in the same places where it appears in these prints. The late Robert Olson was particularly impressed with this irregularity, as was Ed Palma of the San Diego Police Department. (See upper part of Fig. 37.)

Most of the problems of faking these prints have already been addressed, but there are a few more. The most common objection is that this is simply is a copy made from the friction skin of a human foot that has somehow been transferred into these tracks.

Human feet of this size and shape do not exist. While there are a few that reach the 14 inches (30 cm) of these particular tracks, no human foot of this length is as wide—6 inches (15 cm). In a response to an inquiry from Ed Palma, an expert at the Nike Shoe Company stated that when human feet reach unusual lengths, they are invariably no more than one-third as wide as they are long (see Fig. 2). This particular foot is 1.5 inches wider than that ratio would allow. The toe configurations also do not match the human design, as has already been discussed in detail.

It was interesting to discover that very tiny human feet do show some sasquatch traits—flat arch, relatively wide, more equal toes, and toe tips running nearly straight across. I made foot casts of a two-year-old child that show these traits, as well as casts of that same child's feet at nine years of age (Fig. 40). All the human distinctions develop with increasing age and size.

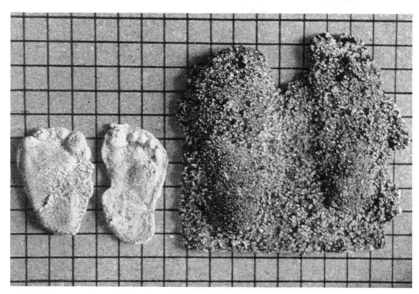

Figure 40. Young human footprint casts. At two years old (left), Jessica Draper's feet showed most of the traits of sasquatch footprints—flat, wide, and a squared-off toe line. The poor casts (right) show that her feet had developed the fully human design by nine years of age.

Transferring imprints of human friction skin in separate patches is also ruled out in at least one of these tracks (middle, Fig. 32). Ed Palma was able to trace faint ridges completely across the entire width of the broadest part of the footprint. This is the one diameter of the foot that is quite impossible to equal with a human specimen.

Of course, even if one could have located a human with feet of this size and shape, how was that person induced to make these footprints in a place that was very difficult to reach? Or were a series of casts made, carried in for miles, pressed into the ground, then carried out again without leaving footprints or other evidence of the perpetrator?

It is possible to make a cast of a human footprint, make a latex mold of that cast, then soak the latex in kerosene which will make the mold half-again larger. This can then be filled with plaster to produce a giant footprint cast, complete with dermal ridges in all the proper places. This method of faking was suggested in print by Donald Baird (1989), and a few others. I responded to the former in the same publication, the essence of which is recounted here.

The biggest problem with the kerosene treatment is that all of the ridge detail will also be expanded to half-again larger. One of the first things the fingerprinters looked at was the spacing between the ridges, and they all found them to be quite normal. Also the shape of the foot is outside the human range in terms of relative width, and its relative toe sizes and orientations do not occur in adult human feet.

An infant's foot mold could be expanded several times with kerosene to the necessary size, but then the ridge spacing would also become several times normal. Any stretching of such a latex mold in particular places will result in corresponding contrasts in ridge spacings in different directions and/or different places. Again, experienced fingerprinters would immediately pick up on these kinds of irregularities, and none has. I have also found by experiment that a latex mold cannot be increased in one dimension or in one part only—it is an all-or-nothing expansion.

The site where these dermatoglyphic footprints were found in 1982 was subjected to rather close scrutiny by the U.S. Forest Service. They brought in a border tracker, who had considerable experience trailing humans in similar environments, and asked him to assess the validity of the tracks. He judged them to be fakes. In fact, he made this pronouncement before he even looked at the tracks, according to three Forest Service employees who told me of overhearing this. Much has been made of this particular investigation (see *Cryptozoology* 1984:128-134), so perhaps it should be answered point-for-point, using the same numbers as in the critic's report.

1. Stride length did not change with slope. If fake feet were being worn, as implied elsewhere in the report, the stride certainly should have changed as the man walked up and down the slope. Only an incredibly strong creature would be able to maintain the same stride.

2. Tracks did not bottom-out in the mud, and those of the investigators sank deeper. This implies a man wearing fake feet, thus not sinking in so far, but it contradicts the finding on the road, six days before, where great weight was indicated. Possibly the moisture content of the ground had increased after the big tracks were made, as this was a swamp-like location.

3. The track series was isolated and with a clear beginning and end, quite unlike bear tracks. Without the proper kind of dirt, sasquatch tracks would be harder to follow than bear tracks because they leave no claw marks. It is also possible that the sasquatch is quite aware of leaving footprints, and plants some of them quite conspicuously as a territory marker.

4. "Toe-print" markings were clear where they should be worn smooth. As noted before, the fingerprint experts found this condition was exactly as it should be.

5. At one track, litter had been scraped away from where the print was found. Forest litter disappears remarkably well inside a footprint when it is stepped on with great weight, as I have observed in my own footprints. The surrounding area was cleared by those who first found the tracks to better examine the ground surface of the track itself.

6. Small toes did not impress deeply as in gripping the ground. Sasquatches do this only on steeper slopes.

7. No sign of heel or toe slippage on steep grades. I would expect little or none considering the deep imprints that were being made.

8a. In several places the foot appeared to have been rocked to each side to impress it. The source of this comment is unclear. If this refers to the footprint with the stone inside it, any possibility of rocking has been specifically ruled out.

8b. The toes on some tracks were wider than on others. This actually confirms that it was a living foot, and not a fake structure.

8c. "Print" marks extend up the side of the foot. This is a normal bipedal trait as may be seen by looking at your own foot, and contrasts with what is seen on the hand. Most people are unaware of this fact (obviously), and a fake track would probably not have been marked so far up the side.

8d. Instep was compressed more than it should be. The meaning of this is unclear, but it may mean that the foot was flat, as is well known.

This report from Rodney Johnson, wildlife biologist, was mostly based on the criticisms that were made by the border tracker (who filed a separate report with almost exactly the same information). Johnson, however, ended his report with some comments on how difficult it would have been to fake these tracks, and how the only method he could imagine was contradicted by other information. He supposed that a cast must have been made of an actual foot to produce these tracks, but thought this should have shown other creases from that foot. He did not address the problem that a separate cast was needed for each footprint, nor how that size and shape of foot could have been obtained.

One of my anthropologist colleagues, Dr. John Bodley, has considerable experience in animal track casting. He was interested enough in this problem to see if he could produce an acceptable fake footprint cast, complete with dermal ridges. He impressed some selected parts of his palms and feet into a clay structure that was shaped like a giant footprint. This included his own heel which he rolled across the back of the structure in order to get a full width of dermal ridge markings. He poured plaster into it for his initial cast, then pressed this object into finely prepared dirt, from which he made a dirty cast that looked much like the real thing (Fig. 41).

I took Bodley's cast, along with another from the Blue Mountains (found years after the 1982 incident) to five different fingerprint experts in California. One of these was a federal agent at Treasure Island who had a visiting colleague from Scotland Yard. In all my visits I explained the situation, saying that one of my casts was a known fabrication and that the other was taken in the forest under unclear circumstances. It took none of them longer than ten seconds to point out Bodley's track cast as an obvious fake. With much further study they could find nothing wrong with the other cast. What they all spotted were the layouts of ridge patterns that were not oriented properly in Bodley's track, but which were correct in the other.

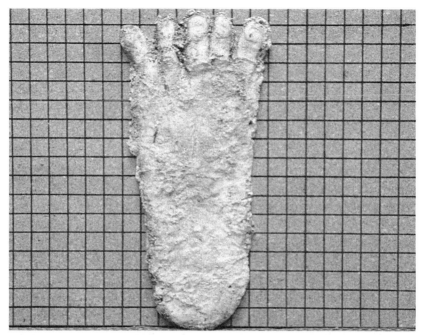

Figure 41. Dermal ridge experimental cast. Dr. John Bodley made this cast, which included impressions of his own skin. It was shown to various fingerprint experts, along with one of those from the Blue Mts. All five authorities immediately picked Bodley's cast as showing anatomically incorrect ridge orientations, but could find nothing wrong with the other one.

Since 1982 Paul Freeman has spent a great deal of time combing the Blue Mountain area for evidence and has found footprints on many occasions. He has made casts of perhaps another thirty of these tracks that I know of, and has loaned twenty of these to me for mold making (all that I asked for to copy). A few more of these also showed friction skin, but none did so as clearly as the first ones from 1982.

Some critics have complained, vocally and in print, that Freeman should not be the only one finding all these tracks unless he is faking them. Actually some other people I know have found tracks there, and many others may have as well, but they are just telling their friends about them and the information only later filters back to me. Freeman was also spending an inordinate amount of time in this effort before a foot injury curtailed most of his searching.

One of the more interesting sets of tracks Freeman cast were from a new individual, consisting of a complete right and left foot (Fig. 42) of rather small size, 13 inches long (33 cm), and the front half of another right foot. These were extensively wrinkled over much of their skin surface, and showed some faint dermal ridges as well, according to the specialists. In these tracks skin detail was clearly imprinted into often vertical and even overhanging side walls, and some of the toe prints spread widest at their deepest impression (Fig. 13). It is also the one whose partial print, moving uphill, had all of its toes strongly flexed down into the ground.

On another occasion Freeman made six casts from a longer trail, all of them showing ridges in many places, but none very clearly. A retired fingerprinter in Salem, Oregon studied the originals of these for many hours (while I watched) without finding anything to make him doubt their authenticity. One more discovery included two casts with fair ridge detail. None of the other Freeman casts showed any dermal ridges, not even the two giant handprints from the stream bank. When the grain size of the soil is too coarse, no ridges will be recorded no matter how carefully they are cast.

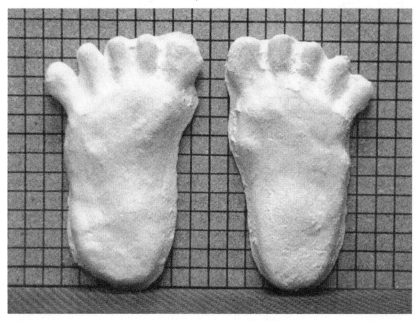

Figure 42. Casts of "Wrinkle Foot." These are the right and left footprints of a rather small individual, cast by Paul Freeman in the Blue Mts. in 1984. Edward Palma and Robert Olson saw small patches of dermal ridges in the casts, but these are almost overwhelmed by extensive wrinkling over much of the foot surface. These tracks are also not very good mirror images in the gross relief of their bottoms. I suspect that this is a very old female individual who is semi-crippled.

Anyone who might have faked these tracks faced the usual problems of getting to the sites unobserved, with the equipment that not only made the footprints but also impressed them so deeply (in most cases), made each of the prints unique and showing flexible foot movements, and left no evidence of his own presence. That faker also was an expert at dermatoglyphics who was able to include the appropriate amount of absolutely accurate friction-skin detail on a reasonable number of footprints. In spite of all this, some skeptics still think that Paul Freeman was able to accomplish the feat. I think not, and raise just one more point. We might ask a simple question, if he has somehow been faking these tracks, why has he never again matched the quality of the specimens that appeared in 1982?

Given the interest generated by the first good example of dermal ridges in sasquatch footprints, it occurred to many of us that there might be other examples already in existing collections. I soon was able to carefully examine all the casts held by Bob Titmus and John Green, but found only a few that showed what at best might be called traces. Titmus thinks that this kind of detail probably was recorded on many footprints that were cast during Tom Slick's expeditions in northern California from 1959 to 1962. Many of these were made in a clay substratum, but no one at the time seems to have paid attention to any such markings. All of the Tom Slick bigfoot evidence has long since disappeared, but there is some chance that it might be relocated. Given the reluctance of the appropriate authorities to accept the Blue Mountain evidence, it is not likely that some more such tracks from California would prove to be any more convincing.

More recently, in May of 1990, a construction worker sent me a footprint cast from southern Indiana (Fig. 43). There are many reports of sasquatch-like evidence from the eastern United States and Canada, but this was the first tangible evidence from east of the Rockies that I have been able to examine first hand. Bob Titmus, who is very alert to the possibility of faked tracks, studied this one carefully and decided it had all the signs of a legitimate imprint from a living foot. I also brought the cast to the San Diego Police Department, where Ed Palma and his colleagues pronounced the several patches of ridge detail as consistent with a real primate foot of that size, almost 14 inches long (35 cm). They all agreed that no human foot could have made that imprint. It also showed the two sasquatch traits that I have never revealed to anyone.

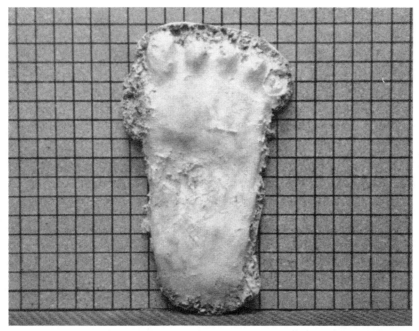

Figure 43. Indiana track cast. This cast was sent to me by a man from Blooming-ton, Indiana, who wanted to have nothing more to do with the subject. It passed all tests for legitimacy by Bob Titmus and Ed Palma and is the best evidence I currently have from east of the Rocky Mountains.

The man who sent this Indiana track provided me with only a brief description of the footprint circumstances, and has since moved to an undisclosed location. He indicated that he wanted nothing more to do with the "damned thing," as he called it, and cannot be reached for any further communication on the subject.

I see no point in pushing this dermatoglyphics issue any further with the Scientific Establishment. I have expended rather enormous amounts of my own time, trouble, and money to make the scientific world aware of the Blue Mountain tracks with dermal ridges, and to no avail. Without any means of confirming the source of the new Indiana specimen, there is no reason to think that it would stir any more interest.

As sort of a postscript to this subject I should mention the dermal ridges in the casts of Cripple Foot. My casts were latex copies of dirt copies of the originals. I showed these to Ed Palma, just to satisfy his curiosity, shortly after this dermatoglyphic investigation began. He looked them over and pointed out three patches where he claimed to see traces of ridge detail. I studied those places intently and saw absolutely nothing, but I remembered their locations. About two years later Rene Dahinden showed me the originals of these casts, which he had located and acquired. In all three places that Palma had indicated I could now see a few faint ridges. Needless to say, this man's professional qualifications are outstanding.

When I first realized the potential significance of dermal ridges showing in sasquatch footprints, it seemed that scientific acceptance of the existence of this species might be achieved without having to bring in a specimen of the animal itself. It was this hope that drove me to expend so much of my resources on it, and of my scientific reputation as well. Having lost this battle almost totally, I am reluctant, and for all practical purposes unable, to pursue this line any further. New information of this kind might be described in future pages of *Cryptozoology*, and I'll tell the news media if they ask, but that's about as far as I can carry this particular load.

4

THE PATTERSON FILM

On October 20, 1967 two young men from Yakima, Washington, were in northern California looking for bigfoot evidence. Roger Patterson was making a documentary film of the area, some footprints, and himself in the role of the hunter. He had a history of intense interest in this creature and had recently (1966) published a book on the subject. Robert Gimlin went along for the ride, being fairly sure that no such animal existed, but he was willing to help his friend in this endeavor. They had discussed what to do if they actually saw a bigfoot, as Patterson preferred to call it, and decided to film it and not to shoot. Years later, Gimlin said that this was a big mistake, and Patterson seemed to grudgingly agree.

The pair were riding horseback along the bed of Bluff Creek in the general area where sasquatches had disturbed the road-building operation just nine years previously. At one point they rode around a large obstacle in the creek bed and saw a sasquatch crouching beside the creek to their left. It reacted abruptly to the men's presence by standing up and walking away, from left to right, and at a considerable angle away from the men. Bob Titmus, who studied the tracks nine days later, told me that the initial confrontation was at a distance of less than 25 feet (perhaps 7 m).

Immediately upon the mutual sighting, Patterson's horse reared and fell over backward on top of him. He quickly extricated himself and retrieved his 16mm movie camera. The sasquatch no doubt had a good look at him during those first twenty seconds before the filming began and apparently saw no great cause for alarm, but decided to depart from the area anyway. The film begins when Patterson is at a distance of 112 feet (34 m) behind the creature, somewhat to the right of it's path, and running toward it about half-again faster than it

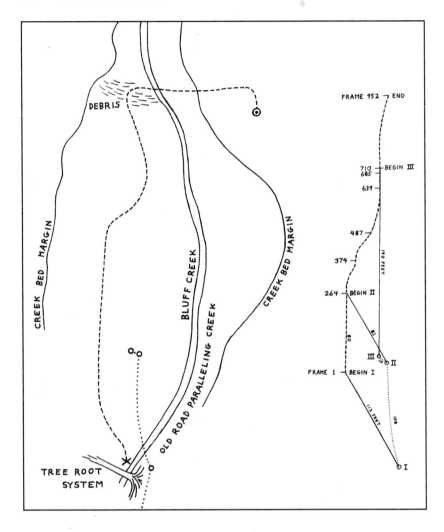

Figure 44. Ground plan of Patterson's Film. On the left is the map drawn by Robert Titmus when he examined the tracks of the participants nine days after the filming. On the right is the author's reconstruction based on study of the film itself. On both maps, X marks the location of the sasquatch at the moment of sighting, and the dashed lines represent its course as it walked away. The lowermost circle on each map marks the location of the two men at the moment of sighting, and the dotted lines represent Patterson's course of travel while filming. The two later circles mark Patterson's two stationary filming positions. The Titmus map includes some of the local terrain; it also follows the subject's trail, after the filmed part, up the hill to where it sat and watched for some time at the position marked by a circle with a dot inside. The author's map includes camera directions at the beginnings of the three filming positions and the actual distances involved. The author's map was plotted by measuring how the subject decreased in size and shifted position against the background. These two maps show reasonable agreement.

is walking. At first the film jumps badly, the small image usually being unrecognizably blurred or completely off the frame. Whenever it can be seen clearly, it is simply walking away. (See Fig. 44 for two versions of a complete ground plan of the filming positions and the movements of Patterson and the sasquatch.)

After Patterson had closed the distance between it and himself to just 81 feet, he stumbled to his knees but kept the camera going. About then the sasquatch turned its head (and upper body) to face him briefly while continuing to walk with long strides. As Patterson told me: "It looked at me with such an expression of contempt and disgust, that I just stayed right there." The way he put it to John Green was "You know how it is when the umpire tells you 'one more word and you're out of the game'; that's the way it felt."

From where he stopped, Patterson was able to hold the camera fairly steadily for most of the remaining filming. The creature's legs were obscured by stream debris in many of the best frames, such as Figure 45, and it was getting progressively smaller on the frames as the distance increased.

Figure 45. Artist's rendition of the classic frame from Roger Patterson's film. At this point in the 53-second movie the subject is in the middle of a turning look toward the photographer, and from a distance of 102 feet. This is frame 352 from the total of 952. It shows how small the figure is within the field of vision.

Near the end of the footage, Patterson quickly moved his position about 10 feet to the left (3 m) for a better view. The subject continued to walk almost directly away (Fig. 46) until the camera ran out of film when it was at a distance of 265 feet (80.8 m). The entire incident was over in less than two minutes, and Patterson had 952 frames of color film of the first and only sasquatch he ever saw.

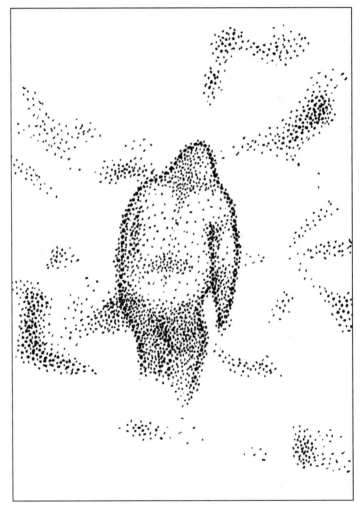

Figure 46. Frame near end of film. This late image shows the subject walking directly away from the camera. It is much enlarged and understandably has lost detail. Drawings based on Patterson's film have been made for Figures 45, 46, 59, and 60. The author's copy of the film may be viewed by serious investigators.

Throughout the event, Gimlin was on his horse nearby, holding his 30.06 rifle, and being rather amazed by what he saw. This was evidently a female sasquatch that I have since determined to stand 6 feet 6 inches tall (2 m) and weighing about 500 pounds (230 kg). They had been seeing occasional tracks of three sasquatches in the area, of different sizes, and they assumed that they were looking at the medium-sized one. Years later, Gimlin told me that at the time he was wondering what they would do if the big one showed up.

After the creature was gone, Patterson and Gimlin measured the stride length and made casts of the clearest right and left footprints they could find. They covered many more tracks as best they could, and then left the area.

Bob Titmus located the place nine days later and plotted the paths of all the participants from their footprints; his map is remarkably similar to what I reconstructed from the film twenty-four years later. He was able to document the event from the beginning, while my study necessarily starts only with the existing film record. He tracked the animal from where it left the movie site, walked up a hill, and back to an overlooking position only 125 yards from the point where the encounter began. There it apparently sat down for some time watching through an opening in the vegetation while the two men were looking at and casting tracks, quite unaware of their observer. Titmus then made casts of another ten consecutive footprints in a row. (I have copies of eight of these; one had been given away many years ago, and I still plan to get a copy of the last one.) Titmus noted that four tracks showed clear evidence of having been cast when he arrived, but Patterson claimed to have cast only two. I can find no one who knows anything about the others.

Throughout the filming incident, and judging from its behavior immediately afterwards, the sasquatch did not seem to be much bothered by the men's presence; one could infer that it just preferred not to be near them. It showed no panic or great haste, and looked at the men only once for a few steps during the filming time. This is about average behavior from what I have heard about other sasquatch encounters. Sometimes they beat a more hasty retreat, while at other times they seem almost to ignore the human presence.

Patterson had the film developed as soon as possible. At first he thought he had brought in proof of bigfoot's existence and really expected the scientists to accept it. Actually only a few scientists were willing even to look at the film, and most of them promptly declared it to be a fake. It was then incorporated as the centerpiece of the documentary film that Patterson had set out to make in the first place. This was taken around and shown in local movie houses all over the Pacific Northwest, and it brought in a fair amount of money that way. Patterson also sold various rights to the film to a number of people. As it turned out later, some of these rights were overlapping and even duplicating in a legal tangle. Patterson himself died in 1972 while public interest was still fairly high, but scientific interest remained negligible.

The Subject

Opinions differ on just what it was Roger Patterson photographed that afternoon many years ago. Most of those who accept the sasquatch as a real animal have accepted the film as authentic; a few are dubious. All of those who deny any reality to the sasquatch obviously have to reject the film as being some kind of hoax. Given the apparent size, posture, and walking stride, the only possible hoaxing method would have to be a large man wearing a fur suit.

Many people have expressed opinions on the details of what can and cannot be seen in the film. Only a few of these opinions are based on technical expertise and careful study of the film itself. The best of these are by Dmitri Donskoy in Moscow and D.W. Grieve in London, who independently studied the film when it was brought to them by Rene Dahinden in 1971. Both of these men are highly respected experts in the biomechanics of human locomotion at prestigious institutions. Their reports are printed in full in Byrne's book of 1975, and Grieve's also appears in Napier's book of 1972. Donskoy found the creature to be a very massive animal that is definitely not a human being. Grieve gave a more qualified opinion—if it was filmed at 24 frames per second it could be a rapidly walking man; if it was at 18 frames per second it "exhibits a totally different pattern of gait" and cannot be human. It is shown below that it was in fact filmed at 18 frames.

Other favorable opinions come from experts with different technical backgrounds: Robert Titmus is a game hunter/tracker and taxidermist, John Green is a editor and newsman, Peter Byrne is a game hunter and photographer, Rene Dahinden is a long-time sasquatch investigator, and Dmitri Bayanov and Igor Bourtsev who have investigated similar phenomena in the old U.S.S.R. On the other side, John Napier, an expert in primate locomotion, decided that either the film was fake, or the footprints were fake, or both. Bernard Heuvelmans, the pre-eminent authority on unverified animals, is quite sure the film was faked. But Ken Peterson, a senior executive with Disney Studios, told John Green in 1969 that their technicians would not be able to duplicate the film. This is a fair sample of the most authoritative opinions, pro and con, by those who have thoroughly studied the evidence.

For the last three years I have tried to find more experts in human biomechanics who could analyze my copy of the film with more modern techniques and equipment. The only one I could locate was Gordon Valient, head research scientist for Nike Shoe Company in Beaverton, Oregon. Using his best equipment, Valient found that the film was too small and unclear for any standard analysis he could perform. He did, however, look carefully at all of the better frames and made useful observations about some rather unhuman movements that he could see. More importantly, he loaned me an old hand-cranked film viewer that illuminates one frame at a time with a ten-times enlargement. With all other avenues blocked for now, I undertook to analyze the film in detail by myself.

To begin with, we have only four items of factual measurement outside of the film itself, as measured at the site or on the retrieved casts:

1. The subject's stride, as from left heel to the next left heel, was typically 81.5 inches (207 cm).
2. The footprints are 14.5 inches long (36.8 cm).
3. The prints' heels are 4.5 inches wide (11.4 cm).
4. The camera was 102 feet (31.1 m) from the subject at the most published frame with its out-spread arms and looking at the cameraman.

A small, dark brown image can be seen walking within a large field of view; at its closest, the figure stands only 1.66 mm on the actual film, inside an area measuring 10 mm wide by 7.5 mm tall. Nevertheless it is possible to measure the image with some accuracy in many places—at 0.1 mm increments on the 10 x enlargement, thus 0.01 mm on the film itself. Further enlargement was not productive because of the vague outlines that appear.

With the above data and measurements, and some simple mathematics, it was possible to determine the following information:

1. Speed at which it was filmed.
2. Height of the subject.
3. Exact course of travel, as well as positions of and distances from the camera.
4. Body shape and dimensions, hence its volume and probable weight.

After obtaining the above information, as the next several pages show, the nature of the subject is easily and clearly established.

Film Speed. Patterson normally had his camera set on 24 frames per second. Some time after the filming he noticed it was set on 18 frames. He did not know when the setting was changed, and it was only a good guess that it happened when he hurriedly pulled the camera out of the saddle bag. This is especially important in terms of Dr. Grieve's analysis, where 24 frames would allow it to be a human subject, but 18 frames would not. This speed also must be known in order to establish the creature's exact course of travel during the filming, and this in turn is necessary in order to find out some of its measurements.

The most obvious way to determine the film speed is to compare it with a human of known height who is walking in the same manner. In both cases, arms and legs swing like slightly modified pendulums, and their periods of swing are directly proportional to the square roots of the pendulums' lengths. The film subject has a ratio of leg length to stature like an average human; Grieve measured this (my measurements and Green's agree), and no one has expressed a contrary opinion. I used myself as the comparative biped.

At a fast walk, clearly faster than the subject appears to be moving, it takes me 1.15 seconds to make a full, two-step stride. At a slow walk, apparently slower than the subject moves, it takes me 1.3 seconds to make a two-step stride. These stride speeds were measured repeatedly over a long course. If the subject was my size, its walking speed was somewhere between 1.15 and 1.3 seconds per stride. If the film was made at 24 frames per second, the subject's walking speed was less than one second per stride (0.9375 seconds to be exact). This is an extremely fast movement, and would require a large person to make jerking stops and starts at the ends of each arm and leg swing; these jerks would not likely be the same with each step. Since the subject is seen to move with smooth arm and leg swings, and they are very regularly 22.5 frames per stride, at this film speed it could not be a person of my size or larger. At 24 frames per second, a normally walking subject, making one stride in 0.9375 seconds, would most likely stand about 3 feet 8 inches tall (112.5 cm). If it was imitating my "slow" pace it could be as tall as 4 feet 2 inches, and at my "fast" pace it should be only 3 feet 3 inches tall; the midpoint of this range is just over 3 feet 8 inches. With normal pendulum-type swings of the arms and legs, as can be seen in the film, this is the size range that is required for this fast filming speed. Such

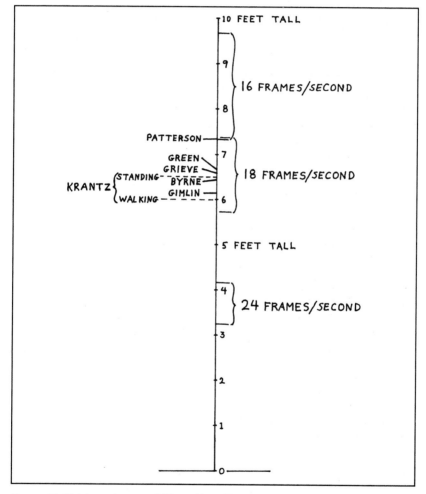

Figure 47. Height estimates of film subject. Two witnesses and four film examiners made the stature estimates shown on the left. At normal walking rates, the three bracketed height ranges on the right are based on the three possible filming speeds. It would appear, without reasonable doubt, that it was filmed at 18 frames per second.

short people are rare to begin with, and the 14.5 inch footprints are incompatible with these statures. In sharp contrast, Patterson thought his subject was 7 feet 4 inches tall, while Gimlin estimated it at 6 feet 1 or 2 inches (223.5 vs. 184 cm). Figure 47 shows this and all other estimates of stature that are discussed here.

If the film was made at 18 frames per second the subject had to be moving at 1.25 frames per stride. This is between my own two measured striding speeds, and somewhat closer to my slower rate of walking. The same reasoning then points to 7 feet 4.6 inches tall if it matched my "slow" walk, and 5 feet 9.3 inches if it matched my "fast" speed. These figures are again based on the pendulum-like swing of the arms and legs at each of these heights. The midpoint of this range is 6 feet 7 inches (175 cm). This figure is at least compatible with all other available evidence.

The possible speed of 16 frames per second has also been mentioned by some writers. At this rate the subject should have been 9 feet 8 inches tall at my "slow" walking speed, or 7 feet 4 inches at my "fast" walk. The midpoint of this range is 8 feet 6 inches (234 cm). This filming speed is not quite so easy to eliminate from consideration, but the midpoint of this size range is clearly out of the question, and even the lowest figure is well above all other estimates except for that of Patterson himself. Given the filming circumstances, and who was doing what at the time, it would seem to me that Gimlin's estimate was probably the more reliable. We may safely rule out 16 frames per second and accept the speed of 18 frames. It necessarily follows that the subject's legs were of a length compatible with those of a man standing somewhere between 5 feet 10 inches and 7 feet 4 inches, and most likely somewhere near the middle of this range.

Further confirmation of this filming speed comes from the Russian investigator, Igor Bourtsev. In the early part of the film he found camera jumps that tended to be spaced at intervals of sometimes 4 and sometimes 7 frames. These were interpreted as movements corresponding to Patterson's running and walking steps. My own frame-by-frame study could not support this in terms of blur spacing, but spacing between the occasional clear frames did follow that pattern in some places. I found spacings of 4, 5, and 7 frames to be the most common, and no other number was evident.

Bourtsev reports that sprinters manage five steps per second. If the filming speed was 24 frames, Patterson must have been running at six steps per second, and this is clearly impossible. At 18 frames he was running at 4.5 steps per second and at 16 frames he did 4 steps per second. Either of these last two are possible, though 4 steps seems more reasonable for most men who are not practicing athletes. On the other hand, Patterson stood only a little over five feet tall (160 cm), so his running pace would be notably faster than for a larger man.

The 7-frame jumps would not exactly represent a walking speed, because at his height Patterson would require just over 10 frames for each such step. At the time it is not likely that he would have been walking at a normal striding gait while he was trying to close the distance to his quarry. Most reasonably he was alternating between a rapid run and a "forced" walk.

Subject's Height. The height of the film subject is determined by comparing the known foot length with the foot-to-height ratio that can be seen on the film. As a foot first strikes the ground at the normal walking angle, it causes the footprint to be slightly extended to the rear. On the other hand, the footprint contours indicate that the longest part of the heel was not into the ground when the foot rested flat. My experiments with real and artificial feet (see Chapter 2) suggest that these two factors exactly cancel each other, so the feet were in fact 14.5 inches long (36.8 cm), just as measured on the casts.

I found ten frames where the full length of the foot can be seen in a vertical position. Casual estimates, by myself and others, are that about six of its foot lengths appear to equal the visible stature. Actual measurement, however, shows that in these ten frames the average is just five of its foot lengths to its height. Five times the foot length is only 6 feet (183 cm) and that must be the actual walking height of the subject. This is slightly lower than the lowest estimate made by any other authority, but it is very close to the one that I consider to be the most dependable.

It should now be pointed out that this reconstructed stature is the subject's *walking* height, not its *standing* height (see Fig. 47). The weight-bearing leg shows a knee bend much more than is usual in humans, and the torso leans forward at the hips. I asked three careful observers to look at blow-up frames of the film and put me in the same pose. This posturing reduced my standing height by almost five inches. Applying the same ratio to the film subject, and allowing for the fact that its feet sunk an additional inch into the ground, we find that it must have had a standing height of 6 feet 6 inches (198 cm). When we speak of sasquatch stature it should be made clear whether we are talking about walking height or how tall it would be standing erect on a firm surface. There appears to be a ratio of 12 to 13 between these two figures; whatever its walking height may measure in feet, the same number of inches should be added to represent its standing height. When Gimlin called it 6 feet 1 or 2 inches tall, it is not clear which of these two heights he had in mind, or if he was even aware of the distinction.

John Green made a different attempt to determine the subject's stature by making a duplicate film of a person of known height at the same place. He was able to position his camera at just the same point, but since this was done several months later they could not be certain of the exact line of travel of the subject. By superimposing the two films—the original subject and Jim McClarin standing 6 feet 5.5 inches wearing boots (197 cm)—he found them to be rather close (Fig. 48). Precise orientation of the two films against each other was not possible, but at least this procedure seemed to establish some limits. One orientation made the sasquatch just over 6 feet 9 inches tall, while at the other extreme it could have been only 6 feet 3 inches (206 vs. 190 cm).

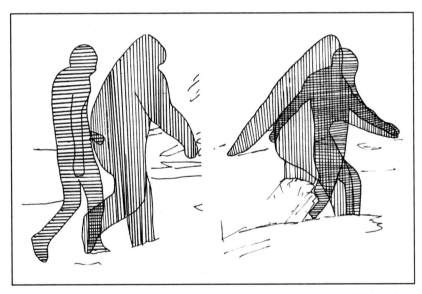

Figure 48. Comparison with a known film. Here are John Green's (1968) outlines from his footage of Jim McClarin superimposed on Patterson's subject. Exact positioning of the two films was not possible, but it set some limits that I interpret as putting the unknown animal somewhere between 6 and 6.5 feet tall. The lowest stature is supported here on other evidence.

In this experiment no one considered that McClarin's walking height was substantially shorter than his standing height. I have compared my own walking and standing heights (with the help of an observer), and made the same comparison by myself on another person. The amount of height that is lost depends to a large degree on the subject's habitual posture. McClarin does not walk with "ramrod" pose, and he most likely lost a good 2.5 inches from his standing height. Making this correction reduces the subject's walking height to anywhere between 6 feet 6 inches and just 6 feet (198 vs. 183 cm). This lowest figure is exactly what I determined from comparisons of foot length to visible stature, so this may be considered to be reasonably confirmed as the walking height of the movie subject.

A final method of estimating stature is to compare the known length of its walking stride with the most likely human stature that would correspond with it. This approach presupposes a stride-to-stature ratio similar to our own, and all observers seem to be in general agreement on this. An old rule of thumb is that a man's standing height is about equal to one full stride (two steps). Actually the stride is usually a bit longer, typically 1.034 times the standing height. (In Grieve's report this was incorrectly given as 1.34 times standing height; the reader might try to walk with steps of this relative length.) Taking the known stride length of 81.5 inches and dividing it by 1.034 gives a standing height of 78.8 inches, which is within one inch of the stature that was otherwise calculated. From this standing height, its walking height should be reduced by 5 inches for posture and 1 inch for ground impression.

Course of Travel. At this point we have established the subject's walking height; we already knew its stride length and the measured distance from the camera in one clear frame. It is now possible to reconstruct its exact course of travel and the camera positions for the entire film. I will not recount every measurement here, but the basic method is fairly simple and, hopefully, easily understood. I was able to make fairly accurate measurements on a series of frames beginning at the point where Patterson stopped running, and including the classic frame that has been the most publicized. The most detailed study involves 111 frames, which represent 110 consecutive short moves.

On a given frame, the observed height of the image in millimeters is compared with the known height of the subject in inches. Ten frames later the reduction in image height can then be translated into how many inches the subject has moved farther away from the camera. This also requires a known distance of at least one frame from the camera, and this is available for the classic one. In the same ten frames, movement of the subject to the right can be measured in millimeters against a background tree. (This was always done from the edge of the tree to the crown of the creature's head.) This amount is then similarly translated into the number of inches the subject has shifted to the right, using its known height as a reference. With such small units as 10 frames (movements of mostly 20 to 30 inches) the two calculated position changes will be at 90° to each other, and can be drawn as two legs of a right triangle.

Starting from frame zero, it is possible to visualize a shift to the right by a determined number of inches, and a displacement directly away from the camera by a different number of inches. The actual movement of the subject was along the remaining, longer side of that triangle, known as the hypotenuse. There is a simple formula for calculating the length of that third side, which works with any units of measurement, English or metric, as long as the same units are used for all three sides of the triangle. The square of the hypotenuse is equal to the sum of the squares of the other two sides. Thus, the length of one side is multiplied by itself, the same is done with the other side, the two results are added together, and the square root of that sum is calculated. We then have a measure of exactly how far the subject had moved along its diagonal walking path during those ten movie frames. We can also calculate the exact angle at which it was moving away in relation to the film plane of the camera. (This could also be given in relation to the line of sight, if one prefers.)

A simple check on the accuracy of this method of triangle building is the fact that we already knew the approximate length of the hypotenuse of all those triangles. Knowing the film speed, and having counted the frames in nine full strides, we also know that it takes 22.5 frames for it to walk one average stride of 81.5 inches. Thus it moves 36.22 inches in every ten frames; that is the typical hypotenuse. The calculated and known lengths of each of the "movement" triangles were in almost exact agreement. I found that it averaged 36.68 inches in the 11 moves (of 10 frames each) that were measured most accurately. This is only 1.3% more than the 36.22 inches per 10 frames that can be calculated from the measured stride. Both methods include variations that are well in excess of this small difference. Since neither method was applied to the entire filmed walk, the two measurements may be considered to be essentially the same.

It should also be mentioned that I used a separate method to correct for possible errors in measurements on the film. The image was always a bit fuzzy around the edges, and an error factor of a few percent was likely. I graphed the many stature measurements, spaced in proportion to the numbered frames that they came from, and drew a careful line averaging their positions. The same was done for the gradual right shifts in the same frames.

As it turned out, the stature decrease and right shift did not always change at perfectly even rates. I reasoned that if the subject made a change of direction along its course of travel in these frames, this should show in a change of slope in both curves. For instance, if it was turned more away from the camera it should show more decrease in stature and less right shift in the same frames. Likewise, if it veered more to the right, there should be less decrease in stature and more right shift in a few frames. The relationship between these two changes in rate should always be complementary, as long as the subject is maintaining a fairly steady walking speed. Some gradual changes of direction were in fact indicated in the measurement data, shown in my detailed map of travel for the best 111 frames (Fig. 49).

Good measurements of stature could be made only occasionally and often not with great accuracy (one point proved to be 3% off the averaging line). As a further check I also measured the crown-to-rump height in all possible cases. Where both measurements were fairly clear, the torso was regularly 64% of the walking height. This served as a double check on the accuracy of each set of measurements. Armed with these data I could then make accurate stature estimates in many more places where the legs were not fully visible.

The procedures described above were applied in detail to the clearest 111 frames, from 264 to 374. Within this stretch I found 15 frames with good measures of its stature and right shift. These were all plotted on a graph, the connecting lines evened out, and then remeasured at regular 10-frame intervals (Fig. 49). This produced the exact relative position of the subject for 12 evenly spaced locations, representing 11 moves of 10 frames each. Connecting these points with a gently curving line gave its course of travel (Fig. 50). This particular stretch also included the 31 frames that Grieve had analyzed in some detail, as well as the classic picture with outspread arms where it is looking at the photographer (Fig. 45).

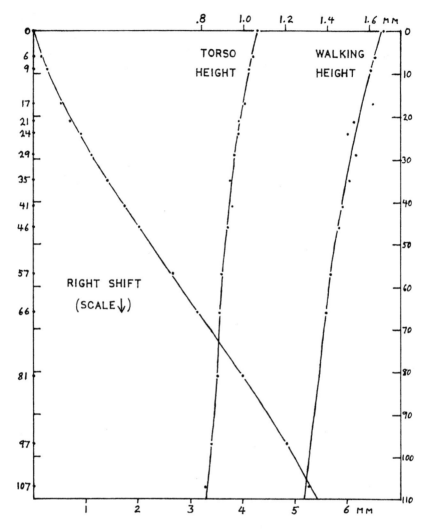

Figure 49. Detailed measurements from Patterson's film. Frame numbers within the closely measured series are marked down the left margin—0, 6, 9, 17, etc.; study segments ten frames apart are marked down the right margin. The more diagonal line connects the measurements of right shift, and their scale is given across the bottom. The more vertical lines connect measurements of torso height and walking height, and their scale is given across the top. The connecting lines were drawn carefully, then the values for every tenth frame were read from those lines. This procedure yields a high degree of accuracy by correcting for individual measurement errors. The two height graphs are also mutually correcting because the torso averaged 64 percent of the walking height—each was used to cross-check the other. Finally, the slight curves in all three lines should and did correspond, thus additionally correcting for slight errors in all measurements.

The course of travel for these 111 frames can now be translated into a more realistic map by correcting for parallax. That means changing the shape of the big square into one with converging sides that point to the camera's location (Fig. 51). In this map it was possible to calculate the actual distances only because we had the exact measurement from the camera to the classic frame.

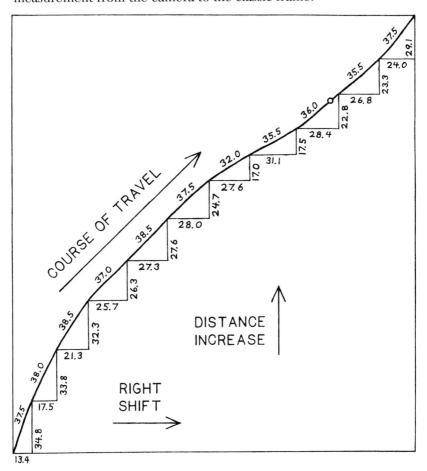

Figure 50. Detailed map of travel. Frames 264 to 374, in groups of ten, show this course of travel, from left to right and moving away from the camera. In this drawing the camera is treated as being located an infinite distance away (down on the map). Each measurement of right shift and increasing distance is given in inches. The hypotenuses, or actual walking course, were drawn and measured between each of the ten-frame positions. These lengths correspond closely with the average stride lengths as measured on the ground. The classic frame with outstretched arms is marked with a circle near the end of this sequence.

Figure 51. Adjusted course of travel. Here the map that was shown in the previous figure is corrected for the actual camera location, which was much less than an infinite distance away. The only direct measurement made at the film site was of 102 feet at the classic frame, and other distances were calculated back and forth from this datum.

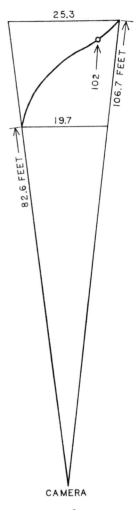

For later parts of the film the same procedure was used to reconstruct the subject's course of travel, but generally with much coarser units. For the part where it cannot be seen behind the trees I simply continued the curves from before and after those frames. For the first part, where Patterson ran while he was filming, only the roughest course estimate could be made.

It was interesting to discover that the first frame was shot from just 112 feet away (34 m), as deduced from the image size of the subject. Since that first frame shows a fairly clear picture, it might be guessed that any earlier footage was all of poor quality and was simply discarded as being of no value. If Byrne was correct in reporting that Patterson had 28 feet of film in the camera when the action began, as many as 185 frames could be missing. However, based on the Titmus map of the site there was no space available for more than a handful of missing frames. Only if Patterson had stayed at the beginning point for a little over 10 seconds could those 185 frames have been exposed. But if he had held his position for that portion, the film should have been of fairly good quality and we would have seen it. I can only conclude that this theoretical footage never existed, and Patterson actually had only 23.4 feet of unexposed film in his camera when the action began.

Subject's Shape and Dimensions. Given a known course of travel we now know by just how many degrees the subject is moving away

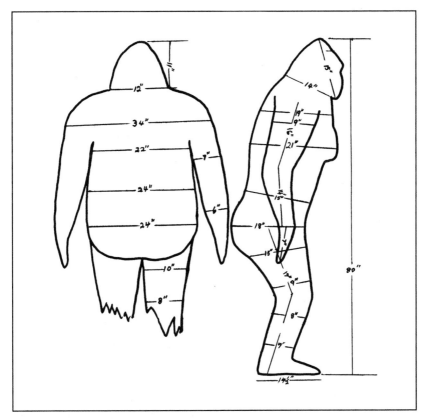

Figure 52. John Green's measurements of the subject. Using what I consider too great a height, Green (1968) made these estimates of various body dimensions soon after the film became available. While these measurements may be reduced somewhat, the general proportions remain essentially as given here.

from the film plane of the camera. This in turn allows us to make some new estimates of its shoulder breadth. John Green had put this at about 34 inches (86.4 cm) and acknowledges that this, like all other width measurements, is only a rough approximation (Fig. 52). Correcting from Green's estimate of its walking height at 80 inches down to the demonstrated 72 inches, this reduces the shoulder width to 30.6 inches (all linear measurements being reduced by 10%). This must again be corrected downward by an additional small amount, as is described in the next three paragraphs.

My own measurements on the film of the shoulder breadth and torso height were made near the end of the film where its back is directly to the camera. In the three usable frames its shoulder breadth averaged 64.4% of its torso height, with only slight variation. Since the subject leans a bit forward, its torso height is slightly reduced from what was earlier measured (along the slant) to compare with stature. With a 2% correction in torso height, the ratio of shoulder to torso now becomes 63.1%. With the torso already established at 64% of the visible height, we can say that the shoulder width is 40.4% of its walking stature. At 72 inches tall, this film subject appears to have shoulders that are 29.1 inches wide.

A more complicated calculation was made that depended on measuring the image width in the clearest frames and correcting these according to the angle from which it was viewed. This procedure involved first correcting the visible shoulder width to the projected line that runs directly from side to side. (The visible image includes an element of chest depth that changes with its orientation.) The straight-line shoulder breadth is then converted, according to its angle of view, to how it would appear from directly behind (Fig. 53). Seven such measurements were obtained from the seven largest and sharpest images, as plotted in Figure 54 on the best-studied frames. They represented different angles of observation, each of which was separately calculated. These all averaged 28.5 inches or 27 inches, depending on which of two designs of shoulder shape that was presumed.

In my opinion, the angled shoulder reconstruction is a little more accurate than the method using rear views, even if it is more complicated. The images that I used were larger, and it is based on the sum of seven calculations that agreed with each other even more closely than did the three more distant views. Accordingly I chose to use the average of the two results from angled shoulders and one from the

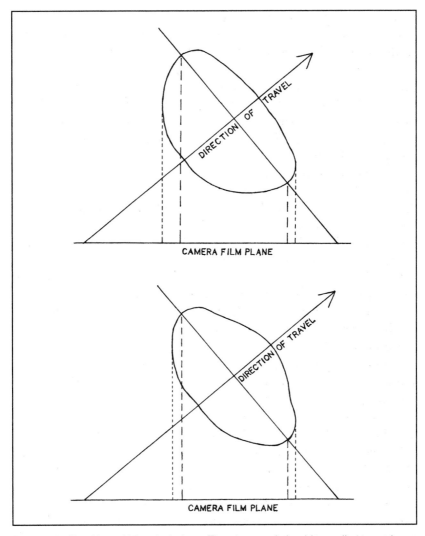

Figure 53. Shoulder width calculations. The chest and shoulder outlines are drawn as viewed from above. The upper picture presumes that the shoulders were rather forwardly positioned; the lower picture presumes the shoulders in a more neutral position. (Calculations were also made with the shoulders in a more back-set position, but the resultant measurements from this proved to be slightly internally inconsistent.) In both drawings the subject is shown moving 40° away from the film plane. Calculations were made for the various angles from which all seven of the measured frames were filmed. The short-dash lines represent the image width that is seen in the film. The long-dash lines represent the actual shoulder breadth from that angle. The difference between these two widths were measured for all pertinent angles for all three likely shoulder outlines. Translating the last measurement into actual shoulder breadth was a simple trigonometric calculation, which was done for all 21 possible positions.

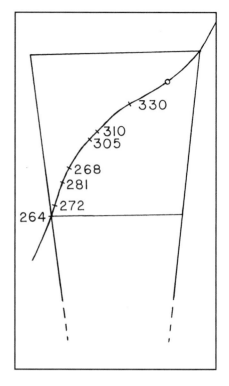

Figure 54. Frames used for shoulder breadth. Clearly measureable shoulders were evident on seven frames within the series where its relative height could also be determined. These frames, numbers 264, 272, 281, 268, 305, 310, and 330, are here located on the same travel segment where the subject's movements were most accurately plotted in some earlier figures.

rear view. These indicate shoulders that are 28.2 inches wide (58 cm), which are then 83% of Green's original width estimate, and 92% of that same estimate as corrected to the new height figure.

At 28.2 inches, these shoulders are 36.2% of the subject's full standing height, or 35.1% allowing for hair thickness at shoulders and head. My own 19.5-inch shoulders are only 26% of my 75-inch standing height—and I am rather broadly built for a man of my size. Human shoulders can be as much as 30% of stature, or even a bit more, but only in rather short men of extreme lateral build, like Eskimos. Most human shoulder breadths are about 25% of stature, or a little less.

Subject's Weight. The body weight of the creature that is seen in the film has been a subject of much disagreement. Grieve called it 280 pounds, Gimlin estimated 350 pounds, Patterson's guesses ranged from 300 to 800 pounds and he told me 500, while both Titmus and Green thought it must weigh at least 800 pounds. (These are, in the same order, 127 kg, 159 kg, 136 to 364 and 227 kg, and 364 kg.) Donskoy referred to it as being extremely massive, but he gave no figure. My own estimate is 500 pounds (227 kg), as based on the procedures that are described below.

The most direct approach is to calculate the body volume from its external measurements and find the weight on the assumption that it has the same density as fresh water. I have made this calculation many times, as has John Green, and we both get somewhat different figures on every attempt. Green always finds it to be far heavier than I do; partly this results from our using different measurements, and also because we divide the body into compartments by different procedures.

The first consideration is how much to subtract for body hair, which could be any where from a half to one inch thick over the body. My preference was to discount half an inch, thus reducing most body diameters by one inch. (Subtracting two inches would make its ankles the same size as my own, and that can hardly be true.)

I divided the body into a series of cylinders—head, torso, upper arms, forearms, thighs, and lower legs, and I made block estimates for the hands and feet. The cylinder diameters (minus hair) were averaged, cross-sectional areas found, and these were multiplied by lengths. My most careful calculation resulted in 7.38 cubic feet of volume which, at 60 pounds per cubic foot, equals 443 pounds.

As a check on this procedure I also took all the same measurements on my own body and calculated my weight using the same cylinders and all the same procedures (but with no allowance for body hair). My actual weight was 13% greater than what my calculations showed. I don't know the source of this discrepancy, but it obviously must apply to my calculations on the film subject as well. Accordingly, I increased my 443 by 13% to get 500 pounds (227 kg) as the subject's most probable weight.

Another method to estimate body weight is from width of the ankle part of the footprint. I described this idea in detail in my 1972b publication, and summarized it in Chapter 3. In short, the square of the heel breadth is directly proportional to the ankle's weight-bearing capacity. Extrapolating from my human data to the footprints at 4.5 or 4.6 inches wide, the film subject who left those prints should have weighed about 500 pounds.

If one studies the body outlines of excessively heavy men pictured in Sheldon's *Atlas of Men* (1954) some approximate matches for our subject can be found, at least in terms of height-to-weight ratios. First there are the extreme endomorphs with moderate mesomorphy (somatotype 7 4 1), where the digestive tract and body fat are overly developed, and the muscular system is about average. The body outlines of the heaviest men, with some added allowance for hair cover, only remotely resemble the film subject (Fig. 55, left and center). If men of this type were expanded to 6 feet 6 inches standing height they would average about 500 pounds body weight. Actually there is one notable difference, these men are clearly much fatter and not nearly as muscular as the figure in the film.

Those men with the highest muscular development, the mesomorphs, never reach the relative weight that we see in extreme endomorphs. The best physical match that I could find was a 5 6 1 somatotype (Fig. 55, right). If he was expanded to 6 feet 6 inches tall he would weigh only 344 pounds; and even he does not equal the movie subject in relative breadth and massiveness of shoulders. Judging from Sheldon's extensive analysis of male somatotypes, the body that we see in the film exhibits a degree of massiveness, combined with muscularity, that does not occur in the human species.

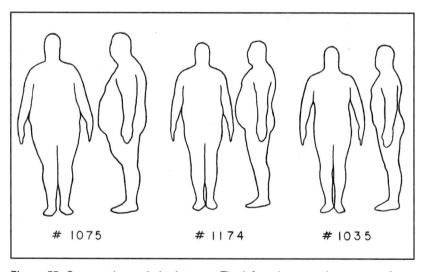

1075   # 1174   # 1035

Figure 55. Comparative male body types. The left and center pictures are of two extreme endomorphs, # 1075 and # 1174, traced from photographs in Sheldon's *Atlas of Men* (1952)—both with somatotype 7 4 1. Their weight-to-height ratios bracket that calculated for the film subject, with # 1075 only slightly exceeding the relative massiveness of our subject. The picture on the right is of # 1035 from the same source—a heavy mesomorph with somatotype 5 6 1. This body is the closest match to the film subject's design, but still not as muscular nor as wide shouldered. Unlike with the very fat men, its weight-to-stature ratio is well below that of the sasquatch.

Locomotion and Anatomy

The manner in which the film subject walks has been a matter of some controversy, but with remarkably little competent study on which to base these disagreements. Most viewers see it as walking in a typically human manner; some say that this shows it is a man in a fur suit, while others say that this is how any bipedal primate should walk. A few observers report seeing certain locomotor differences; some say that this makes it a fake since any bipedal primate should have walked like a man, while others say that these differences clearly indicate a new species. Either interpretation of its locomotion (human or not) is used by various people to support both opinions of its true nature. Until now, the only detailed biomechanical analyses have been the 1971 studies by Donskoy and Grieve.

Donskoy's terse, three-page report is reprinted in full in Byrne's 1975 book. He found that the subject walked in a coherent manner, with all movements properly coordinated in a pattern that indicated great weight and with proportionate muscular development. It showed well-timed arm swings, a long and comfortable stride, and other features that a smaller man simply would not be able to imitate. He implied, and quite rightly, that no man of the indicated size, weight, and muscular development exists. Working with the U.S.S.R. athletics program, he ought to know this more than almost anybody. (I might add that if such a man did exist, it seems unlikely that he would be known to Patterson but not to any anatomists, athletic groups, or the news media.) Donskoy concluded that ". . . with all of the diversity of locomotion illustrated by the creature of the footage, its gait as seen is absolutely non-typical of man."

Grieve's study, reprinted in Napier (1972) and also in Byrne (1975), is much more detailed in terms of providing measurements. Unfortunately many of these are incorrect because he evidently was not told the known length of stride nor the size of its footprints. He also estimated, admittedly for no good reason, that the subject was moving away at 27° from the film plane, when it was actually oriented more like 40° or more away from that plane. Curiously, he viewed the film reversed, with the subject moving from right to left. This fact in itself does not affect his analysis, but the reader is alerted to switch the words "right" and "left" in his report.

Grieve studied 31 of the clearest frames in great detail, which are numbers 285 through 315 of the entire sequence. (Four of these are

unaccountably missing at and near the beginning of his table of measurements.) He correctly notes how the leg movements look rather
like those of a man walking at a forced high speed. Among these
actions are: deep knee flexion when weight is supported, great backward extension of thigh at the end of the support phase, and great
knee flexion following toe-off. All of these unusual movements can
easily be seen in viewing the film. Grieve quantified these by drawing what he said were the axes of each limb segment on the near leg,
and measuring their inclinations from the vertical. He then corrected
the observed angles to somewhat increased values to allow for the
27° at which he thought it was moving away from the film plane.
These can be further corrected to the actual 40° deviation by simply
adding 3° to each of his higher figures, and proportionally less for the
smaller angles. This correction does not change any of Grieve's
observations about how strangely this creature moves—it only serves
to slightly exaggerate them. Backward extension of the thigh changes
from 30° to 33° (but see next paragraph), total thigh excursion
involves two angles and increases from 61° to 67°, and lifted knee
flexion (also two angles) moves from 46° to 52° (see next paragraph).

Grieve made another error here. By studying the frames in question I found that he had measured the leading edge of the limb segments, not the central axes as he stated. This has no appreciable
effect on the lower leg's angle measurements, where the tibia nicely
parallels the shin. But making a correction for the thigh can amount
to as much as a 13° difference, depending on the positions that are
considered. When the thigh is forward, its femur is 13° more flexed
than Grieve's measurements indicate; when it moves far back, it may
be only slightly less extended. The difference can be illustrated by
showing the body profile and its major segments angled according to
the two interpretations, where the thigh axis is the only contrast. In
Figure 56 it can be seen that if Grieve's angle is taken as the thigh
axis (left) the subject is leaning so far forward as to be unsupportable
in a striding gait. Correcting the thigh angle by 13° (right) the body
tilt is just about correct for walking.

Both Grieve and Donskoy clearly saw the major locomotor difference as being the deep knee bend under weight support, often 30°
or more. This is exactly what a particularly massive biped must do to
avoid jarring the body with each step. My own measurements show
this bend to be greater than 50°. This means that the body moves
along horizontally in a virtually straight line, but carried a few inches

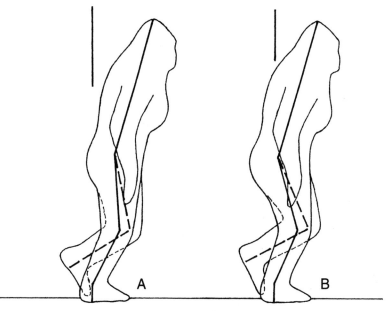

Figure 56. Two indicated body postures. The trunk axis and segments of the supporting leg are shown in solid lines; axes of the swing leg are in dashed lines. The vertical line behind each head is directly above its supporting ankle segment. Picture A shows the limb axes, as given in Grieve's study, when the swing foot is about to pass the supporting foot. Picture B shows the author's correction of thigh flexion by noting that Grieve was actually measuring the leading edge of the limb segments, not their axes. Obviously the pose shown in picture A is leaning too far forward for a walking pace, while picture B is correctly inclined. All other measurements of thigh excursion are consistent only with the interpretation followed here.

lower and closer to the ground than would otherwise be the case. A smaller man who is engaged in rapid movement will walk similarly, but we have already established the size of the subject and speed of the film to positively rule out this possibility.

Given this bent-knee support, the subject must extend its leg slightly farther, both in front and behind, to maintain the same stride-to-stature ratio as in other bipeds. Since the measured stride and reconstructed stature show this human ratio, the observed leg movements correspond correctly. In brief, the stride is notably lengthened in relation to its *walking* stature, but it is quite human in relation to its *standing* stature.

In the swing phase of the stride, one leg returns from a far-back position to reach forward, without any weight bearing in that action. The other leg is in its support phase during that time. In swing phase, that knee must be bent enough for the foot to be lifted clear of the ground as it swings forward. Given the bent knee support, this lift is necessarily exaggerated—the swinging knee must be flexed more than is normal with humans in order to raise the foot somewhat higher. In addition, the relatively longer foot means that it requires even more lift than a human would if it walked with the same supporting knee bend. The fact that the supporting foot is also impressed an extra inch into the ground only increases the need to lift that swinging foot even higher. In this case the knee is regularly bent more than 90°, while the human leg bends less than 70°.

The bent-knee posture on the supporting leg prolongs its time of ground contact at both ends of that phase. When it is extended forward, the foot strikes sooner because the hip is carried closer to the ground; for the same reason it is lifted from its back position just a little bit later than it otherwise would be. This effect is illustrated in Figure 57 where the human striding (above) is contrasted with that of the sasquatch, using the same leg length and stride distance for each species. Our subject's hip is carried only two inches closer to the undersurface of the foot (three inches closer to the actual ground), but this is enough to greatly affect the leg slopes in all positions. It may be seen that the support phases of the two legs substantially overlap with each other.

A striding man has both feet in some contact with the ground for barely 2 percent of the walking stride, while my reconstruction puts both of our subject's feet touching down for over 20 percent of the time (Fig. 58). When the legs are stretched out at maximum angles, front and back at the same time, body support is more important for a relatively heavy biped. In this case the need for support is exaggerated by the lower angles of the ground-contacting legs. Yet it is this same set of low angles that ensures the desireable increased time of double support. It is interesting that in Cachel's 1985 paper she indicated that, for other reasons, prolonged foot contact with the ground should be expected of this animal.

This arrangement means that there is correspondingly less time for the swing phase to move the foot from toe-off to the next heel strike. Excessive knee bending during swing phase serves to shorten the effective pendulum length of that leg and causes it to swing faster than if it had been held straighter. Thus the bent-knee posture both causes a timing irregularity and automatically corrects for it.

The film subject is walking in a manner that differs from human locomotion in several respects. It shows the kinds of knee bends and leg extensions of a much smaller man who is moving at a rapidly forced pace. Yet we know that it was very large and can plainly see it walking with rather comfortable strides. It also shows the motions of an excessively heavy individual, but no man of that weight has the strength to execute such long steps, especially with bent-knee support (Fig. 59). Very fat men instead take rather short steps with minimal knee bending. Judging from the way it walks, there is no possibility that the film subject can be a man in a fur suit.

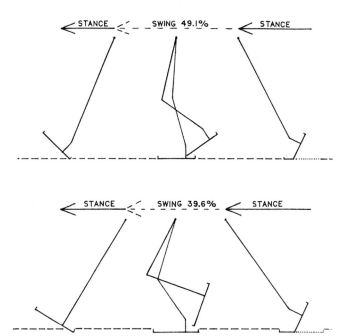

Figure 57. Contrasting striding gaits. A single leg is shown in three positions of the swing phase, and the top dot follows the moving position of the hip socket. At right, the leg is stretched out behind, and its forefoot is just lifting off the ground. In the center, the leg is swinging, with the knee well bent, past the stance leg that is shown only for this position. At left, the leg reaches out as the heel is just striking the ground and ending its swing phase. In the human stride (above) the supporting knee is bent only slightly as the swing foot is approaching it. In the sasquatch stride (below) the supporting knee is bent much more at that position. This difference, plus the impression of the feet into the ground, puts the sasquatch hip several inches closer to the ground than with a human of equal leg length. This also means that the single-support swing phase in sasquatch is a much shorter fraction of the full two-step stride.

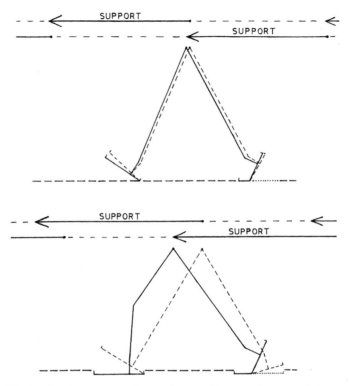

Figure 58. Overlapping support phases. Leg positions at the start of the two-foot support are shown in dashed lines at the moment the lead foot first touches the ground. Leg positions at the end of the two-foot support are shown in solid lines at the moment the trailing foot last leaves the ground. In the human stride (above) both feet are in ground contact no more than 2 percent of the full stride length. In the sasquatch stride (below) both feet are in ground contact for more than 20 percent of the stride length. The hip socket thus travels considerably farther in the sasquatch with double support.

Several scientists claim to see a contradiction in how the creature walks in a masculine manner, yet it appears to have the conspicuous breasts of an adult female. This observation indicates a poor understanding of the reason for pelvic dimorphism (sexual differences). Human females generally walk rather differently from males, but there is no such contrast in apes. In our species the female pelvis is relatively much wider at the level of the hip sockets than is the male pelvis. This results from the very large birth canal that is required for our large-headed newborns. Apes are born with much smaller brains, and their two sexes have more nearly the same pelvic design. All of the evident anatomy of the sasquatch indicates an unimpressive head size at birth. The very large body size of their females only further rules out any need for pelvic differences of the human type. If a female sasquatch were seen to walk like a female human, this would imply a head size at birth far in excess of the human condition. This in turn would lead to an adult head size (braincase plus jaw muscles) far larger than is actually observed, and one might also expect intelligence at or above the human level. Of course the female sasquatch walks more like a man than a woman, and that is exactly how she should walk. If a "breasted" sasquatch walks like a woman, as I have seen in one other film, the most obvious inference is that it is actually a female human wearing a costume.

Most critics still insist that it is only a large man in a fur suit. If that were the case we have an interesting problem of bodily proportions. A man standing six and a half feet tall (2 m) could wear a bulky suit and produce at least some of the visual effects that are seen in the film. But when we see the subject directly from behind it has a chest

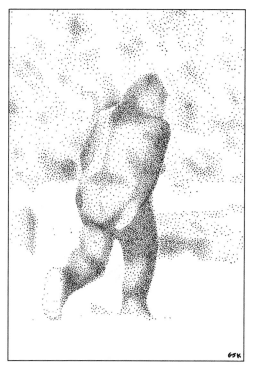

Figure 59. Bent knee support. Artist's rendition of this frame shows the supporting leg in its strongly flexed position.

that is 18.3 inches wide (46.5 cm). The inside edges of his upper arms must then be at least 18.3 inches apart from each other, and that does not allow for any suit thickness on these upper arms. At 75 inches tall, my own chest width at that level is only 13.6 inches (34.6 cm). I can confidently state that no man of that stature is built that broadly.

The only alternative is that the man in the fur suit had his elbows sticking straight out to the sides into the shoulders of the costume. This means his hands were at the "elbows" where he held onto sticks that supported the forearms. But this would require that from one outstretched elbow to the other he measured less than the observed 28.2-inch shoulder width. No man who stands two meters tall has shoulders and upper arms that add up to such a short span; my own is 42 inches, and a man who is 3 inches taller than me could not have an elbow span almost 14 inches less. This also seems to be ruled out by observing frames 61 and 72, shown in Figure 60, where the right hand can be seen with clearly different wrist bends and finger curls. The observed shoulder width requires that a new joint be introduced

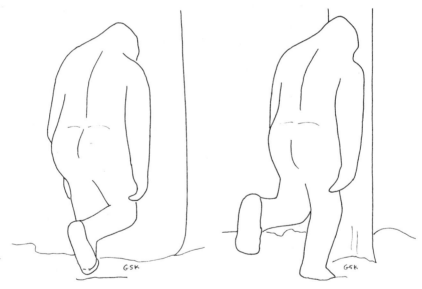

Figure 60. Subject's hand positions. Artist's renditions of two rather critical frames from Patterson's film, 61 and 72, show the right hand in about the same position, but separated by a full step. The earlier frame (left) has the wrist bent outward slightly and the fingers somewhat curled. The later frame (right) has the wrist extending straight and the fingers a bit more straightened out. Exactly this interaction between wrist-bend and finger-curl is normal in the hands of all apes, but not necessarily in humans. These are also two of the ten frames where the foot length may be compared directly with the visible walking height.

into about the midpoint of the man's upper arms. We can safely rule out any sophisticated surgery of this kind. What we are left with is that no human body can possibly be fitted into the shoulder proportions that have been observed and measured.

The film subject shows two large bulges on the chest that are almost universally assumed to be breasts, hence identifying the individual as a female. These are fully hair covered, which is taken as an objection by some primatologists. That the species should have enlarged breasts at all (a human trait) is also a point of contention to some critics. Since this is the only case of a nonhuman, bipedal primate, I would not be so rash as to presume what its breasts *should* look like. But that they would be hair covered in a temperate climate seems perfectly reasonable to me. It has also been noted that nipples are not visible, a very unprimate condition. But at the filming distance, and allowing for a constant color pattern, none could be seen if they were there.

Many years ago I suggested another possible explanation for those prominent bulges; they might be laryngeal air sacs of enormous size, and about half inflated in this film. Most apes have varying degrees of out-pouching from the trachea where extra air circulates. They are at least partly developed in some humans who are glass blowers or trumpet players. In orangs they spread out, under the skin, reaching over the shoulders and often for a short distance down the front of the chest. If the sasquatch had an exaggerated version of these pouches, they just might extend anteriorly and some distance down the chest. These could be inflated, then abruptly deflated (perhaps by pressing down on it with the hands) while exhaling a lungfull of air at the same time. Such a volume of air passing the vocal cords could help account for the extremely loud sounds they are reported to make. Actually I do not find this to be as likely an explanation as that they are breasts. I just think it is a good practice to look at every reasonable possibility—with this and with any other phenomena.

Two observers have suggested that the two hairy lumps might represent the head and rump of an infant that is clinging horizontally to its mother's chest. This is not a reasonable possibility. (The originator of this idea is an erratic individual who ought to be ignored, but since he has influenced at least one scholar to consider the same interpretation, it deserves some response.) Only a newborn human has bodily proportions even remotely approaching two bulges of equal size, and even it would not have such an extraordinary constriction in its midregion. A sasquatch who was old enough for this relative size would have a chest and shoulder region larger than its head, and no constriction at the waist. Further, there is no possible way for such a large infant to cling horizontally to this surface; only the "uphill" limbs could be used for grasping, and that ability is dubious for the hind limb in this species. This idea deserves no further attention.

Is It Real?

Much of the argument for the film's authenticity has already been discussed, but we should consider that if it was a fake, Patterson himself was responsible for concocting it. I came to know the man fairly well in his last few years, and even appeared with him on the Merv Griffin television show as his scientific back-up. In my judgment of his character, Patterson might have tried to fake a film of this kind if he had the ability to do so. Also in my judgment he had nowhere near the knowledge or facilities to do so—nor, for that matter, had anyone else.

After watching the film many times I told Patterson about some of its technical consistencies that were evident to me. With most of these he already knew what was involved or quickly caught on. But when I talked about some of the more technical details of biomechanics, he soon showed the familiar blank look of a student who had lost the drift of the explanation, but was still trying hard to pay attention. Yet he must have known all of these details in order to create the hoax. For instance, he could see the anterior position of the front of the shin, but how that related to foot leverage was quite beyond his understanding. Also, he had originally estimated that it weighed only half of what was settled on later, yet all the details were calculated to fit with the greater weight. I think that a hoax is most unlikely on these grounds alone.

A few years after the film was made, Patterson received a letter from a man in Thailand who assured him a sasquatch was being held captive in a Buddhist monastery. Patterson spent most of his remaining money preparing an expedition to retrieve this creature; I was to be part of the operation. Then a man who was sent to investigate on the spot found out that it was a hoax. At the time Patterson knew he was dying of Hodgkin's disease and firmly believed that with enough money he might be cured. Instead of making another bigfoot movie, which he could have done if he had faked the first one, he spent almost everything he had on a wild goose chase. Then he died.

Shortly after Patterson's death I looked up his partner, Bob Gimlin, for his input on a few particulars. He had received none of the money that was generated by the film, though he thought he was entitled to perhaps one-third of it. If the film was a fake, he ought to have known this; he could have evened the score by publicly announcing this, and probably gotten considerable money for his story. Since he hadn't done so I wanted to explore the implications with him. Gimlin assured me that there was nothing he could say against the authenticity of the event, the tracks, and the film. He could not imagine any way that Patterson could have set it up without his knowledge. He saw no way that it could have been a set-up at all; there was no doubt in his mind that it was a real animal.

If Patterson had somehow managed to prepare such a hoax without Gimlin's knowledge (impossible on the face of it), the man in the fur suit would have been in serious danger of losing his life. The two searchers had agreed not to shoot if they encountered a sasquatch, but there was no guarantee Gimlin would honor that agreement if and when the event occurred. No one in his right mind would play the part of a sasquatch in front of an armed hunter who might act impulsively to protect his friend.

Before my conversation with Gimlin, Patterson had given me a copy of one of the footprint casts from the site, with his permission to copy and distribute it as I saw fit. He had reasoned that its value was dependent on identifying its source, so any copies I sold or gave away would only add to his own reputation. When I visited with Gimlin, we discussed some aspects of this track. I gave him a copy of that particular track because he said he didn't have one. He commented that the cast was the only thing he ever got out of the whole event.

John Green took another approach. He talked to some experts at the Disney Studios for their opinion on how it could have been done without the animal being real. They told him flat-out that they would not be able to duplicate it with all of their facilities. It would seem unreasonable that Roger Patterson, a small rancher and part-time rodeo rider, was able to produce an animated film that even Disney could not make.

Peter Byrne, who studied the film site carefully, noted that this would have been a rather poor location to stage a hoax. This place could easily have been observed by other people traveling through the area. On a Friday afternoon it was especially vulnerable to visits by weekend sportsmen. Not far away in the same creek bed were other suitable photographic sites that were much more secure from casual visitors. If it was somehow faked, it certainly would have taken at least a few weeks to prepare in great detail. It is incongruous that they would have been so careless about picking the location for the actual filming.

John Green pointed out another aspect that was inconsistent with any possible faking scenario. Immediately after the filming Patterson made telephone attempts to get skeptical scientists and tracking dogs to the scene. Had it been a hoax, such an investigation would probably have exposed it right then and there. Several years later a truly fake sasquatch film was made by another man who was far more qualified than Patterson to pull it off. When the site of that film was discovered somewhat later, that it was a hoax was easily established.

Current Status

No matter how the Patterson film is analyzed, its legitimacy has been repeatedly supported. The size and shape of the body cannot be duplicated by a man, its weight and movements correspond with each other and equally rule out a human subject; its anatomical details are just too good. The world's best animators could not match it as of the year 1969, and the supposed faker died rather than make another movie. In spite of all this, and much more, the Scientific Establishment has not accepted the film as evidence of the proposed species. There are several reasons for this reluctance that are worthy of some discussion.

Most of the analyses of this film and its background were made by laymen; their studies and conclusions were published in popular magazines and books, not in scientific journals. Most of these investigators did not know how to write a scientific paper or how to get one published. If they had submitted journal articles, these probably would have been rejected simply because that subject was not taken seriously by the editors, no matter how well the articles may have been written. Thus the potentially concerned scientists were simply unaware of the great quantity and quality of evidence. Most of them had heard about the movie, but were reluctant to look into it until someone else verified it. Since they all took this attitude, preferring not to risk making themselves look foolish, nothing much ever happened.

Patterson's was the first movie film ever produced purporting to show a sasquatch in the wild. Since that time many more films have appeared. I have seen eight of them and they are all fakes. A few of the most absurd of these are available on a video cassette. (One other shows a distant, non-moving object that could be a sasquatch, but there is no way to find out for sure.) Given that such faking exists now, it is not surprising that scientific interest in supposed sasquatch movies is even less today than it was back in 1967.

In many popular publications about the sasquatch there are claimed connections with the truly paranormal, and even fewer scientists want to deal with this. The lunatic fringe has the sasquatch moving through space-time warps, riding in UFOs, making telepathic connections, showing superior intelligence, and the like. All of these enthusiasts try to capitalize on anything new that comes out on the subject. Most of them will eagerly latch on to any scientist who shows an interest, and attempt to lead him/her down their own garden path. It is tantamount to academic suicide to become associated with any of these people.

Finally, and most important, there is the absence of any definitive proof that sasquatches exist at all. If this had been a known species, the Patterson film would have been accepted without question. But without the clear proof that biologists are willing to accept, a strip of film is of little persuasive value. Of course a film like this would have been accepted as fairly good evidence for a new species of cat or skunk, but even then the type specimen would still have to be collected to make it official. For something so unexpected (at least to science) as the sasquatch, the degree of proof that is required rises proportionally.

What is said here about scientific ignorance regarding the Patterson film is equally true for the footprint evidence and the testimony of eyewitnesses. None of this is normally published in the scientific journals, hoaxes do occur, and the lunatic fringe is all over the place. I don't know of a single scientist who has firmly denied the existence of the sasquatch on the basis of a reasonable study of the evidence. Instead of this, most scientists deny it because, to the best of their knowledge, there is no substantial body of evidence that can be taken seriously. It is my hope that the publication of this book will make a modest contribution toward improving that situation.

Some of the Russian investigators, not part of their Scientific Establishment, have pushed hard for further study of the Patterson film. Their hope is that such work might establish the existence of these creatures without the necessity of collecting a specimen directly. I wish this were true. Scientific knowledge of the mechanics of bodily motion certainly has advanced in the last twenty years since

Donskoy and Grieve studied the film. There are experts in sports medicine, anatomy, athletics, running-shoe design, special effects, and prosthetics who could probably make informed judgments on this film. Dmitri Bayanov has urged me and others to pursue these experts, but what efforts have been made along this line have produced no useful results. I can't afford another full round of expert-chasing after my episode with the dermal ridges, but at least I have tried. Perhaps someone else will pursue this more diligently in the future. It is not likely that further study of the film can extract any more information than I already have, but it would make an enormous difference if a neutral expert with more appropriate credentials could just confirm what has been presented here.

A few years ago Rene Dahinden set about to produce a book that would fully document the Patterson film and all the circumstances surrounding it. He enlisted the aid of Bruce Bonney for photographic work with the original film, and for the actual writing. That project showed great promise of lifting the veil of obscurity that has surrounded many aspects of the film and its history, and perhaps to arouse a new ripple of scientific interest. Unfortunately the project has been scrapped, and the two men are now in conflict over who did, or did not do, various things that were required.

Until recently it was difficult to obtain a copy of the Patterson film. There have always been bootleg copies available, if you have the right contacts, but these are of poor quality. The original is virtually inaccessible to anyone. There are a few good copies around—I am holding a third generation copy myself. The legal rights to use this film had long been tied up in litigation, then in private hands of those who were unwilling to allow its use by scientists or anyone else. Even though it is now apparently in the public domain, there is still dispute, and for this reason, drawings instead of photographs have been used for Figures 45, 46, 59, and 60.

With any luck this film will be analyzed by more scientists and technicians with modern techniques. If and when such studies turn out to support the film's authenticity, I still doubt that this would lead to scientific acceptance of the species. Such results would have the same effect as my pushing of the dermal-ridge evidence; experts in some specialized fields would come to accept sasquatch as a real animal, or at least have an open mind on the subject. The main body of the Scientific Establishment will continue to deny or ignore the evidence.

5

OTHER EVIDENCE

While we have no definitive remains of a sasquatch, lesser bodily scraps have often been reported and offered as evidence. Those that I am aware of include hair, feces, skin scrapings, and blood. The usual fate of these items is that either they receive no scientific study, or else the documentation of that study is lost or otherwise unobtainable. In most cases where competent analyses have been made, the material turned out to be bogus or else no determination could be made. The record should be set straight on some of these, just to be sure that no incorrect accounts are circulating.

Hair samples are the commonest of what I call bodily scraps. Some of these have been examined by hair experts and pronounced to be of an unknown animal, and in a few cases even pinned down to being from a higher primate. Unfortunately for these earlier studies, the science of hair analysis is rather inexact and the competence of the investigators varies greatly.

The normal procedure is to look at the hair under optical magnification and to compare its various characteristics with hairs taken from known animals. These characteristics include shaft diameter and degree of flattening, size and continuity of fusi (hollowing within the shaft), size and shape of scales on the surface, and the type and distribution of coloring pigments. If all of these characteristics match an available sample, the identification is assumed. But slight differences that one expert might fail to notice could also make that identification incorrect. Slight hair differences usually mean correspondingly slight taxonomic differences, but not always; sometimes distantly related animals have very similar hair. When a hair cannot be matched, labeling it as an unknown species is not necessarily warranted. Hair characteristics vary on different parts of the same animal, and no comparative collection exists of all types of hair of all mammals. A hair that is unlike anything in a North American collection might be from the armpit of a bear or from an escaped llama. As one expert once put it, the only way to positively identify a sasquatch hair is to match it with a *known* sample.

In spite of these problems, and more, there are likely a few valid hairs presently available. Walter Birkby at the University of Arizona has some that he got from Bob Titmus, and is fairly sure they are sasquatch. The hairs are of a higher primate, in his judgment, and cannot quite be matched with any known species. Birkby takes the sasquatch possibility quite seriously, but he is a careful worker who is not inclined to over-enthusiasm, and has ruled out most of the hairs that have been submitted for his analysis. No matter how competent the expert and how secure this identification may be, hair constitutes no serious evidence in the minds of most biologists.

Zhou Guoxing, at the Natural History Museum in Beijing once gave me a reddish hair that he was told came from a yeren, or wild-man of China. Birkby examined it and informed me that it was human—a blond Caucasian hair that had been artificially dyed red.

Another approach was tried by an ill-informed enthusiast who had three or four hair samples from different parts of the United States analyzed by a competent authority. When these were all found to be not only unknown, but similar to each other, he thought he had a good case. The first problem here is that we have only his word that the hairs were from different sources; for all we know they were all taken from the same original sample. The second problem is that we don't know to what degree these hairs were studied and selected before submission. Third is the simple fact that this kind of evidence would never be accepted as proof by the authorities no matter how well all the circumstances were controlled and documented. Trying to push this kind of evidence is not only a waste of time, but it also tends to cause other, more serious investigators to be seen in a poor light.

A large amount of what looks like hair has been recovered from several places in the Blue Mountains since 1987. Samples of this were examined by many supposed experts ranging from the F.B.I. to barbers. Most of these called it human, the Redkin Company found significant differences from human hair, but the Japan Hair Medical Science Lab declared it to be a synthetic fiber. A scientist at my university first called it synthetic, then looked more closely and decided it was real hair of an unknown type. Lonnie Somer, a graduate student in my department, subjected some of these "hairs" to a number of physical tests that included cutting and burning under close observation. He decided it was synthetic without question, and read a paper to that effect at the Cryptozoology Annual Membership Meeting in 1989. Final confirmation came when E.B. Winn, a pharmaceutical businessman from Switzerland had a sample tested in Europe. The fiber was positively identified as artificial and its exact composition was determined; it is a product known commercially as Dynel, which is often used as imitation hair.

Clearly someone was planting samples of Dynel fiber in many places in the Blue Mountains. I personally watched some of it being collected from snapped-off small trees and out of what appeared to be beds of branches. As recently as January, 1991, more of this artificial hair was brought in. This ongoing fiasco only further illustrates the problem we have of sorting out the fake evidence from what may be real.

Bob Titmus also collected hairs from broken trees, in this case from northern California and mostly many years earlier. He found only occasional strands, not the clumps of "hair" that occurred in the Blue Mountain case. A sample of these was given to Walter Birkby at the University of Arizona. Titmus saved only a few hairs, which I much later sent to Jerold Lowenstein, a biochemist in San Francisco. Lowenstein was able to compare the protein structure and found it similar to humans and African apes; it was less similar to orangs, thus eliminating them and all other animals from consideration. Differences in protein are better indicators of relationships than are visible structures because these are nonadaptive—the differences simply accumulate over time at a fairly regular rate since the last common ancestor of the species that are being checked.

Lowenstein's test was not fine enough to say "yes" or "no" to the closest matches (human, chimp, and gorilla), or whether it was a new type within this group. Titmus, a taxidermist of long experience, feels he could confidently rule out human as the source. It can also be stated with some confidence that no African apes are living wild in the mountains of northern California. This is good evidence, but at present it cannot be confirmed by another scientist because the hairs were consumed by the testing process. Even if this, or some other test on hair, were to be replicated by other established scientists, the results would be of interest only to a few specialists. The vast majority of skeptical scientists would be no more impressed by this kind of evidence than they were with the dermal ridges.

It is now possible to extract DNA from a hair sample to determine the species, or even the exact individual if there is a known specimen for comparison. This is easiest done with a follicle, but just a hair shaft will often suffice. Thus far only one hair sample has been sent in for this test, and it was immediately rejected as being an artificial, man-made fiber. I am looking for more material, but we must be careful not to swamp the testers with fakes, or eventually they will stop this kind of testing.

There are many reports of fecal deposits that resemble those of humans, but which are said to have the volume of as much as an ordinary bucket—ten quarts (liters). In some cases samples have been brought back for analysis, though only a few scientists are willing to look at such material when they are told its suspected source. Vaughn Bryant, at Texas A&M, has examined some of these, but he could determine only what foods had been consumed. So far he has not been able to positively eliminate such sources as human, bear, or even cow.

I have been told that if a sample is collected and frozen within three hours of its deposition, the digestive enzymes can be examined. Bacterial action normally destroys these in any greater amount of time. More recently, methods have been developed to extract an animal's DNA from its feces, and this can be separated from the DNA of all the plants and/or animals it had been eating. Since finding out about this possibility in early 1991, I have been awaiting the next sample for testing. Again, if we did get some definitive answers by either of these approaches, they would be convincing only to the concerned specialists. But if enough enzymes and DNA sequencing eventually support the existence of another higher primate, this might stir at least a little more scientific interest than there is at present.

In 1986 one of the sasquatch hunters in the Blue Mountains provided me with a few scraps of what appeared to be calloused skin. He said the skin was found on a low rock outcropping where he presumed that the sasquatch must have scraped it off the bottom of its feet. The man had been tracking a sasquatch and said that there was no sign of human presence in the area. He is a fairly experienced animal tracker, so I found him easy to believe.

Lowenstein was kind enough to test this skin fragment for protein similarities. Because of its size (0.1 cc) and composition, the identification was much closer than with the hairs; it was human. I pressed Lowenstein for how much lee-way there was in this; given a human-chimp separation at five million years, how far back on the human line might this set of proteins have separated? He would allow one million years at most, but there was no reason to think that there was any separation at all. That would make our subject a member of the human genus, either *Homo sapiens* or *Homo erectus*, and not anything more distantly related to us. This limitation proves to be incongruous with the conclusions that are reached in Chapter 7 as to its most probable identity.

The same hunter brought in a tiny blood sample in late 1988 that he claimed to have found along a trail of sasquatch footprints. He said it could as easily have been the blood of an animal being carried, or of the sasquatch itself. I saw the rock he brought back, with a thumb-nail-sized blood spot on it. He scraped off about half of this into a small jar for me. About one-fourth of this, an amount barely visible to the naked eye, was analyzed by Mark Stoneking, who was then working in Berkeley, California. He sequenced enough of the DNA to determine that most of the sample was human blood, and part was the blood of some lower mammal that he did not specifically identify.

A simple comparison of the proteins of this mixed-blood sample would have given a reading of close to, but not quite, human. Since the hunter knew the general theory of protein comparisons, this would be an obvious way to create a piece of false evidence that might look convincing. Needless to say, I am now dubious of the skin fragment he provided (it was most likely his own), and any other evidence that he has found is being looked at with much more skepticism than before.

Shortly before I came to Washington State University in 1968, a local person brought a lower jaw to our Anthropology Department for identification. He thought it looked rather human, but it seemed far too large. One of my colleagues easily identified it as the jaw of a fairly normal, adult male Native American. Since then I have heard many such stories of people finding jaw bones that they thought were far too large to be of human origin, thus possibly from a sasquatch. A common description is that the jaw fitted around the outside of their own, and that it rose up as high as their ears. Actually with any two jaws of the same size one can fit at least partway around the other. Rising up to the middle of the ear is quite normal, because your own jaw goes up that far.

I have spent a good deal of time trying to track down stories of enormous jaws and other bones, only to find that the specimen either was quite normal or else it could not be located. Other investigators with whom I have compared notes have had similar experiences. Any time one hears of such a specimen—something that looks like a human bone but is much too large—it is almost certainly a normal bone of a human or some other animal. I say "almost" because there is always a small chance that some day it will be the real thing. So I still chase down such stories no matter how slim the odds may seem.

The Ice Man

In the summer of 1968 the frozen "body" of a humanoid form appeared as an exhibit in the Minnesota State Fair, and continued to be shown in various other fairs and carnivals for several years. The object was encased in ice and much of it could not be clearly seen, but it resembled a rather powerfully built human body almost 6 feet tall (180 cm), covered with hair, and with a somewhat apelike face. Obviously it was either some kind of primitive hominoid or else an elaborate hoax. Its size and general characteristics were consistent with those of a not-quite-mature sasquatch. It has never been thawed out for scientific examination and its whereabouts are presently unknown.

No government officials took any notice of the Ice Man; the possibility that it might be an actual human body was not seriously raised. The scientific world might also have missed it but for the efforts of a young man, Terry Cullen, who told Dr. Ivan Sanderson about it. In late 1968 it was examined, as far as was possible under the restrictive conditions, by Bernard Heuvelman, along with Sanderson. Photographs were taken and measurements made, as well as could be done through a layer of ice that was often thick and cloudy. The man who was in charge of the object, Frank Hansen, allowed this limited study and no more.

Hansen first said that the creature had been obtained in Hong Kong, already in its ice block, and that it had originally been picked up in the Bering Sea. Another story, that it had been shot in the woods in northern Wisconsin, soon surfaced and was attributed to Hansen. Heuvelmans has reason to believe it came from Vietnam and was shipped here under suspicious and perhaps illegal circumstances. If it could be properly examined, and if it proves to be an actual body, its point of origin would be of relatively little importance; its mere existence would be the biological/anthropological discovery of the century.

The Ice Man's legs are of human length for his height. His feet seem to be relatively rather large, being 6.3 inches (16 cm) across at the human-looking toes. The rest of the foot is scarcely visible, but was estimated to be just over 10 inches long (26 cm). The arms seem longer than human normal, the hands are also large, and the very long thumb is especially unlike those of apes. One arm is held over the head with its hand on the other side of the head; it has an obvious break in the middle of the forearm. The torso is like that of a powerfully muscled man; it is 14.5 inches wide at the hips (37 cm) and much wider across the shoulders. The face is very large, with evident brow ridges and little forehead, but the muzzle does not have nearly the protrusion that is found in living apes. The nose stands forward by only a small amount, and seems to have deep wrinkles arching across its bridge. One eye is out of its socket and lying against the cheek. Evident male genitalia determined the name Ice *Man*.

Sanderson publicized the Ice Man with an article in *Argosy* magazine (1969) that included many errors of measurement. The whole subject was so sensationalized that most scientists refused to take it seriously; what little interest there was at that time went almost exclusively to Patterson's film. Heuvelmans co-authored a large book, with the late Russian scientist Boris Porshnev (1974), that dealt with the whole problem of what they considered to be living Neandertals. (This is the correct spelling. See Chapter 7.) The Ice Man was a centerpiece of that book and its description and, based on Heuvelmans's direct study, was as accurate as could be made. Because this was published in French, and has not been translated, all of this information is unavailable to the vast majority of North American sasquatch investigators.

My first reaction to the Ice Man was the same as with Patterson's film: I wanted to believe it but it seemed unlikely to be real. Hansen later said that he had some artists make a copy of the original body, and this was what he was then showing. With that revelation it seemed obvious that it had been a clear case of a fraud from the outset. Then Bernard Heuvelmans told me how he could clearly see, in places where the ice was clear, individual hairs, pimples, flecks of dirt, and all the mundane details that are found in real skin of a wild animal. He also showed me photographs of the face from before and after it was supposedly thawed out for a short time; one can see a slight change in the orientation of the lips that could not have occurred within a block of ice. Now I'm inclined to think that what Heuvelmans examined might have been the real thing, but I still want to see it for myself. One aspect that grates on me is that if I had walked just a little bit farther at the Minnesota State Fair in the summer of 1968 I would have been the first scientist to see the damned thing.

Terry Cullen, who first brought the Ice Man to scientific attention, recently gave a detailed account of those events of 1968 in a public talk at Washington State University. This was part of the Eighth Annual Membership meeting of the International Society of Cryptozoology in 1989, the same occasion where Lonnie Somer presented his analysis of the artificial "hair." Cullen has no intention of publishing his remarks, and insisted he was making no argument that the Ice Man was a biological reality. Nevertheless, all of his listeners certainly came away with their opinions moved in that direction (if they were not already there).

Behavior

There are many reports of people hearing loud drawn-out screams that they assume were made by sasquatches. The typical account is from the hunter or camper who heard a startling cry that he/she was unable to identify with any known source. Obviously, many of these noises were made by normal animals whose vocalizations were unfamiliar to that particular person. Elk bugling comes as a bit of a surprise the first time it is heard; coyotes can produce quite a variety of noises; even a police siren can echo through a canyon with an overlapping of sounds. To the overly enthusiastic investigator these all become sasquatch screams.

To the best of my knowledge, none of these reports includes a believable observer who actually saw the sasquatch making the sound. If experienced hunters hear only one type of animal cry that is unidentified, and there are reports of only one unidentified large animal in the area that would be capable of making them, then the connection between the two phenomena appears to be more reasonable. The association between footprints and sightings is much more direct than this; many hundreds of cases are on record where footprints were found right where the sasquatch was seen. If these footprint associations were spurious, why haven't people made up hundreds of similar associations between sightings and vocalizing?

It is notoriously difficult to convey the quality of animal sounds with written words. "High-pitched" is a common description, but just how high is not clear. "Prolonged" is also a relative term unless it is actually timed. We also hear about vibratos, rising and falling pitch, multiple tones simultaneously, and a wailing sound (whatever that means). Comparisons with the vocalizations of known animals doesn't help much either. They generally do not sound like dogs barking, cats screeching, or elephants trumpeting, but where does that leave us?

Loudness of sound presupposes a known distance from the source. If there is no possible source within a given distance, then some estimate might be made about the minimum volume of sound that was generated. I was once driving with a friend along a back road where we had at one point a fairly clear field of vision for about one hundred yards (meters) in all directions. Just then a sound like a donkey braying resounded inside the car. We both reacted by turning to the other assuming that he had suddenly yelled out loud. This was immediately ruled out because we showed the same reaction at the same time, and each of us could see that the other had not made the requisite motions to make such a loud bellow. We did see what looked like a mule standing by a building at least fifty yards away. That animal would have to have stood just outside the car in order to produce the sound that we heard. There are many similar accounts to be found in the better books on this subject, and I have interviewed a few such listeners myself.

There are some tapes that supposedly record sasquatch cries. Again, no one who made these tapes claims to have seen the source, at least not during the taping occasion. It should also be remembered that the listener to these tapes has no secure knowledge of the actual time, place, and loudness of the recorded sounds. I have listened to at least ten such tapes and find no compelling reason to believe that any of them are what the recorders claimed them to be. There is one, however, that was recorded more than fifteen years ago near Puyalup, Washington that made me feel noticeably nervous and uncomfortable when it was played. The same feeling of apprehension came when I heard it again years later, but less intensely. Some people had the same reaction, others did not.

Another recording of some interest, but for different reasons, was a videotape made by three men investigating some fresh tracks in the

Blue Mountains in 1987. We see the forested mountain background and the men looking at the footprints; their conversation is also being recorded on the same tape. At one point they pause and look up as a wailing sound comes on, seeming to echo in the distance. The video-taped conversation is then briefly directed to the sound and to the probability that it was from a sasquatch. I find it difficult to believe that this scenario could have been staged because the men's reactions were just too natural.

One of the most widely publicized sound recordings was suppos-edly made at a remote hunting camp in the Sierra Nevada Moun-tains in California, the location of which was known only to the hunters who used it. They brought in another man who taped a long sequence of noises that were quite unlike any other reported sasquatch sounds. None of them claimed to have seen the creatures, but they did show me photographs of numerous tracks in the snow at the camp. These were some of the most obviously faked tracks I have ever seen. The tape was analyzed by some university sound special-ists who determined that a human voice could not have made them; they required a much longer vocal tract. A sasquatch investigator later asked one of these experts if a human could imitate the sound characteristics by simply cupping his hands around his mouth. The answer was yes. I do not know what these recordings actually repre-sent, but given the circumstances they do not seem to merit any fur-ther investigation.

Except for spoken words, auditory orientation in humans generally is depended on much less than is visual orientation. Our vocabulary for describing natural sounds is far less than it is for what we see. Sound memories are less dependable than sight memories. Scientific analysis of sounds is newer and less developed than that for sight. Unless some of these problems can be overcome, the evidence for sasquatch vocalizations will continue to be one of the least produc-tive lines of research.

No matter how acute sasquatch vision may be, if they are to be aware of each other's locations and circumstances at great distances they almost certainly communicate by sound on some occasions. Given their relative dispersion in forested, often mountainous terrain, one would expect that their vocal communication would have to be very loud to be effective. For this reason we could argue that the sup-posed sasquatch sounds fit our logical expectations. This is better rea-soning than just matching unexplained sounds with an unexplained set of sightings, but it is hardly conclusive. If this is correct, we would want to know just which individuals are communicating what information; when and where do they do it; and what is the reaction on the part of other sasquatches that hear these signals? It would also be interesting to know how other animals react to these presumed sasquatch cries. At present we draw a total blank on all these questions. The only thing that might be suggested at this point is that they seem to deliberately avoid vocalizing in the presence of humans.

Another commonly talked about sasquatch characteristic is their supposedly foul and overpowering odor. There is little that can be added to this from the work done in the last twenty-seven years, except to note that only a small fraction of reports include any mention of a smell. People sense, describe, and remember odors even less clearly than they do sounds. There is no practical recording device to preserve odors, and there is almost no scientific methodology to study what people say they have smelled.

The clearest account given directly to me was that it smelled like an equal mixture of the odors of feces and sweat; most other descriptions are similar. Interestingly, George Schaller describes wild gorillas as having the same combination of odors, and whenever he smelled it he knew he was within a hundred yards of them. If the same rule applies to the sasquatch, I was once much closer than that to one of these animals. On a hot day while driving on a dirt road in likely sasquatch country I was abruptly overwhelmed by the above-mentioned stench. My first thought was that one of my sphincters had failed and I was engulfed in odors originating from my own body. This proved not to be the case, though I was certainly sweating. Evidently the odor had originated outside of the car and I just drove slowly into it. This incident occurred only a few miles from where my friend and I heard the extraordinary sound about a year later. Again I may have been fairly close to a sasquatch without seeing it. There is no way to determine for sure whether either event was caused by a sasquatch. The case for the smell is somewhat less convincing because some people describe the smell of a bear in rut with similar terms.

Some possible explanations for the rank smell are scent glands, carrion eating, and unclean personal habits; and perhaps more than one source is responsible. If this is a generated scent, at least in part, it would help to explain why the smell is noted by only some observers. The scent may be exuded at will, or automatically in response to particular circumstances. On the other hand the nature of the odor is very much unlike that of any other mammalian scent (except the bear in rut). Whether this serves as a signal to other sasquatches is anybody's guess. It could, and in fact does, function to repel humans. It did not likely originate for this purpose because humans were not a significant threat to them—at least not until recently, when firearms appeared on the scene.

James Hewkins, a retired naturalist in western Oregon, thinks that much of this odor can be explained by their habit of eating carrion. His studies include several cases of dead farm animals being moved by a very powerful agent, and being eaten over a period of time. That this is a factor seems certain, but how much of the odor can be explained this way is quite unknown. We have no independent information to indicate whether carrion is a rare or common part of their diet.

Given the sasquatch's posture, bodily wastes certainly pose something of a problem of cleanliness. Excretia will automatically fall down along the legs on at least some occasions, adhere to the hair, and be the source of some of the odor that is reported. We have no reason to think that they practice what we would call personal hygiene, but immersions in water could remove this filth occasionally. Perhaps this is even done deliberately.

Dogs are universally reported to be terrified when in the vicinity of a sasquatch. This has long been noted by the major writers, and I have run across dozens of such reports myself. Often in these encounters no one actually saw the sasquatch, but from sounds, smell, footprints, and/or other evidence the people were sure that one of the creatures was nearby. Obviously there is no assurance that it was a sasquatch that frightened the dog in each case (or in any case for that matter) but that is what the people say, and I'm inclined to believe most of them. Few of these people had previously heard that dogs were afraid of sasquatches, and it is hardly likely that they all would have picked up on an obscure bit of information like this.

This fear is common to all breeds of dogs, of both sexes—from ratters to bear hunters, from lap dogs to bloodhounds. Even the most devoted companion dogs have refused to follow their masters in the direction of one of these animals. I have heard of only one partial exception to this rule where two canines found a fairly fresh sasquatch trail. According to the human at the scene, one dog was quite apprehensive about something in the air, the other, who was half wolf, was not at all concerned. The part wolf was also rather young, and I have no information on the ages of many of the other affected dogs. Maybe it is something that does not bother wolves, or it is activated only with maturity.

I've never known a dog to be repelled by any foul biological smell, so they are probably not frightened by the same odor that people find so repulsive. Another biology researcher, Diane Horton, has suggested to me that a pheromone may be involved, this being one that works differently between distantly related species than the way it acts among conspecifics. This would involve an airborne chemical that can alter the mental state of the recipient at an unconscious level. This fits the observed reactions of many dogs who just seem to be afraid of an immediate area, and not necessarily of any particular thing within it.

Certain people also report that they became uneasy or frightened in the presence of a sasquatch, and often distinctly *before* they had any direct perception of it. Equally impressive is the fact that most people had no such reaction until they became consciously aware of the sasquatch. One could speculate about variable inheritance of a gene that gives sensitivity to the sasquatch pheromone, a gene that is inherited by all dogs. Such a speculation is well beyond the realm of testable knowledge, but it may be more believable than telepathic powers. Like many other lines of reported evidence, little or nothing can be done with this one. Its only practical upshot is to let people know that they cannot count on any hunting help from their dogs.

Bob Titmus noticed over thirty years ago that sasquatches in northern California would sometimes snap off the tops of small trees as they walked by. Little word of this behavior leaked out, and it was not until 1987 that a major instance of this kind of damage was reported in the Blue Mountains. What is not known for sure is whether any of the recent breakage was done by sasquatches, or if it was all done by humans.

I have examined many of these breaks that were shown to me by Paul Freeman. Some of the saplings could easily have been broken by a strong man, others could have been done with mechanical devices that were padded so as to leave no marks. But there are a few breaks that were also twisted, and the twist-and-break action occurred in two places only a few inches apart, with both twists in the same direction. Some of these involved young conifers over two inches in diameter (6 to 8 cm), and often higher off the ground than a man's head. How this could have been done artificially is beyond my own skills; but I remember the boy who ran downhill with his fake feet put on backwards, and wonder what kind of ingenious machine someone might have invented. Titmus assures me that he can duplicate this breakage, and even more, with the help of just one additional man. Clearly, this evidence is far from convincing.

Two other reports of tree damage reached me in 1988 from widely separated parts of Oregon. A call from a young man on the eastern slopes of the Blue Mountains told of broken saplings and other sasquatch evidence. I was not able to investigate this first-hand at the time. It is significant to note that all of the other sasquatch reports, including those of Paul Freeman, were all on the western slopes of that mountain complex, perhaps 10 miles away (16 km).

At about the same time a lady called from the Mount Hood area, 170 miles west of the Blue Mountains, to tell about her observations. These included many footprints of presumed sasquatch origin. She had also noted a pair of trees that stood about four feet apart (1.2 m) on either side of a well-used trail, including supposed sasquatch use. These had recently been pushed down in opposite directions, directly away from each other as if someone stood between them and just shoved them both out. The trees were large enough that several men with ropes would be needed to move even one of them. Again I was unable to go there and check on the actual scene.

Many cases of tree scratching and scraping have been reported, and I saw one of the more notable cases that was found in the Blue Mountains. The scraping was indeed impressive, and it was centered 11 feet (3.4 m) above the ground. It was a flat scraping, not wrapping around the trunk, and I could see no obvious way it could have been reached with a horizontally applied scraping device. On other trees the scraping is located lower down and was no doubt easier to fabricate. But why would a sasquatch be scraping his arms against a tree 11 feet off the ground?

Bedding sites have been reported on a few occasions, and I have seen two of these. One consisted of thumb-diameter branches torn from fir trees and laid out in many random layers as thick as a man's body, and extending about eight feet long and half as wide. It was located only fifty yards from a gravel road in the Blue Mountains of Oregon that is well travelled in the summer, and it contained many of the hairlike strands that later turned out to be artificial fibers. These facts raise suspicions that suggest it was not legitimate. This "bedding" was found near where many tracks and tree breakage had just appeared a few days before, and sasquatch-type noises had been reported. The association might have been no more than coincidental, because the "bedding" branches had been torn off some months previously. If it was all part of an elaborate hoax, some of it was constructed the previous autumn; then the footprints, tree breakage, and noises were added in April at the time of its "discovery." Somehow this doesn't make much sense to me either. We do know that fake hairs were planted at the site, but how much of the rest of it was real, if any, is not now determinable.

The other bedding site was simply a large area of flattened grass, about the size a sasquatch would make if it slept there and rolled over a few times. The spot was on fairly soft dirt, but the grass cover precluded our being able to see any body imprints. No one would have paid it any particular attention if it hadn't been for some sasquatch tracks crossing a stream right next to the spot. One of these footprints was quite clear, and local people from Tollgate, Oregon made a cast of it (Fig. 61). The foot which made that imprint was almost certainly the same individual that Paul Freeman saw on the road four years earlier and about 20 miles (35 km) to the north. The people who found this evidence had no connection with Freeman, and they had never seen the U.S. Forest Service casts or any of the other track casts that were made later. These facts are worth recounting because of the wide-spread belief that much, if not all, of the evidence from the Blue Mountains is part of an elaborate hoax. It should also be noted that if it is a hoax, no one is profiting from it— least of all the investigators themselves who have lost much money, time, and reputation for their efforts.

Sasquatches are often credited with picking up and throwing objects of great weight. Back in 1958, newspaper accounts about the road-building crew in northern California included stories of oil drums, culverts, and huge wheels being thrown about. I read about this event at the time, but didn't take it very seriously. Since then I have picked up much more information about that event and talked with a few of the people who investigated the matter. There is no doubt that fresh footprints at the scene were those of sasquatches. It was here that Bob Titmus, an experienced animal tracker who did not then believe in bigfoot, followed some of his first trails and decided that a real animal was in fact involved. He also investigated the reports of large, man-made objects being thrown around, and found out that none of these stories were true. In the first draft of

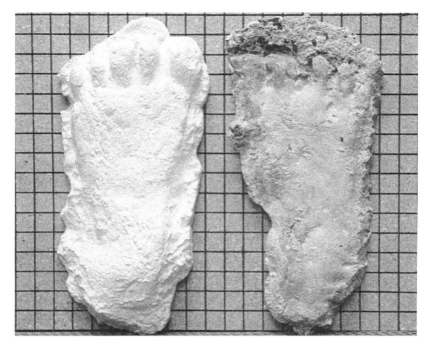

Figure 61. Track from Tollgate, Oregon. A local person made this footprint cast (left) a few miles north of this small resort town in 1986. It appears to be the same individual (right) that was seen and track-cast four years earlier and 20 miles to the north by U.S. Forest Service workers.

this book I dutifully repeated these same stories that appear in almost every bigfoot book. Titmus read that manuscript and corrected (among other things) what seems to have been a combination of rumor and newspaper sensationalism.

Since then I have seen evidence of only two more cases of thrown objects of great weight. These were both in the Blue Mountains where downed tree trunks had been lifted by one end and tossed aside. The required six or eight men would have left many of their own footprints (which were not seen) and should have marked up the trunks with hook marks (which were not there). Still other events of this kind are occasionally reported, but I have no first-hand knowledge of them. Since this kind of destructive activity is fairly visible, especially when human property is involved, it would seem that sasquatches only occasionally indulge in it.

A final item of behavioral evidence is a piece of elk hide that supposedly was chewed on. The story is that an elk was dressed by a local hunter in the Blue Mountains, and the skin was just left at the site. According to my informant, a sasquatch picked this up and dragged it some distance, bit into it once, and then discarded it. The part that showed crush marks was cut out and turned over to me for study. It did appear to have a semicircle of indentations when it was held up in front of a light. I removed the hair to observe the marks more closely and found that they could not be oriented to match the dentition of any likely animal, including sasquatch. My best guess is that the skin was placed on a hard surface and struck repeatedly with another object or objects until the desired result was achieved. The piece of skin was returned to the finder with my opinion being offered, and I'm still not quite sure what really made those marks.

Indian Accounts

Native Americans in the Pacific Northwest have many stories of what sounds rather like our sasquatch. Many of these stories have been faithfully recorded as folklore by anthropologists who felt sure that the indicated animals did not really exist. In one sense this is correct, the hairy bipeds are described as having some undoubted human traits and also a few supernatural powers as well. What these same anthropologists failed to note is that all animals in Indian folklore have human and/or supernatural traits added to them as well. And it is obvious that ravens, coyotes, and beavers are real animals.

Native folklore often uses images of animals who are engaged in humanlike behavior as a vehicle for their cultural traditions and myths. The purposes of these stories can range from explaining origins to making little children behave. (More complex civilized societies have similar stories, though because we are more divorced from nature, the participants mostly have human forms.) If one removes the obviously added human and supernatural aspects from the native mythology, some perfectly real animal descriptions are there to be observed. If one removes the same kinds of aspects from their sasquatch tales, what remains is just what is so often reported by recent Euroamericans. With other folklore characters, removal of these same aspects may leave nothing, in which case it was truly a mythological being.

There is one notable difference between native tales of the sasquatch as contrasted with their tales about other animals, and this may relate to the frequency of encounters. There ought to be somewhat more leeway for variations in the physical descriptions of the sasquatch, as they are not so often being reconfirmed by direct observation. This is indeed the case, and these descriptions vary somewhat from place to place—the most common variation being that a particular feature is simply missing. Since the names also vary, there might be a temptation to think that different species are being referred to.

What I call White Man's accounts are quite different; the animal is simply described as well as possible, and the story usually stops right there. No attempt is made to fit it in with the rest of our cultural traditions; only we anthropologists do that, along with the lunatic fringe. My most interesting source of information to illustrate this contrast was a man whose relatives had told him the native stories when he was a child on the Northwest Coast. He moved out into an academic career in the dominant culture and later, when visiting his home area, saw one of the creatures himself. Thus one man was able to relay to me, and seriously compare, his personal experiences from two very different cultural perspectives.

Figure 62. Indian-carved stone heads. On the left is a representation of a distinctly monkey- or apelike head. It is one of many such heads made by prehistoric natives along the Columbia River. Recent people there have no knowledge of the origin of these objects. At right is a carving of a bighorn sheep by the same people, and it is obviously not the same. (Photos courtesy of Maryhill Museum of Art.)

Native stories that can confidently be related to the sasquatch occur throughout the Pacific Northwest. Their distribution closely corresponds with the area where White Man accounts are concentrated. Attempts have been made to relate native stories from other places to the same phenomenon, but with little success. Arctic stories of the mythical Windigo mostly describe natives who have turned into cannibals; it is only with some difficulty that a sasquatch image can be read into this. In the eastern part of North America there are stories of the "stone clads" who strike with lightening from their fingers. To me this sounds more like an exaggerated version of early encounters with armed and armored Vikings, if it has any physical referent at all.

The pertinence of all this to folklore studies might now be evident. It may be worth reconsidering all native stories about mythical creatures to see if any others may have a physical basis as well. Yeti stories in the Himalayas would be an obvious possibility, which should be compared with their accounts of other animals that certainly do exist. Someone once suggested that applying this reasoning to the Dracula story might lead to an untenable inference. That is not a problem because the Dracula monster was the invention of an English writer who "located" it in Transylvania; the natives there have no such story. (The local history of Count Dracula is of a biologically normal man who just behaved in dreadful ways.)

A final piece of native evidence consists of several carved stone heads that were found along the Columbia River where it separates the present states of Washington and Oregon. These are archeological relics, about which almost nothing is known except that they are many centuries old. The heads are just under human size and are carved to represent what is clearly a monkey or apelike face (Fig. 62). Roderick Sprague, an anthropologist at the University of Idaho, showed these heads to some biologists who positively identified them as representing higher primates. When told where they were found, these biologists then pointed out how clearly they represented bighorn sheep. At the Maryhill Museum, where some of these heads are displayed, there is also a carved stone head from the same source that does represent a bighorn sheep, and it is obviously different. Whoever carved these heads had a good knowledge of what an ape's face looked like. How they gained that knowledge remains to be determined.

6

WHAT IS IT?

There is a considerable quantity of information indicating that a large, bipedal, wild primate is native to certain parts of North America. Science does not recognize its existence, but many individual scientists are interested, and at least a few of them think that it is real. At present, most of the serious investigators are from the lay public; the Scientific Establishment does not encourage, nor offer any funding for, studies of this phenomenon. Those who pursue the sasquatch (bigfoot) investigation do so strictly on their own time and money. Those scientists who take the subject seriously, do so at considerable risk to their professional careers. Most scientific journals will not publish articles on this subject, and many lay investigators jealously withhold their best information. Despite these and many other hinderances, a fairly complete picture of this species is now available. Much of this description was published years ago, notably by Heuvelmans, Sanderson, and Green, but it is worth repeating and updating in the light of the most recent discoveries and scientific studies.

Sometimes people ask me if sasquatch is the "missing link." My usual response is that if they would define that term I would be glad to answer. As it turns out, no one who talks about missing links has any clear concept of what that means. It can mean a morphological intermediate between two species, being halfway between them in all characteristics. It can also mean an intermediate creature with a mixture of characteristics, some like one of the species and some like the other. It can even mean the common ancestor of the two species in question, and it might not be morphologically intermediate at all. Only the second of these three definitions (a mixture of traits) comes close to the truth in this case. In terms of its locomotor adaptations sasquatch appears to have the basic human design; in most other respects it is essentially an ape; and in some ways it is unique and different from both.

Another common misconception is that sasquatch is a "mutation." In the first place, that term implies that there is just a single individual, a common misconception in itself that is very far from the truth. In the second place, every characteristic in which the sasquatch differs from us is the result of a mutation, in their line or ours, that occurred since we last shared a common ancestor. Thus it and we are both mutations, hundreds of times over.

One more version was presented by a member of the audience at the First Annual Cryptozoology Membership Meeting in Vancouver, B.C., in 1982, and stated with an air of complete certainty. We were told that sasquatch is the result of breeding experiments between apes and humans being conducted by Chinese scientists. We were not told how the resulting offspring got loose, or how they reached North America. Nothing was said about when these experiments first began, but it was implied that the current regime was responsible. This opinion may safely be ignored.

What we apparently have here is a perfectly normal species of higher primate that is not especially unusual. All of its characteristics can be matched or exceeded by other mammals, and all but its size can be found among living primates. Its combination of traits is unique, but every species is unique in some way, many of them are much more so than is the sasquatch.

For purposes of this chapter my description is based on information from the Pacific Northwest area. This is where almost all of my own investigations have been conducted. What occurs along this line in other areas is touched on in a later chapter.

Anatomy

We are dealing with reports of an upright creature that walks on two legs, approximately in a human manner. These legs constitute about half of its height, and its two-step walking stride amounts to the same as that height. Bipedalism is its normal mode of locomotion, and individuals are rarely seen in any other pose. They swing their arms front to back in an alternating pattern—right leg forward, right arm back, etc., just as we do.

The size of the sasquatch is perhaps its most remarkable feature. By my calculations, the adult males typically stand 7 feet 8 inches tall

(2.34 m) and weigh about 800 pounds (365 kg). Females are somewhat smaller, standing 6 feet 6 inches tall (2 m) and weighing only
500 pounds (225 kg). With both sexes, their walking heights are
reduced by at least 8% from the above figures because of their posture. These figures also represent something like a consensus of estimates by many observers under good circumstances, but usually with
a correction for weights that are here based on height and body
build. Other anatomical deductions that are described in an earlier
chapter point to the same general sizes. Bob Titmus, one of the most
competent observers I know, accepts these measurements as minimal, but he would estimate as much as 15% upward for statures and
50% more for weights. He may be right.

The body build is very heavyset. A normal human expanded to the
sasquatch height would weigh barely half as much as the estimate I
have made. This redesign is a necessary consequence of absolute
size, which requires different leverage ratios in the musculo-skeletal
system where strength is not otherwise keeping up the increasing
weight. And these changes, in turn, mostly add to the relative weight
at a given stature, much as with elephants. A mechanically impossible situation is soon reached where further adjustments would add as
much weight as they would compensate for. One of the most obvious
of these is the expanded pelvis for attaching leg muscles that correct
for body tilt; the more massive the body, the relatively larger the
pelvis and its musculature must be.

At a given standing height, the sasquatch appears to have a foot
length 1.23 times that of a human of the same stature. Within each of
these two species this ratio should hold for all body sizes. At any
given length, the sasquatch foot averages about one-third wider than
the human foot. Combining these two factors we find that at the
same stature, sasquatch feet have just a trace over twice as much sole
area as occurs in human feet (Fig. 63). Thus if the sasquatch weighed
two times more than a typical man, it would put the same weight,
per unit surface area, on its soles. Since the sasquatch actually seems
to weigh just over twice (2.071 times) as much as a man at the same
stature, it therefore puts very nearly the same weight, per unit surface area, on its soles. In short, the relatively greater sasquatch body
weight, at a given stature, is just made up for by the same increase in
relative foot size.

As absolute size goes up, foot area increases with the square of the
linear increase, while body weight increases with the cube of that same

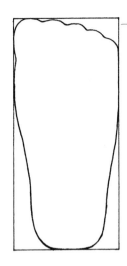

Figure 63. Contrasting foot out-lines. A typical human foot (left) is compared with a typical sasquatch foot (right), set for individuals of the same stature. The sasquatch foot is 23 percent longer than the human, as indicated in the Patter-son film. It is also about one-third wider for the same length (as based on many observed foot-prints), so with the increased length this becomes an actual 64 percent wider. Thus the sasquatch foot, at a given stature, has just a trace over twice the surface area of a human foot.

linear increase. In both species, human and sasquatch, the increasing area of the sole fails to keep up with the more rapidly increasing body weight. Compared with our 5-foot 8-inch athlete, a 6-foot 6-inch man presses down with 15% more weight per unit area, while the typical female sasquatch at that height presses down the same 15% harder. At 7 feet 8 inches, a man presses 35% harder than our standard athlete, and the same-sized sasquatch also presses 35% harder (this would be a typical male of the species). Moving up to 8 feet 2 inches, a man would press 44% harder than our athlete, and the very large sasquatch like-wise presses 44% harder. It appears that there is a limiting factor of just half-again times the relative foot pressure of a normal-sized man versus the largest likely sasquatch. In order to double the weight on a given area of foot surface, the sasquatch would have to be 11 feet 4 inches tall (3.45 m) and would probably weigh 2,650 pounds (1,205 kg). When a sasquatch footprint is two times deeper than a typical man's (or more), this excess must be explained by different walking motions and/or changed soil conditions.

The failure of increasing foot size to keep up with increasing body weight will put limits on how big a sasquatch can get. Compression of the skin and fat of the sole increases toward the theoretical limit of half-again greater, but this is not a serious problem within the pre-sumed size range. Human body weight is transmitted to the ground through no more than 25% of the sole area. Redesigning the sasquatch foot to increase that support area to 38% of the sole would easily handle that problem. The flat arch alone may accomplish most of this redesign. More serious is the tendency for increasing weight to impress the foot ever more deeply into the ground. I would think that as the limiting factor of half-again human is approached, their ability to walk on many kinds of substrates will be seriously impeded. It is not likely that the feet can be made any larger in relation to stature without introducing major walking problems.

The sasquatch body is covered with hair, much like in other mammals, but estimates of its length are quite rarely made and are not very dependable anyway. Perhaps 2 to 4 inches (5 to 10 cm) over most of the body is an estimate that most observers would agree with. For purposes of calculating body volume in the Patterson film, I assumed that the hair surface stands out half an inch (just over one cm) on average, which is not impressive by mammalian standards. If a thicker hair cover is presumed, the calculated body weight is substantially reduced; and any lower weight would be inconsistent with the footprint depths.

Hair is absent on the palms and soles, and it appears to be quite short on the backs of the hands, upper foot, and over most of the face. They do not have a bare patch on the chest like gorillas, nor anywhere else on the body, which is reasonable considering their temperate-climate habitat. A few people claim to have seen rather longer hair on parts of the head and/or neck. No consistent pattern is evident here, so it is no more than an interesting possibility. Cranial hair as short as two inches (5 cm) would probably be enough to conceal the ears, which are almost never noticed.

Hair color is described as dark, dark brown, or black in over half of the reports. The most common variants are a medium or light brown, or even reddish brown. Some observers describe them as being much lighter in color. I have personally heard two accounts of white sasquatches, and there are others on record. One of my "white" reports also had it standing by the side of a road and being notably thin; I think this is an error of some kind. White specimens could be albinos, and there is no good reason to deny this possibility. The coat color is always solid; it is never described as having shading, spots, or stripes.

The arms are commonly reported as being extra large in relation to the rest of the body. They certainly are large, but their diameters in Patterson's film hold about the same relationship to those of the legs as in a very muscular man. Reports of arm length vary greatly, some would have them at about human proportions, and others have the hands hanging below the knees. The film shows that the shoulders are carried very high, as with apes, and the hand seems to swing only a little bit low as measured against the thigh. If the sasquatch happens to be leaning rather far forward at the time its hand swings past a knee, the fingers could easily be at the level of that joint. Many people would see this nonhuman position and understandably report it in exaggerated terms.

Some of the impression of arm size is a reflection of the massive, high-set, and excessively broad shoulders. Instead of being about 25 percent of the stature as in humans, these shoulders are 40 percent as wide as the animal's walking height in the Patterson film. It is quite possible that male sasquatches have relatively wider shoulders than those in the film subject. All front and back sighting reports include similar ratios. The chest and hips appear to be equally broad in relation to stature.

It does not follow, however, that the hip *sockets* would be proportionately wide-set. Their spacing is determined by the size of the birth canal, which could be even smaller than ours. Their great pelvic width results from hip musculature and the bones to which these muscles attach. In order to walk bipedally, especially at this size, the hip sockets should be as close together as possible. At each step, when the entire body weight is supported at only one socket, much effort must be expended to prevent the body from tilting over to the unsupported side. Keeping the hip sockets as close as possible to the midline of the body will minimize this tilting tendency.

There is no visible constriction at the neck. Muscles run diagonally (almost horizontally) from the high-set shoulders directly to the base of the skull, thus filling in this large space that is so conspicuous in human anatomy. The high shoulders, relatively short neck, and a very long face descending from the skull all combine to put the mouth as a level well below the tops of the shoulders. This is the condition found in the larger apes, and contrasts sharply with the human mouth's location that is well above the level of the shoulder tops (Fig. 64). Just as with apes, the sasquatch cannot turn its head very far to the side without its jaw being stopped by contact with the shoulder. In order to turn farther, an ape either tips its head back so that the jaw clears the shoulder, or else it partly turns the torso in the same direction as its head. Patterson's film clearly illustrates the latter action.

One person reported a close observation of a sasquatch, face on, and said it had no mouth and was breathing through a hole in its

Figure 64. Contrasting shoulder levels. In living apes (left), the mouth is located well below the level of the shoulder tops; in humans (right), the mouth is much higher than the shoulders. Apes have taller faces that project the mouth rather lower, and carry their shoulders much higher in relation to the rib cage. According to many reports, clear views of sasquatch faces indicate the same relatively low mouth position as in the apes.

chest. The actual relationships of these parts could conceivably lead to that conclusion by someone who knew nothing about ape anatomy, and who was trying to fit his observation into the human body design. This particular report should not be taken too seriously because Russell Gebhart, who followed up the study, found enough other discrepancies that it all sounded dubious. Still, that was an anatomical description that did make sense in an interesting way.

The face is most often described as being apelike, but frequently with the qualification that the mouth area was not greatly protruding. The nose does not stand out far, but it may be slightly more protruding than is normal for apes' noses. Perhaps the most apelike trait would be the overhanging brow ridges with the sharply retreating forehead above them. The facial structure can be clearly seen in the Patterson film by viewing some adjacent frames stereoscopically. (There was only one camera involved here, but as the subject turned its head slightly from one frame to the next, the same effect can be obtained by viewing them in pairs.) What struck me most in these stereos was how the face was almost vertical, and the forehead so nearly horizontal, that the brow ridges formed a surprisingly prominent angle between these two surfaces.

Teeth have been described by only a few observers. Most often these are said to be humanlike, or "even" teeth. There are a few reports of projecting fangs, but these could easily be exaggerations by overly frightened observers, or else elaborations that were added to fit with the overall impression of a "monster." It is possible that both descriptions could be true if the sasquatch is the species that I think it is, which is known from the fossil record.

Hand-to-foot size ratios are the same as in humans, judging from tracks and the film, but they both appear to be rather large as compared with length measurements in the rest of the body. A foot length of 15 percent of the stature is normal for men, and 14.8 percent for women, while here these are over 18 percent and well beyond the human range of variation. A maximum relative foot size makes sense when one considers the pressure that is put on the sole. There is no obvious reason why the hand should be comparably large, but the same genes could be affecting the size of both extremities. Given their relative foot size, the name "bigfoot" is actually rather descriptive. I had long resisted this name because it seemed to put undue emphasis on just one part of an overall big anatomy, and preferred the name sasquatch instead. Now I am willing to use the two names almost interchangeably.

On the basis of hundreds of recorded footprints it can be stated that the toes are more nearly equal to each other in size than are human toes. Among those casts that I have available for study, there seem to be three variations, with two or more individuals in each type: (1) toes are all nearly equal in size; (2) first toe is slightly larger than the rest, with the latter being nearly equal to each other; and (3) first toe is substantially larger, but still not as much so as in human feet (Fig. 65). The second category is by far the most common.

Relative toe lengths also vary, which can best be compared in terms of their degree of anterior projection, and again I find three categories: (1) all toe tips are about equidistant from a point at about the center of the foot, thus they arch evenly across the front of the foot; (2) the first toe is the most anterior, and the line of toe tips runs at a slight diagonal across the front, with the outside toe being behind the first toe by about one-seventh of the total foot length at most; and (3) the toe tips line up with a more diagonal slope, putting the outside toe tip about one-fifth of a foot length back (Fig. 66). In human feet the diagonal slopes only a little more than in this last type. Here too the second category is by far the most common.

On the basis of full handprints from three different individuals, we see the finger equivalents of the most common toe types. In all three cases the four fingers are almost equal in size, and the thumb does not have the extra width that is seen in human hands. The third digit is the widest and longest, but exceeds the fifth digit by only about 10 per-

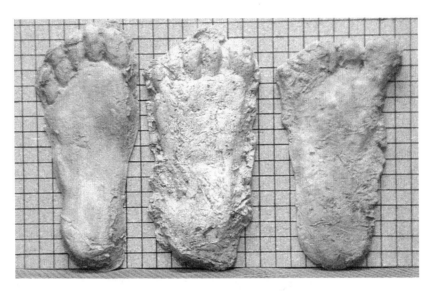

Figure 65. Three sizes of first digits. Sasquatch footprints include three variations in relative toe size. Left: the toes are all nearly equal, center: the first toe is slightly larger than the others, and right: the first toe is substantially larger. The "slightly larger" category is the most common.

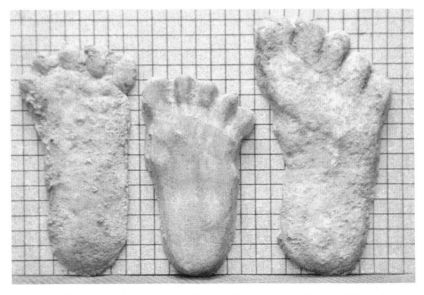

Figure 66. Three slopes of toe tips. Sasquatch toes show three variations in how their toe ends line up across the front of the foot. Left; all toes form an arch at the end of the foot, center: the first toe is ahead and the others form a slight diagonal, and right: the toe tips form an almost human diagonal. The "slight diagonal" category is the most common.

cent in linear dimensions, while these two human fingers differ from each other by more like 25 percent in length and 15 percent in width.

The foot is relatively much wider than in humans (typically 33 percent at the same length), which is especially unusual for such long feet. I don't know of a good instance where the width is less that one-third of the length, which is always the case for large human feet; their width sometimes approaches, but does not reach, one half of the length. The hands are disproportionately broad to the same degree. Judging from prints of typical male sasquatches, both their hands and feet are roughly twice as wide as mine and half-again longer.

Absolute toe lengths, like those of fingers, are difficult or impossible to read from their imprints. In the chapter on print anatomy I showed how the toes could best be interpreted as being quite short as compared with the length of the foot. There are no equivalent landmarks in the hand, like the double ball or the side bulges of Cripple Foot, which might help to indicate where the ends of the metacarpals are located on the palm. But in the fingers themselves we can see indications of flexion creases for the last two joints. These creases show that the last two phalanges are quite short, so it is a safe guess that the nearer phalange is short as well. The knuckle imprint shows the length of only the middle phalanges; an imprint of a closed fist would have been more informative.

The bottom of the foot is flat; there is no longitudinal arch, nor a transverse one. In the human foot these arches are maintained by ligaments between the bones, and by muscular tension on tendons that descend from the lower leg. In extremely heavy people these structures do not have the strength (surface dependent) to support the weight (volume dependent). There is no obvious way that any foot arches could be maintained with the weight of even a female sasquatch. This is an academic point anyway, because we can observe many sasquatch footprint casts that are quite flat. In walking, an arched foot always leaves an arched footprint, and this arching is usually exaggerated over what occurs in the actual foot. In walking, a flat foot sometimes leaves a flat footprint, but this is more often altered into a slight arch shape from the mechanics of imprinting.

The anterior shift of the ankle joint has already been described in some detail as a biomechanical requirement for a bipedal walker of this size. One of the most interesting results of this redesign is that the foot should appear to have relatively little forward extension beyond the shin. In spite of a foot that is a bit elongated relative to stature, the ankle should be far more thickened, front to back, so as to make the forefoot look short. Exactly this condition is seen in several frames of Patterson's film, where the front of the shin lines up with the midpoint of the foot length. Figure 67 gives my reconstruction of that foot compared with a human foot.

The nonopposed thumb has been described in some detail and can be seen in hand casts of four different individuals from two locations. It should be noted that this is not called an unopposable thumb, a term that means it cannot be turned against the finger tips. We know the thumb orientation in five instances of the hand being applied to the ground (two casts are of one individual); how the thumb worked at other times is not directly known. The absence of a thenar pad, however, indicates that it would have had no strength in an opposing move, even if such a move were possible. Given such a large hand that presumably does heavy work, it does not seem likely that rotational flexibility would have been retained.

The thick fat pads on the soles and palms have also been described. The most common evidence of this comes from the variation in footprint sizes and shapes of the same foot in repeated steps. It is also indicated by some vertical or overhanging imprint walls, especially where skin detail can be seen in these walls. The most vivid evidence comes from the two footprints on top of sole-intruding stones. From the side imprint of one thumb we get a direct measure of the pad's thickness. The near absence of flexion creases under the fingers and toes may be ascribed to this padding. The virtual absence

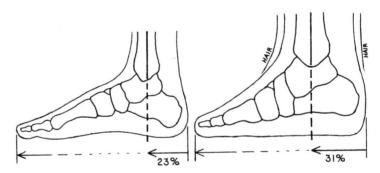

Figure 67. Foot design in Patterson's film. The anatomy of a normal human foot (left) and the author's reconstruction of the foot from the film (right) are compared here. In the film, it can be seen that the front edge of the shin lines up exactly with the midpoint of the sole. Allowing for probable hair thickness, the ankle still is relatively far forward. My estimate is that 31 percent of the total foot length is behind the ankle joint, compared with only 23 percent in humans.

of nail marks would also be, in part, a result of this great pad thickness. Wearing of the nails is the other reason for their absence.

There are clearly two sexes of sasquatches. Sightings often include female breasts and sometimes male genitalia, though most observers are so overwhelmed by the overall phenomenon that they do not notice, or remember, details like these. Where breasts are reported, standing statures seem to be around 6.5 feet (just under 2 m); where a small penis and scrotum are reported, statures seem to be more like 7.7 feet (2.34 m). Since most of the footprints fall into the two size groups of 14.5 and 17 inches (37 and 43 cm), and assuming both of these to represent 18.6 percent of their statures, we seem to have a rough measure of their sexual dimorphism. The corresponding body weights would be at the ratio of the cubes of these linear measurements. Most of my calculations indicate that the males are about 60 to 65 percent more massive than the females. This degree of dimorphism is much more than in humans, where males average 30 percent heavier, but it is less than in gorillas and orangs where the males weigh twice as much as the females.

The reported small size of the male genitalia is consistent with other higher primates, while humans have by far the largest. The vagina must be able to expand to accommodate the newborn head size. Given a similar rate of postpartum contraction of the vagina, penis size would have to vary in a corresponding way to provide comparable stimulation to the females of each species. Thus we find a correlation between the sizes of brains and penises among higher primates, and sasquatch evidently is not in the human category in either respect.

In the absence of any data to the contrary, we may safely presume that all parts of the life span of the sasquatch are about the same as in apes, and there is some evidence to support this conclusion. Life spans may be divided into four major parts: gestation, growth, maturity, and old age. Apes and humans all have nearly the same gestation time of thirty-six to thirty-nine weeks; we may safely presume the same for sasquatch. All apes and humans have a mature, reproductive life span of about thirty years if nothing cuts it short, as is often the case; we may presume the same for sasquatch. Age data on known primates used here is from Schultz (1968) and is shown in Figure 68.

The growth stage of humans lasts about twenty years, while apes reach the same degree of maturity in just half that length of time.

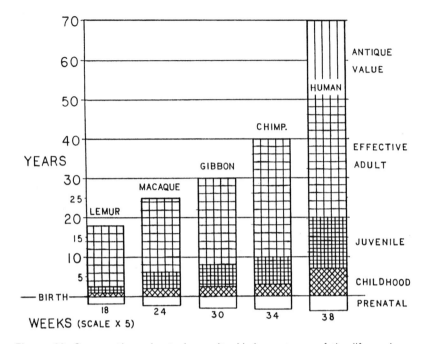

Figure 68. Comparative primate longevity. Various stages of the life cycle are shown here. Prolongation of the human life span is in our doubled growth stage and in the added old age. Since both of these relate to our over-developed brains, it may be presumed that the sasquatch life cycle most likely matches the chimpanzees' and other great apes' longevity.

Human growth is prolonged because of the nutritional requirements of feeding the growing brain in early childhood, and the effects of this early slow-down continue until full adulthood is reached. Our growth delay ensures that twice as much food is consumed while growing up, thus providing a greater store of proteins to draw upon for brain development. This also means that a nutritional shortfall of a few weeks represents a smaller fraction of the prolonged developmental time. As I pointed out in 1981, our slow development is not in order to give us time to learn our culture, as is generally assumed. If that were true, then our culture must have become much simpler in the last few centuries while our children have been maturing at ever younger ages. Instead, improved nutrition has recently reduced the need for the maximum prolongation of growth.

The significance to the sasquatch of this digression is that they would not have any reason for the slow growth rate of humans. We have already seen from the requirements of pelvic design that the sasquatch probably did not have a human-sized birth canal, and the small male genitals point to the same conclusion. With a small brain size at birth, and a large maternal body to tap for its nutrition, there would have been no biological advantage for their childhood to be prolonged any more than it is in apes.

Old age in apes begins by forty years when their biological deterioration seriously begins. At this age eyesight and hearing start to fail, strength significantly reduces, and many other ailments tend to impede their effectiveness. Under natural conditions death normally occurs at this time (if not before). The same physical debilities occur in humans ten years later—an extra ten years of development, plus the same thirty years of adulthood, puts the human life span at fifty years under natural conditions. New methods of age determination show that among all the ancient human fossils, up to and including the Neandertals, not a single one reached fifty years of age. Recent humans who live beyond this point do so because of what I would call their "antique value." Older people generally acquire cultural knowledge and skills that allow them to continue socially useful lives into much greater ages. Sasquatch shows no indication of cultural behavior, and almost certainly does not have enough brain to do so. Thus there is no reason to think that their lives were at all prolonged by antique value, as in humans.

In summary, sasquatch life expectancy is probably about the same as for the apes—forty years if nothing serious intervenes. Given the virtual absence of natural predators (only the grizzly bear comes close), accidents or disease are the most likely reasons for terminating life at an early stage. It is always possible that their teeth may fail, and they die dental deaths as elephants regularly do. If this occurs at all, it may relate to the local ecology and its effect on tooth wear. At our present stage of knowledge no serious suggestion like this is warranted.

Without significant predators, and presumably having a reasonable food supply, the sasquatch may be expected to suffer very few losses other than natural deaths related to age. This is the situation for the great apes as well, and their reproductive rate is correspondingly low. If the apes lose only about half of their offspring, and these mostly in infancy, the sasquatch likely has at least an equally low death rate. With natural selection taking out no more than 50 percent, this leaves them with an extremely high survival rate as compared with most animals. As a consequence the amount of individual variation should also be very high. This is true of the great apes. There is as much morphological variation in a single band of gorillas as there is an entire species of most monkeys. The considerable differences that are seen in various sasquatch footprints are thus fully expectable in a species that is under very low selection pressure. We might expect to find a similar degree of individual variation in many other anatomical traits, like tooth projection and arm length, for example.

Ecology

The manner in which the sasquatch fits into its environment is only roughly known. Some information can be gleaned from the many direct observations, but there is always the possibility that some of this information is incorrect due to exaggeration, distortion, or even fabrication. To some degree this can be tested by the number and probable quality of reports, and also by how well the information fits in with other lines of evidence. We can also learn something from the distribution and particular circumstances of footprint evidence. Finally we have a logical approach of figuring out the needs and capabilities of an animal of this description, and matching them to the resources and opportunities that are available in their known environment. We do have the analogy of bear behavior that serves as something of a guide.

The sasquatch is clearly a nocturnal species. John Green's records show about the same number of sightings by day as by night. Outside of cities, the number of people moving about who might see a sasquatch at night is perhaps one-tenth as many as during daylight hours. The field of vision of these night-active people is also much restricted, they can see only within the range of their artificial illumination (or occasionally by moonlight), and this is certainly less than one-tenth of what they could have seen by day. If we multiplied the night sighters by ten times, and gave each of them the ability to see ten times more area, then they would have seen a hundred times as many sasquatches as they actually have reported. Given the current sighting totals, this means that sasquatch activity is a hundred times more common by night than by day. The one-tenth visibility by night is probably much too large a fraction, so the preponderance of nocturnal activity is probably well over 99 percent. I see no way around this conclusion; if they were equally active by day and night we should be seeing them at least a hundred times more often by day, yet the numbers are about equal.

Nocturnal behavior would presuppose night vision to some degree. This is not directly demonstrable, but it can be inferred from their anatomy as well as from their behavior. Sasquatch eyes have often been observed, and no one has suggested that their size is anything other than in normal proportion to the body in general, and the face in particular. Actually, primate eye diameters do not vary quite as much as overall linear dimensions of the body. My estimate is that the sasquatch eye is only about 1.3 times greater in diameter than ours. This means their retinas have 1.7 times the area of typical human eyes. Since light-receptive cells are about the same size in all primates, it follows that the sasquatch retina has 1.7 times as many receptors as ours has. The human eye contains 7 million cones that respond to bright light in color, and 130 million rods that respond to dim light without being color sensitive. If the number of cones is the same in sasquatch, they would have the same daylight vision as we have, and that is consistent with the many reports of mutual observation. Then if the excess receptors are all rods, their night vision should be 1.74 times better than ours, all else being equal. All else may not be equal, and a greater range of pupillary opening is one possibility, which could add to their night vision capability. There are also many reports of light reflecting from sasquatch eyes, but these are so contradictory I will not attempt to make sense of them. Suffice it to say that strong reflections of yellow, orange, and red are the most common descriptions. Stories about "glowing" eyes may safely be discounted.

A large, warm-bodied animal will require a correspondingly large amount of food. Because of its great size, a sasquatch has less surface area, per unit volume, than have smaller mammals, and thus it is losing to the environment a smaller proportion of the heat that its body is generating. Since most food is used in maintaining body temperature, it requires fewer calories per kilogram than most other mammals in the same environment. Although this represents a considerable savings, the absolute amount of food that is consumed by each individual still would be among the highest of North American mammals. The fact that their major activity is by night, in lower temperatures, may substantially reduce this economy that results from great size.

The kinds of foods that are consumed by sasquatches have been reported by many observers; how many of these reports are accurate is a matter of diverse opinion. They have been seen eating berries off bushes and digging for some kinds of roots; the nonopposed thumbs give them four good interdigital spaces for raking berries and five digging instruments. At least one observer saw a sasquatch digging out rodents who were hibernating under rocks, and the thumb was not seen in an opposed action. They are often seen to pull up fern stalks and eat the base of the root—apparently with a wrapping around, grasping action of the hand. All of these feeding behaviors involved making good use of the hands to accomplish what a bear would do somewhat less effectively with its claws and teeth. For tearing into rotten logs after small animals, the bear's equipment would be just as good or better than the sasquatch's hands.

Many people claim to have observed sasquatches eating food that was provided by human activities. This includes taking fish off of drying racks, picking apples, and stealing chickens. I have heard two accounts of hunters who shot a deer, only to have it grabbed by a two-legged, hairy monster that walked off with it. This might be a good excuse for why you didn't get a deer that season, but making up a story about a bear taking it would have been much more believable. Jim Hewkins is convinced they scavenge carcasses that result from any and all causes, and try to put these into places that are less accessible to other scavengers. It is also possible that they catch and kill elk on many occasions. Bringing down an elk sounds like a very difficult undertaking for an animal that is not designed for a high-speed chase, nor with any indication of cooperative hunting. But human activity has reduced the large natural predators, and these humans take only the prime adults themselves, so the resulting stock of sick, lame, injured, and older elk might provide rather easy pickings.

It is at least possible that the sasquatch has a hind-gut fermenter where less nutritious plants are broken down by bacterial action over a long period of time. Almost all mammalian herbivores in temperate-to-cold climates have such fermenters, which allow them to extract more usable energy from poor quality winter foods. In North America bears are the only large mammal that does not have this adaptation, presumably because they sleep through the winter. Such a fermenter would not be unusual for a primate in this climate, and the sasquatch abdomen is certainly large enough. But given their bearlike diet and their longer feeding nights in the winter, it may not be necessary.

In general I would describe the sasquatch as omnivorous. It is probably mainly a vegetarian and what might be called an "opportunistic carnivore." Meat may be its preferred dietary item, but it has no obvious specializations toward any particular game, so it grabs what it can, whenever and however it can. As long as the quarry does not fight back in a damaging manner, any species is fair game.

Skeptics often assert that there is no ecological niche for the sasquatch to occupy. It is pointed out that the food supply for a large mammal is notoriously small in temperate forests. This is true, but numerous bears live in that same environment quite successfully. The available food is rather broadly distributed, so vast herds of large omnivores would not be practical. Bears forage individually over large areas, and are seen together only in mating or when a mother is rearing her young, or else when the food supplies are very abundant. Congregations of bears, such as in their salmon fishing sites, are rare and circumstantial. The most reasonable expectation would be that sasquatches similarly distribute themselves over the countryside, with groupings only of the same general kinds. This accords with the sighting reports, 90 percent of which are of single individuals; the vast majority of footprint events are likewise those of solitary travelers.

Sasquatches and bears are probably competing for mostly the same food resources in the same areas. However thinly these species may be distributed, occasional encounters would occur and could be damaging to one or both of them. This happens between brown (grizzly) and black bears, with the latter generally getting the worst of it. Black bears would likewise be little threat to any sasquatch except the very young, but they could be annoying at times. With grizzlies there would be a much closer size match, and any encounter is potentially threatening. The nocturnal behavior of the sasquatch serves to minimize such meetings, both species of bears being diurnal. It was Ivan Marx who first pointed out to me how they divided up the clock between them. He described bears as keeping lazy human hours, rising late in the morning and continuing to forage for a short time after sunset, while sasquatch activity seems to be mostly from near midnight to just past dawn. This may be a very old adjustment for mutual avoidance that just happens to keep their activities separated from those of humans as well.

Current estimates of sasquatch numbers would place them in the low thousands. How many thousands depends mainly on how large a part of North America is considered to be inhabited by them. Judging from the relative numbers of footprints that are encountered, it is safe to say that there are at least a hundred bears for every one sasquatch. It follows that they constitute only 2 or 3 percent of the combined biomass of those species. The Pacific Northwest contains at least two hundred thousand bears; there could easily be two thousand sasquatches in the same area. If the sasquatch is actually as widespread over the continent as current reports would have it, we could easily postulate that there are anywhere from ten to twenty thousand of them.

Another indication of population would be the fact that my present collection includes tracks of twenty different individuals. These have come from only a tiny part of the habitable area for this species within the Pacific Northwest. Most of the rest of this area has produced many reports of sightings and tracks, but none of the latter have reached my collection. It would be rash to think that I have track casts of more than one percent of the individuals, thus their total population in the Pacific Northwest must be at least two thousand. One could also argue that my casts span at least two generations of sasquatches, with many of the track makers now being dead. This line of reasoning serves to double the population estimate in my area of familiarity to four thousand—a figure that Titmus would accept, but which sounds a bit high to me.

Winter survival is a problem for most species in temperate climates, and there are many ways that this is handled. How the sasquatch manages is not directly known, but some pertinent observations can be made. They do not hibernate for months like some rodents, nor sleep soundly like bears, because they and their tracks are encountered year around. John Green's records show a decrease in reports by about one-half during the months of January, February, and March. That decrease more likely represents a reduction in human activities than in sasquatch behavior. It is true that trappers are active in the winter, but they are much less likely to talk about their observations than are the usual vacationers and explorers. The time of low reports is shifted to almost a month later than the time of most severe winter conditions. Again I think this is a human variable. As winter begins we seem to be out in it as much as possible, making preparations for difficult weather ahead, or engaged in sporting events. As winter ends and the snow is melting, transportation is greatly impeded and few people are in the places where sasquatches are usually to be found.

During the winter months the sasquatch's most direct competitor is asleep and eating nothing. During winter the feeding "day" of a nocturnal animal is greatly lengthened, thus giving the sasquatch a greater share of the clock than any of its diurnal competitors. Whatever food may be available in winter, the sasquatch's access to it is maximized by these two simple facts.

Pine trees alter their physiology in the fall to increase the sugar content of the needles as a kind of natural antifreeze. This is a potential source of nutrition for any animal that can utilize it, and the sasquatch apparently does so. Long ago a serious investigator told me that sasquatches are found only where some kind of pine is part of the natural vegetation. This turned out to be true for almost all of the reports that I have mapped out. More direct evidence comes from the observation by Bob Titmus that sasquatch scat contains pine needles whenever he finds it during the winter. He told me this only after I had discovered the other information and asked him what he thought about it.

There may be much more to sasquatch winter survival than just food supply. They likely put on a thick layer of fat in the fall, both for insulation and as a calorie supply to draw upon later. They would migrate seasonally to more acceptable winter climates to the degree that they can. The greatest distance I have heard of is 90 miles (145 km) as the bird flies, along a north-south line within northern California. At other locations the best they can do might be to shift to the lowest accessible altitudes and, if possible, near to large bodies of water. Increasing their raiding of human resources would be an obvious recourse, but this seems not to be frequent or we would know more about it.

Some investigators have stressed the ability of the sasquatch to swim, and there are many reports to this effect. When they are seen in water I would wonder how the observer was able to identify the animal. A clear view of the face and/or the hands might be convincing, but little could then be seen of body shape or leg length, and certainly not the posture that is so distinctive. My hesitation on this aspect is only because none of the eyewitnesses I have personally talked to had seen them swimming. There is no doubt that they freely walk through smaller bodies of water as though they were not there. One of the top archeologists at the Smithsonian Institution saw a trail of undoubted sasquatch tracks in northern Canada pass straight through a substantial pond that any human certainly would have walked around. When Cripple Foot left his longest trail back in early 1970, his tracks came out of a large lake and eventually went back into it. Their reported existence in many of the off-shore islands in western Washington, British Columbia, and the panhandle of Alaska would seem to demand at least occasional interchange of personnel with other islands and with the mainland. With such a low population density as is indicated, most of these islands would be too small to maintain a successful breeding population over a period of several generations. These islands have been isolated for hundreds of times that long.

The panic reaction to the sasquatch on the part of dogs might be looked at as an ecological adaptation, but it doesn't make much sense by itself. Even the largest dogs would pose no serious threat to the safety of any sasquatch beyond infancy. A pack of wolves might be able to take a half-grown youngster, but that's about as far as it goes. Bears and puma would constitute much more serious threats to their safety than dogs, but we have no information about how these other species react to the presence of sasquatch. Perhaps their odor evolved as a repellent to bears, and dogs (being fairly close relatives of bears) inherited the same reaction for no reason that applies especially to them. On the other hand, there are many stories of sasquatches going out of their way to kill dogs. If these are true, there must be some conflict between these two species that has no obvious significance at our present state of knowledge.

The subconscious fear reaction of some humans was discussed above as a possible pheromone effect. Pheromones usually function to attract mates within a species. In sasquatch a pheromone might have evolved that functions to repel individuals of the same sex, particularly males, from each other. This would serve the double function of discouraging mating competition and also to help maintain a good foraging distance between them. Just how these could become so individualized is another problem. Since humans are no doubt close relatives of theirs, it should not be surprising that some of us get a similar reaction. At present, this is speculation on my part, but when more evidence is available it might be looked at more seriously.

Society

The social relations of this species are the basis of much speculation, but we can safely postulate some limits within which sasquatch life must be organized. We know that they do not form social units where the individuals are physically proximate, like the foraging bands of other terrestrial primates. Neither is it likely that they form monogamous pairs, even of a few years duration, otherwise the sight-ings and footprint occurrences would have indicated this. (Mo-nogamy is pretty much restricted to small arboreal primates in tropical environments, and sasquatch is about as far from that as it is possible to get.)

There does appear to be a high degree of the same individuals recurring in the same general areas. The clearest case of this is from northern California. Bob Titmus often found tracks of the same five individuals in the Bluff Creek area during part of each year, and again some distance away during the other part. Occasionally two or more lines of footprints would be more-or-less together, but it was not always clear if they were placed at the same time or were hours apart. A small social group is indicated here, but close physical prox-imity of its members was not the general rule.

Paul Freeman reported finding tracks of the same four sas-quatches in the Blue Mountains from 1982 to 1987, and some of us dubbed them "the gang of four." In 1987 three new sets of tracks appeared, one was of twelve-inch feet that could represent a young individual who was just starting to travel on his own, and two were of full-sized adults that appeared to be intruding into an established territory. A local farmer in northeastern Washington assured me that he had seen Cripple Foot's distinctive tracks in the area twenty years before the big flap in 1970, and six years later an excited college stu-dent told me of just seeing exactly the same tracks about forty miles south of there. Similar clusters of reports have been checked out by other investigators, with varying degrees of reliability.

In my two best cases of what appear to be diffuse social groups, there was only one adult male in each of them. This suggests that we are dealing with a single male or harem type of organization that also commonly occurs among primates and many other mammals. Orang utans have this system, where an adult male forages over his area and excludes all other adult males from it. Within his area several females will have their own exclusive tracts separated from each other where they forage, meet the male, and occasionally rear a young one. These one-male orang units typically cover 6 to 8 square miles, with about 2 square miles for each female unit within it. (These are 15 to 20 square km for the male, and 5 square km for the females.) If sasquatch social organization follows this pattern, it is on a far grander scale, given their larger size, terrestrial limitation, and sparser distribution of food resources. Their equivalent areas might be more like 200 square miles, with 40 square mile subdivisions (500 and 100 sq. km).

A variation on this organization would be that all sasquatch females and their young share equally in the territory of the single male. The evidence is too sketchy and undependable for us to distinguish between these two models, but I would be inclined toward the idea of free foraging. There are a fair number of double-track events where both of them could easily have been adult females or adolescent males; either interpretation would rule out exclusive female home ranges. Only if all such cases are of adult females with their adolescent male offspring, can the model of separate female areas be maintained. It also seems to me that with unpredictable variations in winter severity and occasional resource failures, the more flexible system would be the most efficient.

In either variation of the small, one-male social group there would be a surplus of males every generation who must be accounted for. As each young female matures, she either stays with the group to mate with the dominant male, who is often her father (though he may have been replaced), or else she moves to some nearby social group. In either location she will normally replace an older female who recently died. As each young male matures, he must either replace the dominant male of his group, again often his father, or else he goes to a nearby group to see if he can displace the dominant male there. Assuming an equal sex ratio at birth, and an average of four females per social unit, this means that only one-fourth of the maturing males can find places in the social system at any location. What happens to the rest of them?

If the above model is even approximately correct, the surplus males would have to be rogues, wandering from one social unit to another looking for an opportunity to displace the lead male in one of them. One consequence of this should show in the geographical distribution of different kinds of sasquatches. Consort couples and mother-child pairs should occur mainly in the more inaccessible safe areas of regular habitation, while single individuals of large size should be almost randomly distributed over the habitable countryside. I checked this possibility with published maps of land use in the greater Pacific Northwest and mapped the locations of about five hundred sasquatch reports from John Green's files. Safe areas were outlined on the basis of minimal human commercial use of any and all kinds. Out of all the sasquatch reports, I separately marked those that included two or more individuals (consort pairs?), obvious females, and those of notably small size (young?). It turned out that these multiple, female, and small sasquatches had a strongly marked tendency to be located in or near the areas of minimal human use. Almost all of the reports that were located well away from such places sounded like what we usually call adult males. I think this is a good indication of what is happening to the rogue males.

One would presume that sasquatches have methods of locating one another in addition to chance encounters. Their presumed loud calling voices would be one such method, though the available evidence suggests that this system is only occasionally used. We have no idea whether these calls are mating signals (from males or females), male-to-male threats, mother-child locators, or just social noises in general; maybe there are different calls that serve each of these functions.

Given their good vision and probable intelligence, sasquatches may be looking at more than each other's bodies for recognition. It is at least possible that they are quite aware of footprints, including their own as well as each other's. With or without an associated odor, they may be able to recognize each individual by his/her distinctive footprints. The high variability in foot details could be a distinct advantage here that would serve to enhance individuality. By knowing where various other group members have recently traveled, one sasquatch has at least a slightly better picture of where they may be at the moment. How well they can see footprints by night is another problem. I should think that most of their footprint information would have to be gathered during the two or three hours of activity after first light in the mornings. If other species can recognize individuals from scents, it would require no more intelligence for the sasquatch to do the same from visual cues.

Assuming that they are equally aware of their own footprints, it follows that they should also know the physical circumstances where footprints are made or not made. They should be quite able, if they chose, to walk in a manner that leaves as few footprints as possible. They should equally be able to deliberately leave many and/or clear footprints for other sasquatches to see. On some occasions footprints have been found so neatly planted in just the best spots of loose or moist dirt, that it seemed as if they were deliberately planted. To most minds that translates into human fakery, but this is not necessarily so. It could just as easily have been deliberation on the part of the sasquatch itself.

In the spring of 1987, tracks of one or two new adult males were found in many places in the Blue Mountains, where only one adult male had been noticed during the preceding five years. (The two new foot designs are so similar to each other that it is even possible that only one individual was involved.) Unlike most of the previous track situations, many of these were obviously planted to assure high visibility. I saw a few of these lines of tracks, and there is no doubt in my mind that their locations did not result just from casual walking. What the skeptics failed to notice in this situation was that it was only the tracks of the newcomers that were so conspicuous. The tracks of the previous four inhabitants continued to be found only on rare occasions. The newcomers' tracks were in conspicuous locations in general, especially on paths that followed along ridges; the residents' tracks had rarely been noticed in places like that before. If a new male, or a pair of them, had just intruded into this area to challenge the resident-in-charge, this seems like just the kind of activity that might be expected. Along the same trails we found much of the tree breakage that has been mentioned.

It is true that artificial fibers were introduced into some of these tree breaks, and this raises considerable question about the entire scenario. I find it easy to accept that some hairlike material was added to enhance the picture, and on one occasion I know who did it and when. It is even quite likely that all or most of the tree breakage was done by humans as well, but I'm somewhat less sure about this. I still find it difficult to see how all of the footprints could have been faked in these situations.

If my reading of the 1987 Blue Mountain evidence is correct, one or two adult males came into the area to attempt a take-over of the dominant male's position. If there were two, they were likely brothers (or half brothers) because they apparently were not in conflict with each other. Their footprints were also very similar, both having the rare toe design that arcs across the end of the foot. One has toes that are all about the same size, the other has a conspicuously larger and longer first digit; I've named them Earl and Big Toe. If adult male sasquatches have pheromones that are mutually repelling, these two might have inherited exactly the same chemistry, thus enabling them to get along with each other.

While we have seen what may be interpreted as a "show of force," we have no idea what the outcome was. By that time Paul Freeman was almost out of action from his injured foot, and no one in my circle of contacts was able to put in the amount of searching time that he formerly did. Most of my information flow from this area had now stopped. Freeman was also getting increasingly irritated by people who claimed that his data was all fake. None of his critics could show how the tracks could have been made, nor how the larger saplings could have been twisted off. Just like most of the serious investigators, Freeman knew full well that only the retrieval of body parts would prove that sasquatch is real. Casting tracks and gathering other evidence would not get him any closer to the goal, and his interest along these lines has reduced.

Trying to interpret the evidence of a social disruption is very hypothetical in the first place, and it is not something that can be verified in any case. Maybe Earl and Big Toe were able to displace Big Daddy; they might even have killed him. Or maybe Big Daddy was the winner and drove the intruders away. What does seem to be evident is that this contest of wills, if not of bodies, was probably over within the year. Even the less determined investigators should have found evidence of the foot stamping and tree breaking if it had continued. If anyone thinks we ought to concentrate on looking for the body of one of the adversaries of this contest, he obviously has no concept of how nearly impossible the task would be.

Most primates do not have a seasonal breeding cycle, but in a climate with severe winters this might be desirable. Other mammals who breed in any season in the tropics often have closely related species in temperate or arctic climates who are seasonal breeders. Pregnant females and their young offspring are especially at risk, and the optimum season for the end of gestation is usually in the spring. This is when the food supply for the mother is at maximum, and the climate for the newborn is acceptable and improving. Breeding is timed in order for births to occur at the most advantageous time.

When the same reasoning is applied to sasquatch we get no clear answer. With a developmental rate about the same as for apes, a spring birth would still leave them with a relatively small child by the time the next winter begins, and it would again be at severe risk. The mother would also be taxed by a late pregnancy in the worst season, though other temperate-climate mammals are able to handle that problem. If the mother is in some kind of denning circumstance, birth and infancy could be in the winter, even if at some risk, and the infant would have a few extra months of growth before the following winter sets in. This same reasoning could be used to set the birth time still farther back until the whole year is covered. No matter how its birth is timed, there are going to be at least two winters that will put the infant, and to some degree its mother, at considerable risk of not surviving. Juggling the birth time simply shifts the weight between the two winters, and between threatening the infant directly, or indirectly through its mother's health. Given no indication of what may be the best birth time, we have no hint of the mating season, which ought to be nine months earlier.

Intelligence

There is considerable evidence, as the reader has seen, that sasquatches are probably the most intelligent animal in North America outside of man. Without too much difficulty we can set some rough limits within which their mental abilities must lie. The simple observation of their broad-shouldered anatomy automatically puts sasquatches in the superfamily of Hominoidea that also includes apes and humans. Intellectual abilities of the various great apes have been intensively studied in recent years; they are second only to man among the primates, though the gap between them and us is still great. Gorillas, chimpanzees, and orang utans can be ranked as about equal to each other, thus almost certainly representing the same intelligence level of their common ancestor. Since the sasquatch is also derived from that same common ancestor, we can safely presume that there was no loss of intellect in any of its descendants; such a loss would be selectively disadvantageous. This alone would argue for a mental capacity at least on par with the living apes. The question is whether their intelligence goes any further than this.

There are a few people who assert, and some who at least imply, that sasquatch mental abilities are equal to or beyond those of humans. The people who make such claims usually can be ruled out of serious consideration from other observations they make. For instance, one well-intentioned man visited me because of his concern for the safety of these supposedly highly intelligent beings. He also told me that he was personally acquainted, or at least familiar, with all six of them. These constituted three couples, one of which had a sixteen-year-old daughter who somehow did not raise the total to seven. Even if there had been no other reason to doubt his descriptions, his population figures alone were enough to cast serious doubt on anything else he said. Another man told me how he had sneaked into their underground schools and watched the young ones studying at their desks. Yet he knew these were "prehistoric" creatures because their heads were elongated, front to back, like all other prehistoric animals. He was quite unaware of any contradiction between his descriptions of their evidently advanced vs. primitive condition; his testimony can be discounted on other grounds as well. Superhuman status, including various paranormal abilities, is ascribed to them by several people; yet these people are among the most vociferous about how we must not shoot one of them. Just how a gun might pose any danger to such incredible beings is never explained.

On a more serious level the status of sasquatch can be tested against the three most basic traits that distinguish humans from animals—tools, society, and speech. There are no believable accounts of any sasquatch using a man-made tool, nor of them picking up or even touching such objects except in a few rare acts of destruction. That they might use tools of their own manufacture is not even up for consideration. Their manipulation of natural objects apparently includes tossing aside rocks and tree trunks; breaking saplings; pulling up fern stalks; picking up fish, chickens, deer, and other food objects; digging into the ground; and scratching against trees. Their often-reported making of beds from broken branches is comparable to the branch nests that apes make in trees, and requires no more intelligence. The available evidence for the structure of their hands is consistent with this limited range of uses, but it would take little added intelligence to throw stones and swing sticks as weapons. Despite a few claims to the contrary, there is little indication of such weapons use.

Humans organize themselves into social groups with divisions of duties that are arbitrarily decided. Nothing of the kind has been observed with the sasquatch. The only social units of close interaction are mating pairs and mother-child relationships. This amount of social organization is characteristic of bears and other lower mammals. The loose associations of four or five individuals within a definable area, as mentioned above, do not presuppose any special intelligence. Baboons and wolves have much more complex societies, though in their cases it is at least partially genetically programmed. With sasquatch we find no indication of inherent social groupings, nor of any voluntary associations beyond the simplest kinds.

Humans spend a great deal of time mumbling softly to one another with coded symbols that convey meanings. Again, nothing like this human speech has been reported for sasquatch. The loud cries that they apparently make on some occasions may convey emotional and locational information, but most mammals and all primates have call systems just as complex as this.

On all three measures of a human level of intellect the sasquatch is found lacking. Brief observations of humans out in natural environments might fail to show one or more of these human behaviors, but with maybe twenty such human sightings all of these behaviors would have been seen at least a few times. With a hundred times as many observations, these behaviors are yet to be seen with sasquatches. Unless the sasquatch carefully conceals its tools, society, and speech, we must assume that they are absent. To propose such concealment on the part of sasquatch logically opens up the possibility that any or all other animal species are equally intelligent and have managed to hide this fact from us. Speculation of this kind leads us everywhere and nowhere simultaneously, and is obviously a waste of time.

Higher intelligence requires a large brain. The body itself requires a certain amount of brain tissue to coordinate its animal functions; any surplus beyond this is available for higher mental functions. Orang utans have brains of 400 cubic centimeters (just under a pint); at twice their body weight, gorillas have 500 cc; if that body weight is again doubled, another 100 cc should be added. To maintain a sasquatch body with an apelike mentality, about 600 cc (just over a pint) of brain would be about normal. To elevate them to the human condition, at least another 1000 cc (a quart) would have to be added; this is the same amount by which our brains exceed the 400 cc that is needed to run our orang-sized bodies. With their huge bodies and human intelligence, this would add up to a total brain size for the sasquatch that is larger than is found in most humans. Both the physical requirements of their pelvic design and the size of the male genitalia argue strongly for the minimal brain size of 600 cc, and this size is most consistent with all that we know about their behavior.

If sasquatches do indeed recognize each other by their footprints, and if they sometimes emphasize or avoid making their own footprints, then some level of intelligence over that of most mammals is suggested. The amount of geographical data encompassed by their home ranges would be quite a lot for a small brain to remember. These two items are all I can find that suggest anything along the line of significant intelligence, and even these can be matched by wolf behavior. There is nothing that argues for mental abilities beyond those of apes, and precious little that points even to that level.

The way that sasquatches react to humans ranges from near indifference to considerable caution, perhaps even fear. They almost surely recognize that we are upright bipeds like them, and thus both species are well distinguished from all other animals. When a sasquatch sees another upright biped at a considerable distance, it may have to pay close attention to determine whether it is a human or another sasquatch, while all other species are immediately eliminated from consideration. It is at least possible that they can also see how much we resemble the very young of their own kind, having big heads, high foreheads, and relatively small faces. John Cardinal noted that a sasquatch who shows the most humanlike proportions would be very young and much smaller than a man. It might follow that we are seen by them as young children of a kind of bipeds who are even larger than the sasquatch in our adult condition. Thus they don't want to antagonize us "children" lest one of our grownups should appear on the scene. If we were to see what appeared to be a human toddler, but standing over four feet tall (1.3 m), we probably would feel some concern about how big its parents might be. I am rather dubious that sasquatches see us in this light simply because most other species of animals show the same caution towards us. But it is an intriguing possibility.

There can be no serious question about the intellectual status of the sasquatch on the basis of all available information. It is not human, nor even semihuman, and its legal status would be that of an animal if and when a specimen is taken. The fact that it would be classified in the human family of Hominidae does not alter this. A hominid is not necessarily a human, the two labels are not synonymous—a fact that is missed even by some of my academic colleagues. Inclusion in the zoological family Hominidae is made strictly on the basis of adaptations to bipedal locomotion. The earliest such hominids known in the fossil record had ape-sized brains and almost certainly had the same level of intelligence; they were not human.

An interesting view of the sasquatch's nature can also be gleaned from the way observers report what they see. The usual description begins with the word "animal," then some degree of humanlike attributes are noted. When a description starts out with the word "human," then qualifies it with some animallike traits, it usually turns out to be a false report. Most people who see these creatures have an immediate, gut-level reaction to identify them as animals.

Endangered Status

A rather excitable and vocal segment of the public considers the sasquatch to be an endangered species. There is no evidence to support this view, but then there's not much to contradict it either. Any proper assessment of an endangered status requires that the species be thoroughly studied throughout its habitat by recognized experts in the field. Nothing of the kind has ever been attempted with the sasquatch, and it never will be unless and until its existence is proven beyond all doubt. This requires a type specimen. No government agencies or scientific organizations will make a move in this direction on the basis of the presently available information.

Most of us who have studied the problem would estimate their population to number at least two thousand individuals, and quite likely several times that figure. This is well over the five hundred that often signals the beginning of difficulties due to insufficient genetic diversity within a species. On the other hand, these numbers appear to be spread very thinly over a vast area, and there may be problems in maintaining genetic contacts from one small group to another.

Human activity, mainly farming but also city and road building, has dramatically reduced the forest habitat on this continent, with a corresponding reduction in the range and numbers of all animals who have a forest orientation. In the last hundred years this trend has begun to reverse, with the less-productive farmland being allowed to return to its native vegetation. One could read the history of sighting reports to indicate that the sasquatch had become extinct in most of the eastern United States, and only in the last fifty years has been making a limited comeback. The earlier documentation is so sketchy as to make the first part of this interpretation uncertain, but there certainly are plenty of reports from there in recent decades.

Human interference has not necessarily been a bad thing for the sasquatch in all respects. We have eliminated their only potential competitor, the grizzly bear, from almost half of the continent. Our abandoned farms, forest fires, and clear-cut logging result in many years of second growth that provides an increased food supply for virtually all species. Our intricate network of back roads and power lines lets in strips of sunshine to allow more growth at ground level. The roads themselves, including abandoned ones, provide easy routes of travel.

We don't know what the effects might be from our general disruption of the balance of nature. By reducing the predators we have artificially increased many of the prey species, perhaps making some of them more accessible to the sasquatch. But those same prey species, who are all herbivores, might also be decimating some of the preferred food of the sasquatch. There may be other, less obvious ramifications that would affect a rare species much more than the common ones. We also have no indication if our various forms of pollution might be having some adverse effects.

If an actual specimen of a sasquatch were to become available for study, its existence would be recognized and it would probably be declared an endangered species. This would immediately activate all existing laws for its protection, and this in turn would threaten the economic well being of some major industries. Considering the recent fuss over the snail darter, a tiny fish that delayed dam building for years, and the current strife over the northern spotted owl, the discovery of an animal like the sasquatch would have a devastating impact. Before any specific protection could be recommended, there would have to be a thorough study of its ecology. Given the nature of the beast this investigation could take many years. In the meantime there would be enormous legal and public pressures to play it safe and postpone all commercial activities that even *might* pose a threat to them. This would mean a stop to all logging, road building, and suburban expansions, to name the obvious. I doubt that our economy could tolerate even any significant slow-downs in these areas, but there would be great pressure from the environmentalists to shut them down completely.

It is clearly in the best interests of all the concerned industries that this animal never be proven to exist. I have already suggested that some lumber companies have hired one or more people to lower the chances of this event ever happening. The most effective approach would be for such persons to loudly proclaim the existence of the sasquatch and to offer totally unacceptable evidence to support their contention. In fact, the more absurd the evidence, the more effective it would be to make the whole subject look ridiculous. Just to be on the safe side, the activists should also publicly agitate against any efforts to shoot a specimen by inventing stories that suggest a humanlike status for them. There are several people who's activities fit this description exactly. One such person has had no visible means of support for the last fifteen years that I have known of his antics; if he is not being paid for this, it's rather difficult to explain why he's doing it.

Michael Cohn, of the Brooklyn Children's Museum, pointed out to me years ago that my own work could be seen as a threat to these companies. In this enlightened age they would not resort to physical intimidation to shut me up if they felt threatened, but they could arrange to have me neutralized by getting me far away from the Pacific Northwest. If a lucrative job is suddenly offered to me in the eastern U.S., or even in Europe, I would be very suspicious about how and why it happened.

John Green has raised the interesting possibility that sasquatches suffered a population crash fifty to one hundred years ago and are now in the process of recovery. He suggests that occasional direct human contacts might have passed one or more human diseases into their population, and it/they spread gradually over subsequent years. Such disease transfers between humans and apes are well known. There are many areas that had some early reports when human settlement was new, then no more information until very recently. If this is correct, then sasquatches are not likely in any danger at the present time.

Basically, we have no reason to think that the sasquatch is an endangered species. My best guess is that they are in excellent condition and possibly are now in the process of expanding their range in the woodlands of the eastern United States. But this opinion is based on slender and often unreliable evidence, and it could easily be wrong. My biggest concern is that they might be endangered by recently expanded populations of herbivorous competitors. There is a distinct possibility that the sasquatch is headed for extinction. There is no possibility that anything will be done to find out for sure if a specimen is not produced. Those who speak most strongly against collecting that one individual are making a clear statement that they do not want any protection for this creature and would prefer to risk its extinction.

7

THE FOSSIL RECORD

The fossil record is only one of several lines of evidence for evolution, but it is the one that most concerns us at this point. Before discussing the various fossil forms that might represent the sasquatch (or its ancestor) some discussion of basic evolutionary principles might be in order. My colleagues in the biological sciences have no need for this exposition, but it may be of interest to some of the other readers.

Biological evolution is the process of change in a species over succeeding generations. The laws of inheritance tend to assure that each generation will consist of individuals who closely resemble their parents. In most species, for most of the time, this process is followed with a reasonable degree of success. But changes do occur, sometimes slowly over millions of years and sometimes more rapidly in just tens of thousands of years. In some cases, as with insect pests and microorganisms, significant changes can even occur in a few years.

As a general rule, all hereditary information (DNA molecules) is passed on fairly accurately from one generation to the next. But genetic mutations do occur that introduce novel variations into this heredity. The exact nature of the mutation process is now well understood. Very rarely are mutations advantageous in that they improve the fitness of an individual to adapt to its current environment. The overwhelming majority produce characteristics that are disadvantageous to some degree. These bad mutations are random changes in protein formation that lead to random differences in the growing and adult bodily forms and/or functions. The average human (or other animal) contains one or more original mutations, and hundreds of somewhat disadvantageous mutations that are inherited from his/her ancestors.

Not all individuals of a species reproduce exactly their share of the next generation. That would consist of two functioning children for each couple, whether these be humans, dogs, or clams. Many individuals reproduce none at all, some manage just their share, and others have many more offspring. The genetic peculiarities of those who reproduce the most will thus be more frequent in the next generation. When one DNA molecule manages to make more copies of itself than others do, the minimal unit of evolution has occurred.

Differential reproduction may result from purely chance factors, in which case there is no directional change over time. Migration of some individuals from one breeding population to another will also change the genetic composition of both populations, but this has no effect on the total genetics of the whole species. The only nonrandom factor in evolution is what has long been called natural selection, where some individuals reproduce more, and others less, according to how well they are adapted to the ecological niche of their species. This is analogous to artificial selection, where plant and animal breeders consciously select certain individuals to reproduce the more desired traits. When this kind of unequal reproduction occurs automatically in the natural world, certain variations will become more frequent and others less. With the constant input of new mutations, and the known time scale that is available, then the resulting evolution is inevitable.

Contrary to the common perception, biological evolution does not inherently tend to produce larger and more complex organisms with higher intelligence. Evolution is opportunistic. Animal species will change their adaptations in any morphological direction that may be advantageous for them at that time and place. Some species grow larger, some smaller; complexity may increase or decrease; and intelligence may go up or down over time.

Given the fact that the earliest life forms were tiny, simple, and stupid, the major openings for new adaptations were only in the other directions. Today at the upper end of the range of size, complexity, and intelligence, the major openings are to move still further in these same directions. Among the main mass of living things, changes are about as likely to go up or down on these scales. I stress this point because many people think of evolution as having certain inherent trends; biologists long ago dropped this concept.

Likewise, humans may well be the highest form of life in some respects, but other animals certainly are not evolving in the human direction. In the complex web of natural interactions, it is necessary that every ecological niche be occupied by some species. For any of them to become more human, or even smarter, would not improve their adaptations; and it would leave behind an unoccupied niche if it did occur. The sasquatch has its own ecological adaptations that would not be improved by evolving any further in the human direction. It is not an evolutionary failure because it has failed to become more like us, any more than we are failures because we have not developed sasquatch characteristics.

Primate Evolution

Members of the mammalian order called Primates are characterized by arboreal locomotion by means of grasping hands and feet. All primates show this adaptation, or are obviously descended from a primate that was a tree climber in the past. Our hands are built much like those of other primates; even our feet show all the structures of the grasping design that have been modified for better weight support with terrestrial locomotion.

A particular kind of arboreal locomotion, called brachiation, is found today in all of the apes. Here the body is redesigned to hang by the arms from overhead branches. The apes' arms are greatly elongated in relation to the torso, the shoulders are very broad, and the chest is not as deep as it is wide. The lumbar region of the back is so shortened that the rib cage almost touches the pelvis, and the external tail has been eliminated. There are many additional detailed changes in joint designs in the arms, and some rearrangements in muscular development and attachments. One of the more interesting aspects of this arm swinging anatomy is that we humans share all of these adaptations not just partially, but fully. We do differ from apes in some particulars, but the various ape species differ just as much from each other. What has been observed and described of the sasquatch anatomy fits with this design as well.

All of the apes and humans shared a common ancestry something on the order of ten million years ago. Gibbons probably split off the common line somewhat earlier, and our ancestors separated from those of the chimpanzees only about half that far back in time. The ancestral apes were originally quadrupeds, or four-footed locomotors, and they were developing their brachiating anatomy just when their group was beginning to split up. Fossils of these apes are first known from Africa, their continent of origin, but they have also been found in the warmer parts of Europe and Asia. An early African form, dating back to before brachiation began, is known as genus *Proconsul*. Somewhat later forms from all three continents are called *Sivapithecus*, who were largely terrestrial, but who had begun to brachiate. The latest examples of *Sivapithecus* were full brachiators; some of them were ancestral to the orang utan, while a related genus, *Afropithecus*, was the ancestor of African apes and humans.

Bipedal locomotion is first known from almost four million years ago in the earliest *Australopithecus* fossils. These australopithecines were still largely arboreal brachiators, but they were anatomically adapted to travel on two feet on the ground as well. This bipedal adaptation most likely began only shortly before the time of the first known australo fossils. The biochemical timing of ancestral splits appears to put our separation from the African apes at about five million years ago, so this fits well with the fossil record. The australos shared some close locomotor similarities with us, and their teeth were of the human type, but otherwise they were apes.

The known australopithecines include at least one clear line, *A. robustus*, that separated from the rest and presumably became extinct at a later date. The other line, *A. africanus*, eventually evolved into genus *Homo* at least 1.6 million years ago. The first species of our genus was *Homo erectus*, which showed considerable brain enlargement and other more human traits. Only very recently did they evolve, through Neandertal and similar intermediates, into full-fledged *Homo sapiens*.

Every fossil form was fully adapted to the ecological circumstances of its time and place. As long as these conditions did not change, the best adaptation for them would most likely continue to be just the same as it was then. As might be expected, some species have not altered their anatomy in many millions of years.

Most evolutionary change results from some change in the environment to which the affected population must adapt or perish. Such adaptations can often be very rapid, when the needed characteristics already exist in the genetic load of what had been undesirable variations. What was maladaptive at one time may become the ideal type when circumstances change. Other adaptations may have to await the appearance of suitable genetic mutations.

Environmental change might involve the entire geographical range of the species, in which case it must evolve or become extinct as a whole. Often, however, the change affects the environment of only part of the species. In this case the affected part may success-fully evolve, while the rest of the species is under no pressure to do the same. This is how new species can often appear while their ancestral form still continues unchanged.

Finding Fossils First

It is likely that sasquatch represents a kind of higher primate that is already known in the fossil record. If it is not part of a named species, it probably will relate closely to one of them. Its official recognition, if and when that happens, would then be another case of where we have a living form that was first known from fossils. It is true that sasquatch reports go back in time to well before the discov-ery of any of the fossils that might now be equated with it, but our modern form is still unproven and we do not know enough about the diagnostic details that are needed to classify it with certainty.

Finding living representatives of previously known fossils is noth-ing new. In 1938 the first coelacanth fish was found, whose relatives were known as fossils, and the whole group was thought to have been extinct for eighty million years. In the late 1950s a living species of peccary (American pig) was found in South America that had long been known to science from fossils that were several million years old. There are many other such cases.

Although the world's living fauna has been sampled many times more thoroughly than any earlier (fossil) fauna has been, simple sta-tistical odds would predict that at least a few animals might have been missed. For marine forms it is likely that there are many more known fossil types that are yet to be found living in the sea. This fol-lows from the simple fact that even large stupid animals can easily remain undetected in this environment. By similar reasoning we can predict that among land animals, any large ones that remain undis-covered would most likely be scarce, nocturnal, secretive, and fairly intelligent. The lack of any one of these traits would almost certainly have guaranteed their discovery by now. From this same list of traits, only scarcity will reduce the likelihood of their being known as fos-sils. All of this does not mean that the sasquatch is necessarily real and already known as a fossil, but it should at least defuse any argu-ment that this is inherently impossible.

The reported sasquatch anatomy is that of an erect, bipedal, higher primate; this is the essential definition of the family Hominidae, of which humans are the only recognized living representatives. Living and fossil members of this zoological family are called hominids; this is contrasted with the broader category of hominoids, the superfamily Hominoidea, that also includes all of the apes. Living hominoids are all characterized by adaptations for brachiation, or arm-swinging locomotion. The apes (pongids) regularly use brachiation to move through trees, while we (hominids) have mostly abandoned this form of locomotion in favor of bipedalism. Hominids still exhibit most of the anatomical structures that facilitate brachiation, notable among these being the broad shoulders that are found only in apes and humans.

If people were inventing stories about bipedal monsters they might have made them broad shouldered as well, but they didn't have to. If the sasquatch is a living hominid, it is a hominoid as well, and it must have their characteristic broad shoulders. We test the theory that sasquatch exists by asking whether it has broad shoulders, and it passes the test. Failure to pass this test would have disproved the theory in its present form; passing the test simply fails to disprove it, and the theory remains viable. The idea that the sasquatch is a human invention is not testable by the same method because the inventors could have given it any characteristics. Instead, we could propose that if all sasquatches stories are without biological foundation they must have been independently invented by hundreds of different people. In that case at least some of them should have been narrow shouldered (like standing bears). Since no sasquatch report fits this description, that theory can be considered as disproved in its stated form.

The Candidates

We have fossil remains of at least four clear-cut types of hominoids that might be the sasquatch, or at least its close relative. Three of these are hominids, clearly being members of our zoological family, while the family affiliation of the fourth type is yet to be determined for sure. Their positions in time and in human ancestry are shown in Figure 69. These are all worth examining in some detail to see how well they fit, or fail to fit, the species that is described in the preceding chapter. Only the North American evidence is being considered at this point; the possibility that there are still other living hominids is deferred to the next chapter.

1. **Neandertal** man is known from many fossils that have been found in and around Europe that date from over 100,000 years ago

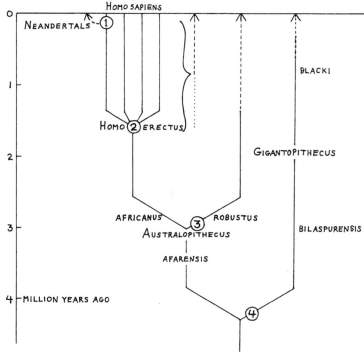

Figure 69. Probable hominid phylogeny. The author's interpretation of human ancestry is shown here, along with the major fossil types that are known. Those labeled 1 through 4 are candidates for being the sasquatch ancestor. Dashed lines and arrows show each of these candidates carried up to the present, during which time certain evolutionary changes must be postulated for some of them.

and continued up to 35,000 years ago. (This name is correctly spelled here; at the time of the first discovery the Germans wrote it Neanderthal, but dropped the "h" around the year 1900 as part of a spelling reform.) The Neandertals had upright bipedal locomotion much like ourselves, with the ex-brachiator's broad shoulders and hanging arms. They were of about average human stature, but more stoutly built than members of any living human population. A typical Neandertal male standing 5 feet 6 inches tall probably weighed at least 200 pounds in prime condition, rather than the 145 pounds of an athletic modern man of that stature. (In metric, this is a male at 168 cm weighing 91 kg instead of the typical human 66 kg.) With that much extra weight to carry, at least in some seasons, it is not surprising that their feet were relatively much wider than ours. Figure 70 illustrates the skull contrasts between Neandertals vs. both modern man and *Homo erectus*.

Neandertals had human-sized brains, often lived in caves, used fire, and made fairly good stone tools. Judging from possible tool uses and the apparent need, they almost certainly made crude clothing of animal skins. Most scientists now include them in our species of *Homo sapiens*, but as a distinct subspecies. Thus they are called *Homo sapiens neanderthalensis* (using the older German spelling). I think this classification is in error, and that they are members of a different species, but that is not an issue here. Being game hunters, Neandertals would have had the human cooling system that depends on sweat evaporation directly from the skin surface. Accordingly, their body hair would have been minimal, like ours.

If we are to equate Neandertals (or their modified descendants) with our sasquatch, some serious objections must be overcome. Their range would have to be considerably extended to the east and north in order for them to reach North America, but a closely related type was living in northern China that could be the source and thus reduce the distance. The eastern-most true Neandertal is from the Teshik-Tash site in "Soviet" Central Asia. From there it is over 6,300 miles (10,200 km) to central British Columbia by the most direct route. From the closest known Chinese fossil of this date the distance is still over 4,800 miles (7,800 km). Distance is not the major

Figure 70. Neandertal and *Homo erectus* skulls. The Neandertal (center) is contrasted with modern human (right) and *Homo erectus* (left). Neandertals are the most recent of the suggested sasquatch ancestors; they lived less than 100,000 years ago. They were fully human in brain size and presumed intelligence, made stone tools and fire, and in general seem much too advanced to be a likely candidate. *Homo erectus* was somewhat less human in all respects, but would still have to lose many human traits to evolve into a sasquatch.

problem; it is the adaptation to Arctic climates that would pose the most significant difficulties.

More problematical is the large brain size of the Neandertals that contradicts the anatomical evidence we have for sasquatch. Associated with that is their presumed intelligence (equal to ours), tool making, fire use, and clothing—none of which are seen in our creature, and which ought to have been too useful to give up. Neandertals would also have to re-evolve a full coat of hair. They would have to select for a much larger body size, with all the appropriate anatomical adjustments, including the nonopposed thumb, in a very short time. Some scientists have complained that the apparent sagittal crest, running front-to-back along the top of the sasquatch head, is incompatible with the smoothly rounded braincase of Neandertals. Actually this is no objection because a suitably enlarged Neandertal would have its jaw muscles so expanded that an attachment crest of this kind might well develop.

There are severe time constraints on the possibility of sasquatch descending from a Neandertal. These fossils are last known from 35,000 to 40,000 years ago, when they evolved into (or were replaced by) modern *Homo sapiens*. The earliest Neandertals date back to about 100,000 years, at which time some of them just might have begun a separate evolutionary career. Neither of these durations seems to provide nearly enough time for the necessary changes to have evolved. Even more problematical is the evidence that Neandertals were ancestors of the Caucasoid branch of our species; they were not a separate line that contrasted with all human races. There were Neandertal equivalents at that time in the ancestry of other races. This fact raises the question of which Neandertaloid is being referred to, or if more than one form might be involved in the supposed sasquatch ancestry.

While some kind of Neandertaloid might have reached North America, most likely it would not have differed much from the known forms. Such a migration, if it reached here, would have been exterminated by, or incorporated into, the population of fully human invaders who soon followed. In spite of their advocacy by several scientists, especially the Russians, Neandertals almost certainly cannot represent our sasquatch. If these hominid forms had survived to the present day, their physical description would not match that of the North American biped. That Neandertals might have been the ancestor of a different kind of unknown biped in Asia is another matter.

2. *Homo erectus* is an earlier, widespread form of hominid that lived in most of the Old World from 1.6 million years ago up to the time of the Neandertals. These people (if the term is appropriate) were of about modern human size, and had the same locomotor design as us and the Neandertals. Like the latter, they had very powerfully built bodies, but most of them probably did not carry as much excess body weight. We have no information on their foot design, but the bones of their legs and pelves are mostly modern, so their feet probably were too. (See Fig. 70 for comparative skull characteristics.)

The *erectus* brain size was between that of apes and humans; they made some medium-quality stone tools and sometimes inhabited caves, but they usually did not use fire and probably did not make any kind of clothing. Their bodies, however, would have been equally reduced in hair cover because they also ran game animals to exhaustion in the heat of the day (persistence hunting).

Almost all of the objections to the Neandertals apply equally well to *Homo erectus*. They are known from northern China (Peking Man), but there is the same problem of how they could have spread so far north as to gain access into North America. The distance involved is the same 4,800 miles as for the later Neandertaloid Chinese fossils. They have a less contradictory brain size, and their cultural level is also less, but even this seems too advantageous to their descendants for them to have discarded it so completely. There would have been more time for them to evolve increased body size with all its complex adjustments, the new hand design, and a hairy coat—but again this represents a lot of change for no apparent improvement in adaptation. To consider *Homo erectus* as the ancestor of sasquatch is very nearly as problematical as deriving them from Neandertals.

In theory, we could propose that a line of *Homo erectus* separated from human ancestry at any time back to its origin at 1.6 million years ago. This allows up to 16 times more evolutionary time available than for even the oldest Neandertals. The time is there, but the reason for the necessary changes is still inadequate.

Roger Patterson toyed with the *Homo erectus* identification, but he had too little scientific background to evaluate its pros and cons. A few serious scientists have also suggested this possibility, but I doubt that any of them would want to be quoted to this effect.

3. *Australopithecus* is a genus of fossil hominids known mostly from Africa that date from almost four million years ago up to the

appearance of *Homo erectus*. They ranged from typical human size down to less than half as massive, depending on which sex of which species is considered. Australopithecines had ape-sized brains, no cultural equipment of note, and not being game hunters they almost certainly had a full coat of body hair. They were well adapted to bipedal walking, but they were at least equally adept at brachiating in the trees. It is their dentition, more than anything else, that closely relates them to the hominid family. Figure 71 shows the skulls of the two forms of *Australopithecus*.

To evolve the sasquatch out of an australopithecine would be much easier than it would be for either of the more humanlike forms discussed above. The required geographical extension involves a somewhat greater distance—9,600 miles from East Africa (15,500 km), or 6,800 miles (11,000 km) if they actually lived in Southeast Asia. The only real problem here is the same one of getting as far north as the Bering Strait. They would also have to evolve the great body size and other adjustments, including the novel hand design. Increased size would automatically cancel active brachiation, but the powerful arms might be retained. There is no problem of reacquiring a hair cover in this case, but that insulation would certainly have to be thickened.

Two species of *Australopithecus* are generally recognized, *A. africanus* that probably evolved into later human forms, and

Figure 71. Two australopithecine skulls. The apparently vegetarian species, *Australopithecus robustus* (right), is thought by many to be the sasquatch source from over two million years ago. They would have to evolve much larger body size, but otherwise look like acceptable ancestors. The specimen shown here is a male from East Africa. *A. africanus* (left) is slightly more human in some of its detailed anatomy, but would make an almost equally acceptable ancestor. The specimen shown here is a female from South Africa.

A. robustus that is considered to have become extinct at about the time when genus *Homo* first appeared. The latest *africanus* had somewhat enlarged brains and they were making very crude stone tools; *robustus* showed neither of these traits and thus is the more logical candidate to be the ancestor of sasquatch. In the anthropological literature it is frequently stated that *robustus* was the taller and heavier of the two species; in fact this has never been demonstrated. They more likely were about the same size, and it is even possible that *africanus* was the larger species.

There are only a few problems with the *A. robustus* scenario—distance, size, and hands—so it must be considered to be a real possibility, as Gordon Strassenburgh (1984) has long argued. In fact, even the *africanus* species has better credentials than either Neandertals or *Homo erectus* for being the forerunner of sasquatch.

The last known *robustus* dates back to well over a million years ago. If it actually survived to the present, it would have had about the same length of time for evolutionary change as did *Homo erectus*. And it had much less change to accomplish. It is also possible that an earlier offshoot of the *robustus* line separated even earlier, perhaps almost as far back as three million years ago. The case for making *africanus* the sasquatch ancestor follows essentially the same pattern. Time is no constraint in either case.

4. *Gigantopithecus blacki* is our final serious candidate. This is a fossil primate known from three partial jaws and about a thousand loose teeth that were found in southern China and northern Vietnam. These date from 300,000 years at the most recent, and extend back to perhaps a million years ago. A related species (*G. bilaspurensis*) is represented by a single lower jaw found in India that is considerably older. We know rather less about *Gigantopithecus* than we do about any of the other types, but much of the missing information can be inferred with varying degrees of certainty. Figure 72 shows the four jaws.

One thing we do know about *Gigantopithecus* is that it was indeed a giant, as its name implies. The one adult male jaw hopelessly outclasses all other primates in size (Fig. 73). Even the young male and both female jaws are larger than those of male gorillas.

I recently made a detailed reconstruction of what the entire skull should have looked like (Fig. 74); a description of this work was published in the 1987 issue of *Cryptozoology*, and is reprinted here in Appendix A. Skull and body size are hard to predict from tooth size

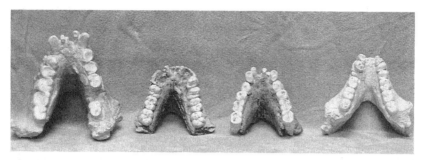

Figure 72. Four *Gigantopithecus* jaws. Starting from the left, these are the adult male, young male, and adult female—all from China. At the far right is the adult female from India. This Asian ape was probably bipedal, and in every known and surmised characteristic is an exact match for sasquatch.

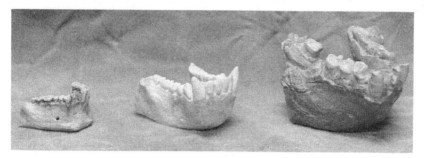

Figure 73. *Gigantopithecus* size contrasts. The adult male from China is conspicuously larger than a large male orang utan (center), which is almost the size of a male gorilla jaw. The corresponding part of a big man's jaw (left) is tiny by comparison.

alone, unless one knows pretty closely the type of animal that is involved, or else a clear indication of how the dentition was used. In this case we have most of the lower jaw, and the dentition is of the hominoid type. By comparing measurements of this reconstruction of an adult male with those of gorilla skulls, it was a routine matter to predict that its body weight should be on the order of 933 pounds (424 kg). Less detailed reconstructions by other scientists indicate even greater size. This is the largest primate that has ever been known to exist, and it requires no changes to match the sasquatch in this respect. One of the jaws is that of a female, and its body size would have been about two-thirds that of the adult male that I reconstructed in detail. Most other anthropologists who have speculated on the size of the living *Gigantopithecus* come to similar conclusions. But some insist that tooth size cannot be used to predict body size, while ignoring the fact that we also have its jaws.

Figure 74. *Gigantopithecus* skull reconstruction. Here is the author's version of what this primate's complete skull looked like (right). For comparison, the male gorilla is shown in the center and the human at the left. (See Appendix A for a detailed description of how this reconstruction was made.)

The fossils consist only of the tooth-bearing parts of the lower jaws, and these diverge toward the rear in a remarkable manner. (See illustrations in Appendix A.) This divergence is so extreme that it would make sense only if the base of the neck was positioned so far forward as to require this spread in order for it to fit between the jaw's rear extensions. Such a neck orientation would have to be vertical, and thus indicates a fully upright posture. The teeth are intermediate in design between apes' and humans', and leaning more to the human type—a condition that is found in no living primate. Much of the human design of teeth follows from the fact that our jaws are also widely spread at the back, and the effect of this divergence on tooth occlusion makes the projecting canine teeth dysfunctional. All of this evidence points to an erect, bipedal locomotion for *Gigantopithecus*. Unlike with the other fossil candidates, there is here no direct confirmation of the posture from skeletal parts. With the teeth being of a clear hominoid design, it follows that *Gigantopithecus* was also a brachiator like all the other hominoids. These animals were much too large for any arboreal locomotion, but they still would have had the broad shoulders of that adaptation.

Gigantopithecus co-existed with *Homo erectus*, the known human ancestor, who was adapted to hunting game animals. It is not likely that two species of hominids would have lived side-by-side with the same adaptation, otherwise one of them would soon have out-competed the other. Thus it is safe to assume that *Gigantopithecus* was not a persistence hunter and had a full coat of hair, just like all the other nonhuman primates.

The first stage of human brain enlargement also can be related to hunting game by persistence of pursuit. The enhanced mental time span would have enabled the early human to remember exactly what he was doing for many hours, and to anticipate the results of success at some future time. Without this function there would not be any need to evolve a larger brain that is metabolically so expensive to build and maintain. It is a safe presumption that *Gigantopithecus* had about the same relative brain size and intelligence as is found in modern apes.

A full description of this giant primate would then match that of the sasquatch in every particular that can be dealt with. Only its thumb remains unknown; one can only speculate on what would be the most useful design for a creature of this description to manipulate its environment.

Compared with the other candidates, the known location of *Gigantopithecus* is intermediate in its distance from North America. In terms of its ability to extend its range sufficiently far to the north it has a distinct advantage over all the others. Its large body size automatically would present relatively less surface area to the environment as compared with its heat-generating volume. It alone is preadapted to inhabit areas of cold winters. Of course, any one of the others would have to reach this larger size if it was to become the sasquatch, but *Gigantopithecus* had a head start by already being that big. And we know it was accomplished in this case, while we can only speculate about what the others might have done.

From the last known *Gigantopithecus* there are only three hundred thousand years to evolve into sasquatch. Both *Homo erectus* and *Australopithecus robustus* had much more time available. But then, it may well be that *Gigantopithecus* did not have to undergo any evolutionary change at all. Sasquatch could have separated from this Asian line at any time within the last three or four million years.

As far as I can determine, it was Bernard Heuvelmans (1952) who first suggested a connection between *Gigantopithecus* and the Himalayan yeti. Ivan Sanderson made the same proposal in 1961, he was soon joined by the anthropologist Carleton Coon (1962), and many others have since agreed. In 1968, John Green made the specific equation with our North American sasquatch, and this has since become a near consensus of opinion.

There are no other known or seriously suspected bipeds in the fossil record of higher primates. If the sasquatch ancestor has not already been identified, then we must postulate the existence of yet another type, perhaps even a separate and independent origin of bipedalism that is without a recognized fossil record. Such a possibility might be an upright, walking version of the orang utan that evolved somewhere in Asia. This would be a parallel to what actually did evolve out of the African ape line to become human. I explore this possibility rather timidly in the next chapter, but not in connection with the sasquatch.

It would require a great deal of evolution to make a biped out of some early version of the orang, then to expand it to the size of a sasquatch. But to change a Neandertal, or even *Homo erectus*, into a sasquatch strikes me as requiring considerably more evolution, and with less time in which to accomplish it. I would not completely discount this possibility of an orang connection, but I see no cogent argument in its favor either.

The ultimate origin of *Gigantopithecus* is not known for sure, and some authorities would relate it to the orang line. If this is correct, then this fossil type is just the deviant orang that has been postulated. There is one piece of hard data, however, that contradicts the idea of relating sasquatch to the orang, with or without including *Gigantopithecus*. This is the hair sample retrieved by Bob Titmus and analyzed by Jerold Lowenstein. It ruled out any close relation with orangs, and putting its affiliation instead with humans and the African apes.

Any other source for the sasquatch would have to be very hypothetical and improbable. The evidence is closing in rather tightly on just a few possible known fossil types. I would put the highest odds on it being *Gigantopithecus*, and that this type is derived from the African group of apes. I would rate *Australopithecus robustus* as a poor second choice because of the changes that must be made, and *A. africanus* is in a close third place because these changes need to be only slightly greater. In a remote fourth place I put a bipedal version of the orang, which is not *Gigantopithecus*, but one that still may have a couple of bits of evidence in the fossil record. In my opinion, no other serious contenders are viable; this is not to say that I would rule them out of modern-day existence, but they just aren't sasquatch.

Scientific Names

Every recognized animal species has a name that consists of two words, the genus and the trivial (or specific) name. Together these are the name of the species. Technically speaking, you cannot name a species without giving its genus name at the same time. That genus is then included within a known family, along with any similar genera; that family is placed in an order, along with similar families; that order is put in a class with its related orders; and that class is one of several in a phylum of the animal kingdom. With sasquatch there is no proper scientific name, and there never will be until a specimen is produced and put on record. In the meantime people may suggest names for it, and these may be placed in the appropriate higher categories. But such names have no legal standing in science.

There remains a remote possibility that some recognition might be accorded in a rather roundabout procedure for giving sasquatch a name. This follows from the fact that footprints and other disturbances made by known species are considered to be material evidence of the species. I made the contention in a publication in 1986 that we in fact have footprints of *Gigantopithecus blacki* here in North America. (See Appendix B in this book.) Unless and until it can be demonstrated that the fossil jaws and the modern footprints stem from different species, both sets of evidence can and ought to be subsumed under the same name. It should be noted that I have not created a scientific name for the sasquatch without having a type specimen to support it, as Ciochon et al. (1990) have stated. *Gigantopithecus blacki* was named by Ralph von Koenigswald more than fifty years ago; I simply attributed some footprints to that species. Paleontologists often attribute footprints to known forms of dinosaurs and exhibit them, as such, in major museums without stirring any controversy.

My argument, much like John Green's, is based on the most probable interpretation of *Gigantopithecus* as a bipedal hominid that has no other human traits, and that same interpretation can be made for the sasquatch from footprint evidence alone. To propose that two different kinds of animals are involved, with essentially the same description, would be unlikely in the extreme. Since there is only a small amount of tangible evidence from either source, and no direct overlap between them in what material there is, it must remain a possibility that there is some degree of difference between these Asian and American giant primates.

It is possible that there might come to be some degree of acceptance for the name *G. blacki* for the sasquatch, so long as any differences that might appear are of no more than a subspecies distinction. If some day they prove to be different species, or even different genera, there is no way at present to legally propose names that will be used in that eventually. But one can make such proposals in print, as I am doing now for the second time, and only hope that they will be used as needed by whomever has the authority to give the official name when the real time comes.

It is my suggestion that if discovered skeletal material shows sasquatch to be a different species of *Gigantopithecus*, it should be named *G. canadensis*. This is a commonly used zoological name for species that are native to northern North America. If it proves to be a new species of the genus *Australopithecus*, I similarly propose to name it *A. canadensis*. If the evidence argues for a new genus, my suggestion would be to make it *Gigantanthropus*, an admittedly cumbersome name, with again the same specific designation. It was Franz Weidenreich who first proposed my generic name back in 1945; he thought it would be more descriptive of the Chinese fossils, at the time only known from a few teeth. Once accepted, scientific names cannot be changed, so Weidenreich's name is still available for someone else to use.

The lower jaw would be the most definitive piece of the skeleton with which to determine the affiliations of our North American species. Its canine and first premolar, the third and fourth teeth from the midline (Fig. 75), are the most diagnostic. A medium-sized canine tooth, associated with a barely two-cusped premolar, would probably make it *Gigantopithecus*. With a big, flat-topped premolar and a canine only half as large, it would be a descendant of *Australopithecus robustus*; but if that canine is as big around as the premolar, then it stems from either *A. africanus* or something in genus *Homo*. A quite different arrangement of tooth sizes and shapes might argue for a new genus. Other traits than teeth can be used for classification, but these will probably be the most diagnostic.

Bernard Heuvelmans privately urged me to go for naming the footprints with the maximum distinction—a new genus and species. There is much to be said for this procedure because if its distinction

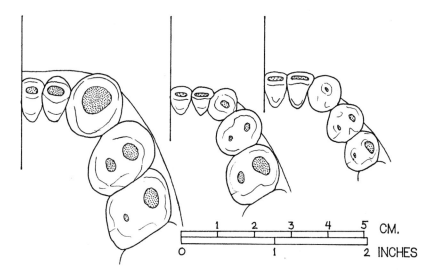

Figure 75. Some diagnostic teeth. These are crown views of the lower front teeth of *Gigantopithecus* (left), *Australopithecus robustus* (center), and *A. africanus* (right). The vertical line is the midline of the jaw in each case, and the first five teeth are illustrated. Each is drawn to simulate the same degree of tooth wear, with exposed dentin shown in stipple. All members of genus *Homo* have teeth like those on the right, but smaller.

fails to hold, it simply will be moved back down to where I named it in the first place. And if its distinction does hold, my name might have priority. I was reluctant to follow this advice for two reasons. It seemed unlikely that a new name at any level could gain acceptance without there being a type specimen consisting of bone, whereas there was at least a chance that assigning it to an existing name would be recognized. Also it struck me as not quite honest to propose a distinction at any higher taxonomic level when I could see no evidence of there being any difference at all.

It could be argued that a footprint is just as valid as a fossil bone on the grounds that either of these is only a modification of the environment that was made by an individual of the species. It should not matter that the bones represent part of the environment (food) that was actually ingested by the animal, after which this food took on a permanent form. It could also be argued that some fossils do not actually contain any of the body substance either; many fossil sea shells are in fact natural casts from which the original material has been entirely removed. It would seem to follow that footprints are equally valid. Surely we are not going to invalidate all names based on specimens that do not now contain some of the animal's original substance.

Several attempts have already been made to assign a new scientific name to sasquatch, even though an acceptable type specimen was not available. All such efforts are futile; the scientific community is not obligated to recognize any of these names. The only name that has any reasonable chance of being accepted, in my opinion, is that of an already named species. Of course it is possible that the public will come to use a particularly catchy name that is easy to remember, and this in turn could influence whomever is someday in a position to assign the official name. The names that I have proposed are an attempt in just this direction, but my names may not be the kind that the general public is likely to remember.

If and when the definitive specimen is brought in, the scientific and publicity hassles will be a major problem. The person in charge will be criticized for everything he/she has done, and will be pressured to do more; contradictory advice will come from every imaginable quarter. There are only a few rewards that would result from this chaos, and one of the most outstanding of these is the right to pick the official scientific name.

8

ELSEWHERE AND ELSEWHEN

Many sasquatch enthusiasts seem to think that by finding more widespread evidence of the species, they are in effect strengthening the argument that the species is real. Up to a certain point this reasoning is valid; if bigfoot had been an isolated phenomenon in a small part of northern California, its biological reality would certainly be in doubt for that reason alone. Including them within the sasquatch type that occurs throughout the Pacific Northwest and adjacent parts of Canada greatly enhances their believability. Since large terrestrial species tend to have the widest distributions, extending their originally proposed range to include most of North America and large parts of Asia does no violence to biological expectations. Wolves, brown bears, reindeer, bison, and horses have (or had) similar distributions. No arboreal primate covers such large areas, but many of the more terrestrial species are nearly this widespread.

But when it is suggested that a wild primate is found native to all continents, including Australia, then credibility drops sharply. Only humans, along with their domesticates and parasites, have distributions that are worldwide; no other land animals even remotely approach this condition. Beyond a certain point, it can be argued that the more widespread a cryptozoological species is reported to be, the less likely it is that the creature exits at all.

I made this point in a recent article (see Markotic 1984), and some investigators took sharp exception to it on the grounds that the available evidence did in fact indicate just such a distribution. The thrust of this chapter is to lay out some of that evidence from the points of view of zoology and anthropology in order to see how it might best be interpreted. Here I am dealing with reports that I had no hand in gathering, and material that I have mostly had no opportunity to examine. However, much of this has been published by seemingly reputable people, and I have met a few of the principal investigators in various countries and discussed some of the evidence with them. It must still be admitted that I am walking on much thinner ice here than elsewhere in this book. The locations of various reported unknown hominoids are shown on a world map in Figure 76.

As has already been indicated, sasquatch-like reports have come from almost all parts of North America. There are few accounts, and in my mind mostly dubious, from parts of the Desert Southwest and the Great Plains. Where they are reported in these areas, the immediate locations are mostly in forested mountains or major river valleys. It could be argued that if sasquatches were to be found anywhere in these vast areas, it is just in these forests (generally including pine trees, by the way) where they ought to be expected. On the other hand, most of the forests in question are small or in long narrow strips, and have little or no contacts with each other or with the major forested areas of the continent. It is difficult to see how sufficient food and concealment could be found to support a breeding

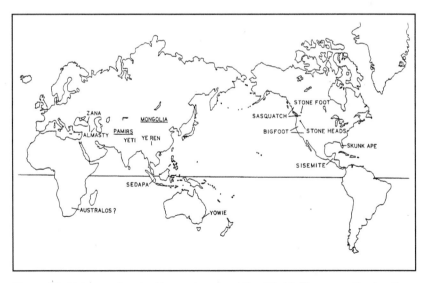

Figure 76. Unknown hominoid reports around the World. These are the locations of the major kinds of unverified bipedal primates that are mentioned in the text, along with some geographical places. The author's area of study is western North America, with its bigfoot or sasquatch. I give much credence to the stone heads and foot, skunk ape, sisemite, and footprints from the Pamirs. The other reported creatures are more difficult for me to evaluate.

population in many such places, especially where there is considerable human settlement as well. Prior to the intrusion of Europeans, this distribution is only a little more logical.

The Sierra Nevada Mountains of eastern California provide a reasonable sasquatch environment; there are many believable reports from there, especially in recent years. I have come across similar stories from the mountainous parts of western Mexico, but have little firsthand information; Titmus saw some tracks there in 1963 that could well have been real. Ivan Sanderson mentioned sightings in Guatemala where it is locally referred to as Sisemite. A few years ago I corresponded with a Guatemalan resident, Barry Wallace, who has encountered some evidence of the animal and thinks that it may be the same creature as our sasquatch. This string of evidence running southward from the Pacific Northwest is certainly suggestive, but for sheer volume of reports it is not impressive. But when one leaves the English-language press coverage of the United States by moving in that direction, this relative silence is just what might be expected. There are no reports beyond Guatemala that may be taken seriously at the present time; only Grumley (1974) has pushed this idea, and rather clumsily in my opinion.

In the eastern woodlands, including part of southern Canada, there are some very old stories followed by a long silence. In the last few decades there have been numerous claims of sightings and footprints in that area. The quiet century could be an artifact of press coverage, but that seems unlikely. We are also missing the accounts that were told by parents or grandparents to a child who is now grown up. This could also be an accident of reporting, but it strongly suggests a long absence, or extreme scarcity, of the creatures for at least a hundred years.

Many of the more persistent eastern reports come from low-lying and/or swampy lands of the lower Mississippi and other major river basins. These could have been continuing habitats throughout modern times. In Florida there are numerous reports of what is locally known as the "skunk ape." Outside of the Pacific Northwest, Florida has more reports in John Green's files than any other state or province. If we were to exercise extreme caution and cut the number of Green's reports from each state in half, then subtract another twenty just for good measure, then all of the middle and eastern U.S. and Canada would be dramatically reduced or eliminated, except for Florida. There is no reason to think that Floridians are more likely than most people to make up or spread these stories. The recent population influx into the state has caused the major cities to expand inland from the coasts at a remarkable rate. This disrupts and displaces all local species. The incoming humans are largely strangers to the area, and are the most likely to report anything unusual. Long-term natives, on the other hand, tend to keep much more quiet about things that might excite other people.

Almost all of the nonswamp land in the eastern U.S. was deforested and farmed by 1890. Since then, and especially after World War II, much of the less productive farmland has been allowed to revert to its natural vegetation and, presumably, its native fauna. At first I paid little attention to sasquatch/bigfoot reports from states like Indiana, Ohio, and Pennsylvania, but they seem to be increasing in numbers and apparent authenticity. Some of this could be attributed to more information becoming available about the phenomenon in the west, thus triggering copycat reports. However, their numbers and internal consistency argue against major hoaxing there, just as strongly as anywhere else. If we were to dismiss all of the eastern reports, then we would also have to dismiss all reports of the same quality from all other places, including the Pacific Northwest. And that would leave us with almost no sightings from anywhere. Some skeptics would support this line of reasoning.

Footprint evidence from the eastern U.S. would be much more impressive to me than eyewitness accounts. Until recently I had seen little of this, and none of it was very convincing. A footprint cast from Arkansas was easily dismissed as a fake, one from Maryland was so vague it could represent almost anything, and an Ohio cast was from a footprint made by a large man. Some photographs of a cast from northeastern Missouri looked good, but I never saw the cast itself. The advocates could point out that just because Grover Krantz has not seen the evidence, this can hardly be counted as an argument against it. True.

In the spring of 1990 a man who prefers to remain anonymous sent me a plaster cast of a footprint from Indiana (Fig. 43), postmarked from the city of Bloomington. It was examined by the tracker Bob Titmus, and the fingerprinter Ed Palma, the two best experts available, and they both thought it looked genuine. The track also passed all of my own criteria, published and private, that distinguish sasquatch tracks from human tracks and from fakes.

With all of the evidence recounted above, and more, it would seem unreasonable to deny that sasquatch occurs in the eastern U.S. There remain many possible sources of error and hoaxing in particular cases, but to dismiss it all as being out-of-hand is no longer possible. At this point I would not hazard a guess as to the density of population, except to note that it must be high enough for most of them (except rogue males) to maintain some degree of social contact with other members of their species.

Most of Canada consists of boreal forests and tundra, and there are almost no sasquatch reports from these areas. There are almost no people there either, and we probably wouldn't hear about it even if they did see sasquatches. On the southern fringe of this vast area, in the oil fields north of Edmonton, I am told that workers there talk about sasquatch sightings as if they were commonplace. On the northern fringe, in the tundra of the Yukon Territory, a Smithsonian archeologist told me about seeing a line of unmistakable sasquatch tracks.

Near the middle of southern Canada, about two hundred miles north of Winnipeg, the Royal Canadian Mounted Police found and

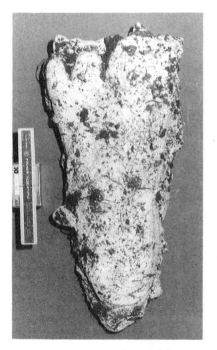
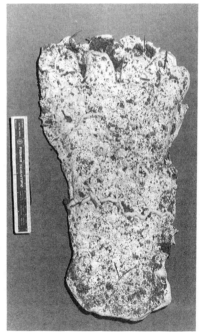

Figure 77. Footprints from Manitoba. These tracks crossed a dirt road in interior Canada in 1988. Such four-toed feet are often reported in eastern North America, but this is the only good evidence I've seen of them. (Photo courtesy of the R.C.M.P.)

photographed a good set of tracks in 1988 that crossed a dirt road (Fig. 77). These photos were sent to elicit my opinion of their authenticity; they passed every test I knew of. The only oddity is that only four toes were present on each foot. The R.C.M.P. report also mentioned that the area ". . . is known for numerous Sasquatch sightings over the years." We may safely assume that the same kind of evidence occurs across the entire area, but it is only rarely seen, and even more rarely reported.

Old stories of sasquatches are recounted in some detail in John Green's major book of 1978. They go back as far as the 1830s. I have also read in the journal of Juaquin Miller, one of the first Europeans to travel in northern California, where he found a long line of giant tracks in snow. He eventually decided, probably erroneously, that they must have been made by a group of Indians who were walking single file in each others' footsteps. Bord (1982) repeated a newspaper account of an apparent sasquatch sighting in New York state in 1818.

An Indian stone carving from near Lillooet, British Columbia is an obvious approximation of the kind of foot that would make a sasquatch track. The heel and first toe are broken off, but the existing part shows some interesting traits. Its underside shows a flat foot of large size, double ball, great width, and near-uniform toes running almost straight across (Fig. 78). The upper surface mostly has a geometric design instead of foot detail, so the item was made on the basis of seeing a footprint, not a foot. Archeological associations suggest that it may be about five hundred years old. It is presently housed in the Vancouver City Museum.

An interesting description of the capture of what may be a young sasquatch appeared in a Victoria, B.C., newspaper in July of 1884. It was described as being wild, hair covered, long armed, and very strong. Reportedly it measured 4 feet 7 inches tall and weighed 127 pounds (140 cm and 57 kg). It was captured on the Canadian Pacific Railroad, near Yale, B.C., while this line was still under construction. The creature was to be taken to England for exhibition. Very little additional information is available on it. Some newspaper follow-ups put the whole story in doubt, but there are some personal records that tend to confirm the incident. Its fate is unknown, assuming that it ever existed at all. (See John Green's 1978 book for full details on this story.)

In 1884 the Canadian Pacific Railroad still had a long unfinished gap through the mountains to the east of Yale, where "Jacko" was supposedly held for a short time. To travel east with this creature

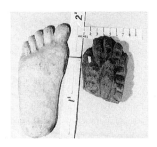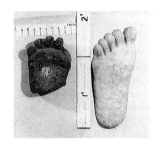

Figure 78. Indian-carved stone foot. On the left and center this object is compared with a large sasquatch track cast; on the right is a closer view of its underside detail. It is over seven inches wide and probably would be at least 16 inches long if the foot shape was maintained in its missing heel portion. The broken-off first toe would not have been conspicuously large. The crease across the ball is the trait that most suggests a sasquatch type of foot. (Photos courtesy of John Green.)

would have been almost impossible, as no wagon road even existed then to reach the other rail head. To travel west by train to Vancouver would mean a long sea voyage around South America, which perhaps would be undesirable for the railroad man who was in charge of the beast. The easiest route would have been a wagon trip south into the United States to reach the Northern Pacific Railroad, which had been completed just that year. Then a train trip east and a short sea voyage would bring them to England.

Traveling east on the Northern Pacific would put Jacko and his keeper in Duluth, Minnesota, where I have been told there was a newspaper account of a strange animal arriving from the west in that year. I could not find record of that news item in the files of the only surviving Duluth newspaper from that time. It may have been in another newspaper that is now long gone. Since two people said they had heard about this news item, and they did not know each other, it still sounds real.

As a further check I visited three towns on the Canadian Pacific Railroad, just to the east of the last gap, to see if there was any evidence that Jacko had passed through there in 1884. This inquiry was made in 1974, and ninety years was too long a time for any witnesses to be found still alive. What I did locate in each town was the oldest functioning person who had lived there all of his/her life. These proved to be interesting visits for their own sake. To each of them I posed the same question: If such a creature as Jacko came though this town fifteen or twenty years before you were born, would you have heard about it eventually? All three were quite certain they would have picked up on such an item, and they all were equally sure that it had not happened. I did not make a comparable test on the U.S. railroad in Montana, but instead followed up another line.

In the 1884 season P.T. Barnum added "Jo-Jo the dog-faced boy" to his circus. Jo-Jo was advertised as having come from Siberia, where it supposedly required several of Barnum's men to subdue the boy's father. Barnum never bothered with telling the truth about his exhibits, but one would presume that Jo-Jo must have been quite powerfully built to have suggested this kind of story about his origin. At the Barnum Museum in Bridgeport, Connecticut, there are no photographs of Jo-Jo from 1884. However there is one, marked 1885, that shows a hairy-faced young man of very ordinary-looking strength and body build. The contrast between the advertising of 1884 and the photograph of 1885 is so striking that it looks as if the first of many replacements probably occurred after that first year.

My suggestion of course is obvious, that the first Jo-Jo was in fact the captured sasquatch youngster, Jacko. Barnum's agents would most likely have picked up on the story of Jacko if he reached Duluth. They would have had a convincing argument for Mr. Tilbury to sell the creature to them. After all, Barnum had just bought Jumbo, the world's largest elephant from England, so he obviously could make the best offer. Such a sale would also save a voyage, as well as the risk of losing the animal that might already be ailing for lack of its normal diet.

If Jacko (Jo-Jo) died during or after the first season, Barnum would obviously replace him with the most hairy-faced man he could find, and pretend that nothing untoward had happened. Jacko's body could have been disposed of in any number of ways, with no prospects now of ever locating it. A friend of mine, Tracy Blair, once suggested that the body might have been buried in the Barnum cemetery where Tom Thumb and others were interred, perhaps under the name of John Tilbury—a synonym for Jacko combined with the surname of the man who was in charge of him. Another friend, Gregory May, checked out the cemetery and could not find this name or any other that might suggest this creature. The tracking of Jacko, tenuous as it was, came to a halt at this point.

China

There are reports of hairy bipeds from many parts of Asia. Russian and Chinese scientists and lay people have investigated these for many years, with pretty much the same inconclusive results as in North America. I was able to discuss the situation at length with Zhou Guoxing, Vice Director and anthropologist at the Beijing Natural History Museum. He has personally investigated much of the evidence throughout China, and he is reasonably convinced that the creatures called yeren, or wildmen, are real. He showed me casts of footprints that came from various places, none of which were as detailed as some of the better ones from North America. With most of them I would defer judgment as to their authenticity, but some looked fairly good.

At the westernmost edge of China are the Pamir Mountains, which also extend into the former Soviet Union, Afghanistan, and Kashmir. From this area Chinese investigators have recovered evidence, including footprint casts, that look to me much the same as those of our sasquatch. Evidence from other parts of China is either undiagnostic, or is clearly from some different source. Since red hair is so commonly described for the wildman in southern China's Yunan Province, and the creatures do not sound especially large, it seems more likely that another animal may be involved. Actually there is an impressive number of possible sources for wildman accounts that can be listed, only the first four or five of which apply to North America.

1. Sasquatches, possibly a smaller version
2. Bears standing briefly on their hind legs
3. A man in heavy clothing, especially at a distance or under poor viewing conditions
4. Natural objects of the appropriate shape that are only briefly glimpsed
5. Surviving Neandertals, as suggested by the archeologist Myra Shackley and many Russian investigators
6. Orang utans, a surviving mainland population
7. Bipedal mainland orangs, a different species
8. Large Rhesus monkeys. There is a rare species in the interior of China that is quite large; the hands and feet of one were saved a few years ago and for a while were thought to be those of a wildman.
9. Golden monkeys. This is a rare Chinese monkey that actually has no similarity to the wildman but is still commonly blamed for reports.

10. Yeti, the Himalayan snowman that made the footprint of the famous Shipton photographs

11. Bearded European men, especially after the story has passed through a few individuals who have never seen one of these hairy-faced giants.

Most of these possibilities merit no further discussion at this point, and one of them (No. 5) is discussed in the next section. Fossil orangs are known from much of the Asian mainland, including almost half of China, but most zoologists think that none survive today; they could be wrong. A bipedal version of the orang was discussed in the preceding chapter, but there is almost nothing tangible to support this possibility. Considering that large parts of southwestern China are densely vegetated, sparsely inhabited, and difficult of access, it would be a bit rash to make pronouncements on what is not there. I think it would be equally presumptuous to assert that unverified animals of a certain description do live there.

In 1951 Eric Shipton obtained a clear photograph in the snow of a strange footprint in Nepal that is commonly ascribed to the Yeti, or "abominable snowman." This shows what appear to be five toes, with the largest on one side and descending in size to the other side. The first two toes both seem to be turned a bit toward the other three, as if in a grasping pose. The footprint is no longer than a human's but is easily twice as wide (Fig. 79). Ivan Sanderson made much of this photo, along with native reports, to build a picture of some kind of ape that was only partially bipedal. Until another photograph or cast of that particular foot design turns up, I see no point in taking it seriously.

At least one bearded anthropologist has had Chinese children point at him and excitedly cry out "yeren." If I had gone to some of the more remote villages, my own anatomy would certainly have gotten the same responses. We can only speculate on how many wildman stories trace back to this source, passed on by word of mouth, then updated to impress some authority from the city. Country folk in America often delight in confounding their city brethren; I see no reason why the Chinese should not also play that game.

The total number of wildman reports from China that are currently "on record," whatever that means, is now three hundred. That is so much smaller than the admittedly incomplete number from North America, that some explanation is called for. Given the relative numbers of people involved in the two areas, a skeptic could assert that Americans are twenty times better liars than are Chinese. I would rather think that it is simply a matter of differences in information-gathering problems and procedures.

A recent British television expedition recovered some supposed wildman hair from local investigators in central China, and had them analyzed by scientists in Shanghai. Some of the sample were eliminated as belonging to various known species. Six remaining hairs were morphologically very similar to human hair, and distinguishable from a sample of other primates, but their chemical constitution was unique. These hairs reportedly contained only 16 amino acids instead of the normal mammalian 17, and their iron-to-zinc ratio was 50 times higher than human and 7 times higher than in the primate sample. The hairs also had a higher acid protein content than in human or other primate hair, and they differed from all these in containing more calcium, chromium, magnesium, iron, cobalt, copper, and strontium. Such distinctions are indeed impressive, but unfortu-

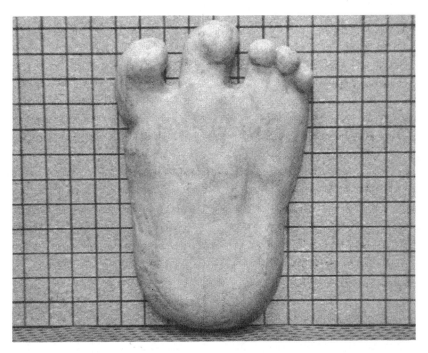

Figure 79. Replica of Shipton footprint. A Nepalese craftsman made this image of what the foot should have looked like that made the famous footprint that Shipton photogaphed in 1951. The original was given to the Brooklyn Children's Museum, where this copy was made through the courtesy of Michael Cohn.

nately they constitute no evidence for a new species. One would expect wildman hair to be chemically closest to human, with these two forming a group in contrast to other primates. Instead, we find human and other primates hair standing together in sharp contrast to that of the wildman specimens. Given its morphological similarity to human hair, this supposed wildman sample has clearly been contaminated by some chemical agency, perhaps dyes or preservatives. What the hair actually represents is undeterminable on present evidence.

U.S.S.R.

(As of this writing the Soviet Union has ceased to exist, but I will continue to use the older geographical terms for the sake of familiarity.)

Reports of hairy bipeds come from many places in the Soviet Union, and these also may represent quite different kinds of creatures. In the case of China, my best guess is that they have sasquatch in the far west, and that no strong case can presently be made for anything else other than known animals (which includes orangs). In the Soviet Union, on the other hand, I see evidence of two types for sure (though one of these appears to be human), and there is at least good evidence of yet a third type.

Casts have been made of giant footprints from the Soviet side of the Pamir Mountains in central Asia. Igor Bourtsev and Dmitri Bayanov showed me two of these in Moscow—one full sized and the other apparently of a child. The large one would easily become lost in a group of adult female sasquatch tracks. The small one shows even more exaggerated sasquatch traits, much like some presumed child tracks from America. It would be useful to see more data like this, but there is enough at least to suggest a sasquatch distribution that runs in a broad and inverted U-shape from the Pamirs, through Beringia, and as far as Guatemala. A long stretch of this area, through eastern Siberia, remains poorly documented, especially for outsiders like myself.

Sasquatch-like accounts come from places scattered over much of Siberia, and some range into the eastern and northern parts of European Russia itself, and far to the south in the Caucasus Mountain region. Many such reports go back to the last century, and comparisons have been made with still earlier accounts from of Europe. It is not immediately clear whether all of these reports can be ascribed to the same species. The most "normal" of these should be looked into first.

When Neolithic farmers first entered Europe a few thousand years ago, they cleared and planted only the most easily tilled lands. Vast areas remained as well-forested refuges in which Mesolithic hunters coexisted for many centuries, often trading and peacefully interacting with the farmers in other ways. Over time, agriculture spread slowly into the forests, reducing the number of hunters and the area held by them. In the 13th Century a new type of tree-felling axe was invented and put into general use. This was the final factor in reducing the remaining large forest lands, and their Mesolithic inhabitants as well.

In most of Europe the last of these hunters would soon be losing their livelihood and giving up in the face of advancing civilization. While the majority of them would expire quietly in the forest, a few (often children) would find themselves alone and were picked up by the farming people. These stragglers normally would be dressed in animal skins, a fact that could easily give rise to descriptions that they "were covered with animal hair."

A close parallel to this situation was well documented early in this century in California, when a native American named Ishi gave himself up to the farmers after all the rest of his tribe were gone. He and his last family members had survived for many years, virtually under the noses of the dominant population, with almost no indication of their existence. Ishi's tribe had been noted earlier, and a member of a related tribe was able to communicate to some degree with him. If it hadn't been for these facts, Ishi might have been described as some kind of wildman, of only semihuman appearance (compared with Euroamericans), and being unable to speak. If one adds "hairy skins" (Ishi came in naked), we have a quite normal explanation for the thirteenth-century wildman discoveries in Europe. In fact, this sort of appearance by the last of the Mesolithic hunters is virtually demanded by the anthropological circumstances.

Forest clearing was rapid in the potential agricultural lands of western and central Europe. It progressed more slowly to the north and east, where the terrain and climate made farming more difficult, and where there was less population pressure. Some areas remain today that are capable of supporting viable populations of *Homo sapiens* who could still be practicing a hunting and gathering economy. Such people are well known in other parts of the world; whether any of them remain in Europe, without being known to civilization, is the big question we face.

The most recent event that seems to fit the description of a Mesolithic survivor was the capture of Zana (or Zanya) in western Georgia of the trans-Caucasus sometime in the mid-1800s. Her description, which included substantial size, a coat of hair, and a frightening face, was probably written long after the fact (Tchernine 1970). Though she never learned to speak (at least not in Russian) she did come to accept her new life, learned to perform simple tasks, and bore several children by her human master. She died sometime in the 1880s.

There is no direct evidence remaining of Zana herself, but a photograph of one of her sons shows nothing to indicate a less-than-human anatomy. The remains of this man have been exhumed, and through the courtesy of Igor Bourtsev in Moscow I was able to examine the skull in great detail. It is a perfectly normal specimen of modern *Homo sapiens*, with slightly stronger jaws and more flare to the zygomatic arches (cheek bones) than is usual. Under no circumstances could this man's mother have been as primitive as a Neandertal; even a grandparent of this type would have left some anatomical evidence of this ancestry, and it is not there. Assuming that this individual has been correctly identified, and I have no reason to doubt it, his anatomy would fit perfectly with one parent having been a late Mesolithic hunter.

There are a few other reports of captured or observed creatures in and around the Caucasus region that might also prove to be Mesolithic people still surviving there. In some cases, however, the amount of inaccuracy in the reported descriptions would have to be truly remarkable to allow for this identification. The clearest of these, recounted in full in Sanderson's book, refers to the capture of a hairy wildman in the Caucasus in late 1941 who was examined by a Soviet army doctor. It was the size of a large man, and with an unusually big chest and fingers. Its chest, back, and shoulders had a hair covering two to three cm long (one inch), but no mention was made that the entire body was so covered; in fact he referred to it as being "naked." The army doctor judged it to have an animal's personality, and thus it was not a disguised enemy spy. There is no record of what was done with it.

The 1941 specimen was probably not a young sasquatch or its hair should have stirred more comment, and I would think that its face, shoulders, and thumbs ought to have been noted as being remarkably unhuman. There seem to be too many animallike traits to easily pass him off as another Mesolithic human, though that idea cannot be completely dismissed. The most obvious remaining possibility is that it was a Neandertal. Many of the Russian investigators favor this interpretation, and they might be right.

Marie-Jeanne Koffman has spent many years studying the evidence of a wild hominid population in rather remote parts of the Caucasus. These creatures are known by many local names, but almasty (or almasti) has become the most commonly used designation by investigators. I was able to examine some tracks she brought back to Moscow, including a series of overlapping photographs of a long trail of them. There is no doubt that these are genuine footprints of a hominid, but they are not sasquatch. In fact, they pass the test of being human rather than sasquatch in most particulars; but they are clearly not human either. The feet would have been somewhat more than normal human length, but of exceptional width, and with little or no indication of an arch. They roughly match the footprints of known Neandertals that were sealed in an Italian cave for at least forty thousand years. The first digit shows an unusual mobility, and in some prints it appears to deviate inward by 20 degrees or more from the next toe; in most cases it is closely set against the other toes. This is an anomaly that can occur in modern feet, so it could occur in a Neandertal or other hominid as well. Alternatively, this may represent a very unhuman trait that removes these creatures from any close relation to ourselves. The circumstances under which these footprints appeared were such that Koffman was able to rule out, to her satisfaction, any chance of modern fakery. I think that she is a careful investigator, and is not given to overstating the evidence.

Koffman has collected over five hundred eyewitness accounts from natives of the Caucasus region who claim to have seen the "wildman." She summarized this evidence in a recent paper that hopefully will soon appear in *Cryptozoology*. From an advance copy of her paper, translated from the French by E.B. Winn, some of the essential points can be recounted here. The almasty (presumably adults) are erect bipeds that stand taller than most humans, averaging 6.5 feet tall (2 m), with both sexes being the same size. They are well covered with body hair about 6 inches long (15 cm), but which is much longer on the head. The hair color is usually given as reddish brown, while the skin is much darker or even black. The neck is short or nonexistant, the shoulders are broad and hunched, and the arms are proportionately somewhat longer than in humans. Some of this arm length is from especially long fingers, while the thumb is described as being notably short. Curiously, at least three reports indicated that they grasped objects with all five digits wrapping around the item in the same direction; one observer even noted the absence of a thenar pad. Leg length is usually described as being of human proportions, though some said they were short and/or bow-legged. Females have pendulous breasts that can be thrown back over the shoulders.

Many of Koffman's witnesses described the head and face of the almasty in some detail. The face is large, they say, especially in its breadth across the cheeks. The braincase is flattened and relatively small, while the forehead is very retreating above the projecting brow ridges. The nose has almost no projection, but is very wide. The mouth is described as being thin lipped and maybe twice as wide as a human's. The teeth are large, and at least two observers commented on its projecting canine teeth, while one specifically denied this condition. Several observers reported some degree of forward projection of the muzzle region—more than the human condition, but not like in monkeys. The eyes are described as being notably slanting (more so than in Chinese) and capable of reflecting red light. The chin is called strongly retreating.

Many of these observations are based on very close sightings, sometimes touching or within touching distance. Clearly the almasty, as described by Koffman's witnesses, do not have the same degree of human avoidance as our North American sasquatch. Their odor, however, is described in similar terms and is equally repugnant to humans. And that odor is not reported in all close encounters. Almasty supposedly enter certain man-made buildings with little hes-itation, handle our artifacts, and sometimes even put pieces of cloth over parts of their bodies. There is no indication that they make or use any of their own artifacts, nor much evidence that they make any use of what they handle of human workmanship.

Almasty sometimes take cultivated crops and other food, but prob-ably not in great quantity or more concern would be evidenced. This kind of eating, their use of empty cabins, and occasional encounters, are about all the physical interaction that they have with humans. Their relationship to dogs presents a stark contrast with the Ameri-can reports. Dogs supposedly show no fear of them; it is the almasty who fear the dogs, and apparently with good reason. Koffman included a report of some dogs pursuing and killing one of them.

Additional evidence of similar kinds has been reported by other investigators from the Caucasus region. Some accounts include the trading of goods with almasty, but I find this rather incongruous with the image of them based on all of the other evidence. There also is a recording of a vocalization from Georgia that I could only describe as "interesting" in that it does not exactly sound like a human voice, but it does not sound much like any of the reputed sasquatch recordings either.

I must reserve judgment on the Caucasus evidence, having been able to examine so little of it. If we leave preconceived notions aside, a case might be made for fitting all of the European evidence into a Mesolithic mold, a surviving Neandertal, or a deviant version of sasquatch. But for any one of these interpretations to be all-encompassing, we would have to postulate that many of the descriptions are exaggerated, distorted, or simply not true in many particulars. We can minimize this problem by deciding that more than one of these types are involved. I would assign all of the Medieval reports to Mesolithic foragers who were dying out, and include Zana as the last of these. The 1941 capture, Koffman's tracks and descriptions, and the sound tape could all be ascribed to sasquatch with the fewest (though still many) contradictions, while many investigators insist that Neandertal is the correct identification.

The proposal of Mesolithic survivors lasting up to Medieval times is not supported by any archeological evidence that is commonly reported, but it is not out of the question either. To extend these Mesolithic people up to modern times in a more remote area should not raise these eyebrows much further. But to suggest survival of the much earlier Neandertals to the present day in the Caucasus region, is indeed contrary to most authoritative opinion.

The case for the almasty being surviving Neandertals is actually the weakest of all, especially in view of Koffman's eyewitness reports. Neandertals have big braincases, and these would still be relatively large even if they had evolved to this greater body size. Their noses were notably large and projecting, not flat as described here. Neandertal facial bones are large, but are especially noted for their height, not their breadth. Their fingers definitely are not long, and their thumbs were of human size and fully opposable, quite unlike the almasty description. It is almost certain that Neandertals had little if any more body hair than modern Caucasoids. They also made tools and weapons that are not evidenced in any of the Caucasus accounts.

While I see no inherent reason why Neandertals could not have survived in some locality, this is clearly not the place.

Myra Shackley, a British archeologist, seriously claimed to have found evidence of living Neandertals in Mongolia, as recounted in her 1983 book. She made surface finds of stone tools of the appropriate Mousterian types, though their implied modern date is not fully assured. She also gathered descriptions from local people of another, rather subhuman population that lived in the area. These sound acceptably close to Neandertals, but a foraging population of the Mesolithic type of modern humans is another possible interpretation. Shackley's "Neandertals" were welcomed by the hominologists in Russia, especially by those who would assign all of the world's hairy bipeds to that group. Most of the scientific world has paid little attention to Shackley's claims.

The late Professor Rinchen (no additional names) sent me a photograph of a supposed wildman footprint from Mongolia back in 1972 (Fig. 80). I don't know if it has any possible connection with Dr. Shackley's evidence, no exact location was given. The Rinchen photo is not very informative; quite clearly it has been altered, and possibly even faked.

Figure 80. Footprint from Mongolia. Professor Rinchen sent me this photograph that he had obtained somewhere in Outer Mongolia. No scale was provided, but he indicated that it was larger than a human foot. Obviously it has been altered by scraping it clear of debris; it might even have been created by such scraping.

Most of the Caucasus descriptions could be fitted into a sasquatch mold, but only with considerable difficulty. The size, and especially the massiveness, of the sasquatch body is not evident here, though it could be a geographical variant in this regard. More problematical is the notable sexual dimorphism of the sasquatch and its distinctively different (and much larger) footprints. The nonopposed thumb is like the sasquatch, but the elongated fingers are not. Its behavior is also somewhat different, especially in its interactions with humans and their dogs.

Quite frankly, I don't know what the Caucasus natives are describing. It is neither human nor Neandertal, and almost certainly not sasquatch. Three of Koffman's written accounts include a brief description of examining a dead almasty. If any of these remains had reached a competent biologist we would know that they were real, and we would most likely have a good idea of just what they were.

Australia

On the face of it, the island continent is one of the least likely places one would expect to hear about reports of hairy bipeds. Nevertheless, Graham Joyner has gathered and published a small book (1977) of collected newspaper articles that seem to be describing just such creatures. These date from as far back as 1871 and can hardly have been stimulated by similar stories from other continents—a few, perhaps, but not many. In 1984 Joyner brought this subject into the journal *Cryptozoology* with a short article about the name "yahoo," though it is usually known in Australia as the "yowie." Collin Groves wrote another article on this for the 1986 issue, and through at least 1989 that journal has published a steady stream of comments by various contributors on the question of the beast's existence.

Having read all of Joyner's book, I was struck by the fact that the descriptions are all of fairly large creatures that show some degree of upright posture, but beyond that they share very few traits. This is quite unlike the North American reports where we get a constant repetition of the same theme, with minor variations in size and color, and little else. One is forced to conclude that these articles were culled from an even greater diversity of published animal descriptions, from which all those of smaller size and/or horizontal orientation were omitted, as well as everything of known identity.

Some of the Australian accounts might be referring to real (accepted) animals, but they may be of unusual size, deformed, or the witness was notoriously inaccurate in his/her description. An unusual proportion of these were reported by children who might not have been very familiar with some of the local fauna. Still, a fair number of them are describing what is clearly a hairy human form.

The humanoid yowies show no resemblance to sasquatch in being truly hair-covered giants. Their descriptions do not seem to cluster around the heavyset Neandertal type either. The only image I can read through these diverse accounts is something rather like an Australian Aborigine, but seen by someone who had no knowledge of them. Just like Ishi in California, some of the Abos may well have survived their tribal destruction and continued to live out their natural lives not far from the Anglo settlements. These reports are not common in the open country, but are concentrated in the Blue Mountains of southeastern Australia. (Yes, the same name struck me as interesting too.) It is also noteworthy that these reports seem to fade out shortly after the turn of the century. Had they all died out by then?

There is one more possibility that could be added, but not very seriously. My own research has indicated that Australia was occupied by *Homo erectus* at an early date. *Homo sapiens* entered about thirty-five thousand years ago in overwhelming numbers, mixed with some of the original inhabitants, and then upgraded the whole population to the modern condition. It is at least possible that a few of the original *erectus* groups survived to recent times. This idea would be comparable to that of Neandertals surviving in the Caucasus and/or Mongolia, but the likelihood seems remote. If there were many reports that mostly clustered around the same description we might take this idea more seriously. At present, I see no need to try to explain a phenomenon that is not known to exist. But then, that's the same attitude most of my colleagues take toward the sasquatch.

Other Places

One person, who shall remain nameless, garnered a lot of stories from the natives in a small area of East Africa. Many of these were so different from each other that at least five types of creatures were identified, plus a sixth that was a catch-all for those that didn't fit elsewhere. The stories, with no supporting evidence whatever, were presented with apparent seriousness at a Cryptozoology meeting; many of us who were present could barely refrain from laughing, and others simply walked out. Needless to say, the natives had figured out how to gain favor with the European person and set about to concoct some whoppers without even bothering to cross-check their stories with each other.

In a more serious vein, J.T. Robinson and C.K. Brain spent some time trying to track down native accounts of a nonhuman bipedal form in South Africa many years ago. Since both men were involved in australopithecine research, the obvious possibility facing them was that there might be living representatives of their fossils. Neither of them has chosen to speak much, or to write anything, about what they did or did not find out. We presently have no reason to think that there was anything of substance to these accounts.

From Malaya and the major islands of Indonesia there are reports of a hairy biped called "orang pendek" or "sedapa," and a variety of other names. Sanderson summarized the evidence, mostly from native accounts and folklore, but a few Europeans claim to have seen them as well. The sedapa is apparently of about human size, walks quite well on relatively short legs, but also climbs trees as adroitly as any ape. This is a reasonably good match for what has recently become the commonly accepted description of the australopithecines. It is still being argued whether some of the million-year-old fossil jaws from Java are of this type or of a more human creature.

If the Javan jaws in question belong to genus *Australopithecus*, they are clearly of the *africanus* species. These should occur in two sizes, the males being about twice the size of the females, and the known jaws from Java are likely of both sexes. There are two very unequal sizes of sedapa as well. Before too much excitement is generated over the sightings by a handfull of Europeans, we must remember that a thousand times as many are on record as having seen the sasquatch and are not generally believed.

At least one good description of a sedapa face indicated that it had somewhat projecting canine teeth. If this is true, it would most likely rule out *Australopithecus*. There are still two other fossil jaws from Java, one upper and one lower, that might fit this description. I have associated the two as belonging to the same species, which has moderately projecting canine teeth, but at the same time has a widely spread lower jaw. Other scientists do not share this opinion, but most of them are unsure of just how to interpret these two specimens. There is no obvious reason for these jaws to be so widely spread in the back unless this is to avoid crowding the neck, in which case it is designed for upright posture. Franz Weidenreich (1945) described many orang-like traits that can be seen in the lower jaw of this pair (he thought the upper jaw was more human). Long ago (1973) I raised the possibility that it might represent a largely bipedal form of this Asian ape.

There are two sets of fossils in Java, either of which might be taken as evidence for a million-year-old ancestor of the sedapa. If one of these fossil types is the real thing, then the other represents nothing living that we know of. Meanwhile, most scientists who deal with these fossils include them all in genus *Homo*, thus ruling out any possible connection for either of them with the sedapa. Without further corroboration I cannot take this situation very seriously, but to deny the possibility that it exists would be rather presumptuous.

If the Minnesota Ice Man actually originated from Vietnam, as Heuvelmans thinks, then yet another type of hairy biped may be indicated. While I am now strongly inclined to think that the specimen is real, it seems much easier to believe that it came from some location closer to the place where it was first exhibited (Minnesota). And this would make it a young male specimen of sasquatch.

Multiple Species

A major point being made in this chapter is that there are different kinds of hairy bipeds that have been reported around the world. I would not seriously argue that any of these are real, beyond the sasquatch itself. I would give this species a distribution that probably encompasses much of North America, and most likely includes some of northern Asia, but no more. I would also summarily remove the Medieval European stories from consideration by assigning them to relatively modern humanity, and some of the more recent Russian reports should go that way too. I find no reason to believe that any of the others are real, nor any compelling reason to think that they are not—only a healthy skepticism.

It is difficult enough to get most of my skeptical colleagues to listen to anything about the sasquatch evidence, and almost impossible to make them take more than a cursory glance at a footprint cast. Still, some of them are curious enough to want to know a little more about the subject, and I am the person they often come to. If I were now to assert that there are multiple species of hairy bipeds out there that have not been demonstrated, then I would lose what little credibility I have now.

Ivan Sanderson "positively identified" four major categories of hairy bipeds, with examples and subtypes spread over most of the world. Some of his readers were willing to believe anything he said; others would accept none of it. There are many scientists who are open minded but cautious; they will listen carefully to the evidence for living *Gigantopithecus* or maybe Neandertals, but not both of them. Bernard Heuvelmans has argued cogently for recognizing any and all possible differences in the reports, because if there are two or more species involved, lumping them at this point would necessarily alter their descriptions in at least some cases. This procedure is scientifically sound, but it is socially impractical in the extreme.

Fortunately for my own credibility I do not see any compelling evidence for more than one type of hairy biped, and find no reason to think it has anywhere near worldwide distribution. In my opinion the sasquatch, known by many names, occurs over most of North America and northern Asia, and that is all. Fully modern people of hunting-and-gathering types have occasionally surfaced at unexpected times and places, thus we have the Medieval European reports, Zana, and most probably the yowie of Australia. I would have to reserve judgment on the possible Neandertals of Mongolia, and the idea (my own) that some yowie reports just might be *Homo erectus*. If there is anything to the reported sedapa of Southeast Asia and Indonesia, it may be a much less human creature for which there are two possible fossil representatives. More evidence must be produced before this tropical form can be taken seriously. The Caucasus almasty does not fit any known mold, but Koffman's collected descriptions come closer to those of the sedapa than to any of the others that are mentioned here. I find nothing to support the existence of a separate Himalayan snowman. If there are any hairy bipeds in these mountains the most economical theory would be that they are simply an extension of the more familiar sasquatch.

The serious sasquatch researcher will note that many familiar items are not discussed here. Most of these are deliberately left out because the information is dubious, it is an isolated report, or I could not find a dependable reference to it. Such omissions should not affect the thrust of this book because, unlike Heuvelmans and Sanderson, it was not my intent to give worldwide coverage. This chapter simply constitutes an effort to put the sasquatch problem into a broader perspective, and to anticipate some questions on these subjects that are regularly asked.

9

THE HUNTERS

North American sasquatch hunters are a diverse lot whose various goals include taking a specimen, capturing one, filming, studying their behavior, trying to protect them, trying to make contact, or just gathering data. The first and last of these goals make sense, while all the others are misguided, to say the least. In saying this I am stepping on some toes, so all of this merits some further explanation that may well step even harder in some cases.

The first category is our hard-core hunters who are trying to bring in the first body. These are mostly ordinary people who have ordinary jobs—not academics, wildlife workers, or government employees. These hunters have seen a sasquatch or know a trusted friend who did, or else they have studied the subject in some depth. Most of them have (or think they have) considerable skills in hunting and tracking big game animals, while some have specialized military experience that seems pertinent to them; few, if any, have both kinds of background. All of these hunters have some regular occupation that has precluded their devoting full time to the hunt.

The motives of the hunters fall into four main areas: fame, money, vindication, and/or science. They almost all expect to become famous if they bring in the first specimen, both for its own sake and because this notoriety is a requirement for obtaining the next two rewards. They generally have little concept of how much this success will disrupt their private lives with legal hassles and media badgering, to name just the two most obvious problems.

Financial reward is the most common motive. The first mounted skin may well bring in a great deal of money, but this presupposes success in three critical respects. (1) The skin must be retrieved in good condition in a timely fashion—an unlikely event to say the least.

(2) A buyer must somehow be found who is willing to pay a substantial amount. (3) The delivery and money collection must be accomplished without someone else getting either the skin or the money, legally or otherwise. The hunter should note that if he openly advertises for a customer, he is just as openly inviting someone to try to take the goods away from him.

Publicity can bring financial rewards if it is well handled—interviews, public talks, story contracts, and product endorsements. But the pressure would be intense, and most of the agents will try to get what they want while paying little or nothing. (Negative publicity can also be a major factor; self-labeled conservationists will harass the hunter for killing a member of a supposedly endangered species, while others will accuse him of murder.)

Personal vindication is a major motive for those who previously have stuck their necks out publicly, especially by claiming to have seen one of the creatures. These witnesses currently get some recognition from others who think the species is real, but much of this support is from the lunatic fringe. Scientist call these sighters fools or liars, the media think it's all just a joke, and the public has mixed opinions, mostly negative. To bring in absolute proof would be to show that you were right and so many others, especially the experts, were wrong. This is a personal motivation that can drive some people as much or more than money.

A few of the hard-core hunters have expressed some interest in advancing science by proving that a new species exists and by providing the body of the first specimen for detailed study. Personally, I think the greater motive in this direction is to figuratively rub some scientists' noses in it. On the other hand, at least two of these hunters have publicly stated their intention of denying any scientist access to the body if they bring it in. The motivation for this latter attitude is not clear, especially when official verification depends on the examination of the body by these very scientists. I sense a certain amount of spite being expressed on this issue, but it is not at all clear against whom it is directed or why, and especially what is to be accomplished by their statements at this point.

All of the hard-core hunters are in competition with each other, and most of them are keenly aware of this fact. There will be a prize of some kind to the hunter who brings in the first specimen, but there will be no second prize. That first specimen will prove the existence of sasquatch. It will promptly be declared an endangered

species, and taking a second specimen would become a serious viola-
tion of law. Even if one did shoot a second sasquatch, none of the
usual rewards could be obtained: no one could buy the skin, you get
jail instead of fame if it becomes known, and vindication is unnecessary at that point anyway. The scientists might appreciate the second
specimen, but it would be confiscated by the authorities without any
thought of payment.

Being aware of these facts, each hunter figures that if and when
one of their number brings in the first sasquatch, the rest of them
will be out of business. Few of them would have any intention of
sharing the credit or proceeds if they succeed, and they assume that
all the other hunters have that same attitude. When deer hunters get
together to discuss their subject it is natural to offer helpful information to each other. If I help you get your deer this year, you might
help me get mine next year. And hunters enjoy bragging about
what they know. In the sasquatch case, however, anything that
might assist another hunter could spoil your own chances—and that
means forever.

Needless to say, it is unusual for sasquatch hunters to do anything
that might help the other guy in the quest. Many of them can't help
bragging about what they have found out, but they often cancel this
by adding false information to throw the others off the track. My
impression is that they spend as much time and effort trying to prevent others from shooting a sasquatch as they do trying to succeed
themselves. Given the circumstances, this is entirely understandable.

I have participated in several attempts to get a working agreement
with a few hunters for cooperation in the hunt by sharing all information, dividing up the areas to be searched, and with an understood
procedure to be followed if one of them were to succeed. No agreement could be reached on how to divide the spoils, and no one was
satisfied that the other hunters would abide by any such agreement
and not just take it all. I think that none of them thought he could
trust the others to circulate accurate and complete information. One
of these hunters privately raised the possibility with me that if two of
them were on the scene of the shooting, maybe only one of them
might return.

There are a few of us, most notably John Green and myself, who
are so publicly extended on the subject of the existence of the
sasquatch, that we win no matter who brings it in. Added to this is
the fact that neither of us is a hunter, and it is most unlikely that we

would ever shoot one. We are also fully aware of the problems involved in handling such a specimen. Green says he would simply deposit it with a competent scientist in the nearest university and let nature take its course. I would want to have full rights and responsibilities for the study, but if someone else had to put up with all the work and trauma that would ensue, I wouldn't be greatly upset.

The hard-core hunters all hope to bring down that first specimen with a heavy rifle. Opinions vary as to the best gun to use, but all agree that a typical deer rifle is simply not powerful enough to seriously damage an animal of this size. Guns that are suitable for elk, moose, or large grizzlies are always preferred. None of these men wants to leave a wounded sasquatch out there; it would be a sad waste of a specimen, and it might be extremely dangerous to follow.

The hunters appear to be using two procedures to locate their quarry: chance and anticipation. They spend many hours or even days moving slowly or just watching in a suitable area, hoping to encounter a sasquatch just like many unsuspecting other people have done before, but they will be prepared to deal with it. At the same time they are making note of all animal signs, especially footprints and other environmental disturbances that indicate when and where the creatures have been, and hopefully what they were doing. In this way the hunter tries to build a behavioral picture that might enable him to anticipate when and where an encounter might be anticipated.

Some hunters have tried to follow a trail in the hope of catching up with the quarry. If it knows someone is following, a sasquatch could easily outdistance any human pursuer, and it possibly might avoid leaving tracks as well. No one is known to have caught up with the quarry in this manner; the trail has been lost, by circumstance or design, or else the hunter was unable to continue for lack of time, strength, food, or whatever. I've heard about cases where novice hunters were diligently following a fresh trail in hopes of catching up, but abruptly quit when it dawned on them to ask who catches whom if they succeed.

Lures of many kinds have been tried, apparently without success. A variety of food baits have brought in other animals or nothing at all. At least one hunter used soiled sanitary napkins with no result. A few years ago my wife suggested that playing a tape of a baby crying might be similar enough to the sound of one of their own to draw them in. Annette and Mike Johnson provided a lengthy recording of these cries from their newborn, and Greg May played the tape once in the Blue Mountains with a classic ghetto blaster. The only result was total pandemonium in the nearest herd of elk. This might be worth trying again.

There are no doubt many other kinds of attraction methods that have been used. Obviously none has worked to the degree that a sasquatch was taken, but we don't know if one was even partially successful. Tracks might have appeared in response to a lure, or one might have been seen too briefly to be shot. Any hunter who has achieved that degree of success would never tell the others about it. The last thing he would want is for someone else to win the prize by using his own technique.

Another variation of hard-core hunting methods is the tranquilizer gun. At least one hunter has openly displayed such a weapon to the news media, and others have publicly stated their intention to use one. This is strictly for appearances, and none of the serious hunters has any intention of even trying to dart a sasquatch. There is much public opposition to the idea of killing one of these animals, so this is used simply to avoid bad press. It might also be used to put public pressure on the other hunters not to shoot a sasquatch, thus hopefully neutralizing some of their competition. This subject is elaborated upon below.

Novices

There is another category of hunter, far more numerous than the hard-core, who are simply "looking for bigfoot" without having any clear idea of what they are looking for or what they would do if they found something. These novices are usually as ill-informed as they are enthusiastic. They try to contact previous eyewitnesses, look for previously discovered tracks, and hope to see new tracks or even the sasquatch itself. They are usually equipped with cameras and notebooks, sometimes with tape recorders and plaster as well. Many of these novices are simply trying to decide for themselves whether these creatures exist; I can sympathize with them because I started out pretty much that way myself.

The novice who is trying to "find bigfoot" usually has given little or no thought as to how his/her potential discovery might be proven to anyone else. Having talked to many of them, I get the impression that they seem to think general acceptance will be automatic when they see the evidence. Others plan to take pictures of the creature on the assumption that this will constitute proof. These people are very naive about the kind of evidence that is required, and they usually have no concept of how much has already been collected.

Some novices talk seriously about obtaining a specimen with a tranquilizer gun. Obviously they have never looked into the subject or they would know that they would not be able to obtain the necessary equipment, and that it wouldn't work anyway. Eventually, all of these novices either drop the subject, or else they shift into one of the other categories of hunters when they learn more of the facts.

Tranquilizers

Most of the public is under the impression that any animal can be rendered unconscious with a tranquilizing drug contained in a rifle-fired dart. They think that this can be done fairly easily, and that it is harmless to the quarry. They have seen this done many times in movies and television programs, and naturally assume that it would be a simple matter to do the same with a sasquatch. It seems obvious to them that this would get around the need to kill a specimen in order to prove they exist. Nothing could be further from the truth.

In order to dart a sasquatch, one must somehow locate the creature and get within range to use the weapon. Only a few people have succeeded in doing that with a good rifle, and there is no reason to think it would be any easier with a tranquilizer gun. In fact, this method requires a much closer approach because these darts travel a much shorter distance than a bullet and are not very accurate. A good rifle might work from as far away as two hundred yards (or meters), but a tranquilizer is effective at only about one-tenth of that distance, and even then one might easily miss. There is no way to call up a sasquatch on demand. Most people who see one never see another. If you are so skilled and/or lucky as to get that one sighting, and you have a weapon in hand, your chance of bringing it down with a high-powered rifle is easily a hundred times greater than for putting a dart into it. If you miss, you probably will never get another chance.

Darting equipment is expensive and difficult to obtain. The drugs that are normally used are narcotics that can be legally obtained only by licensed field researchers. The dosage that is used depends on the size of the animal, so several darts are usually carried with different amounts in each of them. When the quarry is spotted, its weight is estimated, the appropriate dart is selected and loaded, then the close approach is attempted. Most sasquatch sightings are so brief that one has time only to estimate its size, and then it is gone. And without a great deal of familiarity with the species, most hunters would be quite unable to guess the weight with any accuracy. There is little chance that at the moment the sasquatch is seen, the rifle and case of darts would be immediately at hand, with plenty of time to load up and shoot. And this presupposes that the sasquatch is within range, and that the hunter can act calmly and carefully.

There are different tranquilizing drugs whose effect on each species may vary. We have no good information on how the sasquatch would react to these various drugs. Too much of the wrong kind could kill the specimen, in which case a good rifle would have done the same job more dependably and probably with less trauma to the subject. With too little and/or the wrong drug, there are at least three undesirable possibilities. First, the animal simply goes away with the dart and a long-term injury from the enormous needle that was used. Second, it may go away only to fall unconscious at some great distance, and perhaps not survive but never be located either. Finally, it might be aware of the nearby source of that painful needle jab and, perhaps in a somewhat drugged state of mind, decide to retaliate.

If the administration of tranquilizing drugs was as simple as it seems in the movies, then all a doctor would have to do before surgery would be to quickly jab the human patient with a needle and they would be ready for an operation. There is good reason why anesthesiologists get the patient's medical history, check his/her immediate health, give strict preoperative instructions, apply very exact amounts of certain drugs, and carefully monitor responses. If they didn't do that they would often lose patients. The same principles apply to wild animals as well.

When wildlife experts tranquilize animals, they usually know how their chosen drug will work on that species, and how much to use on specimens of known age, sex, and weight. They also know all of the likely adverse reactions to expect, and are trained and equipped to handle them. In spite of this, they occasionally lose an animal that has been drugged, and some will run off apparently unaffected. I have read about one case of a polar bear that did not go down until the third dart was shot into it, then it revived in time to attack the scientists and had to be dispatched with rifle fire. Without all of the necessary experience and equipment, a first attempt at a new species would have only a very small chance of bringing in the subject alive.

Some years ago I made these points in a public lecture in San Diego, where much of the audience was appalled by my advocacy of shooting a sasquatch. They still thought that tranquilizing was the way to go if a specimen was to be taken at all. Two weeks later a hippopotamus escaped from the San Diego Zoo, was darted, and promptly died of suffocation. I can only hope that these objectors were able to see this as a good illustration of the dangers in following the tranquilizing approach.

Educational programs do not show the traumatic failures that occur in the real world of animal tranquilizing. A well-funded, concerted program might succeed in bringing in an unconscious sasquatch this way, but it would probably also result in the death and serious injury of a dozen or more of the animals in the process. A single neat kill with a powerful rifle would avoid this kind of slaughter.

Despite all of the problems indicated above, suppose you somehow succeeded against all the odds and had a sasquatch unconscious on the ground. How do you restrain an eight hundred-pound primate when it wakes up? If you were able to manage this, and you reach a phone to call the authorities, who would believe you? You could measure and photograph the body, take blood and tissue samples, collect parasites, and then let the creature recover and go away. You would then have some interesting evidence that might convince a few more experts. But a type specimen must still be collected and put on record before most scientists will pay it any serious attention.

After the tranquilized animal wakes up, we should also consider how it might react to this experience at the hands of a human. Most likely it would avoid our species very carefully for the rest of its life. It is also possible that the creature might decide to kill every human being it can lay its hands on. However unlikely that last possibility might be, I would not want to risk turning something like that loose anywhere in the world. This scenario of a killer sasquatch on a rampage would certainly result in our obtaining the needed type specimen. After a few attacks it would be diligently hunted down and dispatched. This is hardly a desirable way to achieve the goal.

In summation, the idea of trying to tranquilize a sasquatch is a very impractical approach to the problem. To have any chance of success, trained experts would have to be found to do it—none would volunteer their services at this point and there are no resources to pay them. Such an approach would probably result in the deaths and maiming of many individuals before one is successfully brought in. The operation could be quite dangerous to those who tried it, assuming they could ever gain access to a sufficient number of the quarry. Given the inaccessibility of the animals, even the best staffed and funded operation could not reasonably hope to succeed for many years, tens of years at the very least. If the sasquatches are in any ecological danger, they would likely be extinct before the first one could be brought in by this method.

Recorders

Many investigators are simply gathering all of the information they can on sightings, footprints, and any other evidence that is available. These people usually keep good records of their data, hence the name, but they vary widely in terms of what they gather and what they do with it.

The quality of the recorders' data is not just a question of good or bad, though this is a large variable. Some of them try to filter out exaggerations, distortions, hoaxes, and overinterpretations—all with varying degrees of success. Others seem content to include any and all reports, no matter how atypical and/or undependable they may seem. I remember one recorder on the West Coast who told me she was careful to get confirmation of each report from at least two sources before taking it seriously. I inquired into more detail about one of her better stories, which was reported to her by two people, and it turned out that both of them had heard it from the same original source. That fact didn't bother her at all. For this and other reasons it seemed pointless to investigate her reports any further.

Quality of data depends on the kinds of events that are selected for investigation. Some recorders restrict themselves to animal accounts that broadly fit the description of the sasquatch as given here. Others include stories that include traits of a much more human type, and are in fact probably of human origin. Many are also gathering UFO information, for which I will not fault them, but when they combine this directly with the sasquatch it does not seem to stand up well. I have talked with only two people who claim to have direct knowledge of an association between UFOs and sasquatches; on other evidence it was quite obvious that neither of these people had full possession of their faculties. There are some who would associate sasquatch with almost every paranormal phenomenon that has been reported. This is explored further in the next section.

Recorders vary in how they disseminate their information. This can be in the form of regular publications, privately produced newsletters and small books, or personal access to their files. Hardcore hunters are gathering this same kind of information, but for obvious reasons they are not disseminating their best data in any form. One can safely presume that the hunters' data are strictly of the wild-animal type, and not any of the paranormal interpretations. There are some investigators who are not obviously hunting the animal, and who claim to have extensive files of information, yet refuse to share it with others. Since they do not have the hunter's motive for withholding their data, it would be a fair working hypothesis that they actually have no important data at all.

The novices are information gatherers, but they do not always record it diligently. Those who continue the search and learn more about the subject sometimes develop into recorders of one kind or another. Some become hard-core hunters, others become "professionals" (see next section), but most of them eventually just quit.

Recorders are generally individuals, but sometimes a small group of them will work together, with or without a strong leader. As long as they are not trying hard to bring in the first specimen, dead or alive, there can be as much cooperation in this endeavor as in anything else that they might attempt.

The curious thing about most recorders I know is the great value they seem to place on the reports for their own sake. To my way of thinking, these reports might be valued as a means to an end, but not as an end in themselves. But some people collect baseball cards and other items of no intrinsic value, so why not sasquatch reports? My pet peeve along this line is the investigator who boasts that he has many reports, but is so jealous of them he won't let anyone know what they amount to. For all practical purposes, his reports simply do not exist.

I would propose a subtype of recorders that could be called "chroniclers," who gather large amounts of information that is carefully selected for quality, and publish it for others to use. Most notable among these are Green, Heuvelmans, and Sanderson, who's books have been mentioned frequently here. All of these authors have kept the paranormal out of their works on hairy bipeds, though Sanderson got into some other strange things toward the end of his life. These chroniclers probably like money as much as most people, but that was not the driving force behind their work. John Green is now financially secure for reasons having nothing to do with chronicling the sasquatch; Bernard Heuvelmans is barely making ends meet; and I have no knowledge of how well-off Ivan Sanderson was. For at least the first two of these men, investigating unknown animals cost them far more than it ever earned. They all acquired a certain degree of notoriety for their works (not likely a serious motive in itself), but that publicity proved to be a means of gaining more information on their subject. This also happened to Roger Patterson after he made his movie, and it is happening to me because of the media coverage that I don't always manage to avoid.

There may well be other chroniclers who have large amounts of valid information, but who can't find the means to publish it. There definitely are others with paranormal leanings and, in my opinion, too many of them have found the means to publish.

A final comment must be made about another subtype, the "bibliographer." Most recorders get involved in gathering published works and references, at least to some degree. The usefulness of this activity has not been established in this particular field. To the best of my knowledge only one person has made a major effort along this line. Danny Perez published a respectable book in 1988 consisting solely of bibliographic references on the subject of sasquatch.

"Professionals"

The final category of investigators are those who *do not* want the sasquatch to be proven to exist. These people may appear to be serious researchers and/or field workers, but they all stand to lose their social standing if and when the proof is brought in. They are not hunters and have no realistic prospects of being the one who finds convincing evidence. They all know full well that when the proof is found, the scientists will move in to dominate the field, and they will be shoved aside into obscurity.

These people have made an ongoing profession out of sasquatch hunting. They give public talks on the subject (sometimes for money), write pamphlets or newsletters, give press releases, attend scientific conferences where they try to present their views, and sometimes lead study groups and expeditions. In most cases this appears to be a part-time and largely unpaid activity, but these "professionals" have chosen this route to gain a certain amount of social status. Their behavior does not differ in many respects from that of the serious investigators, but they all share the common trait of opposition to shooting a specimen. These people are not stupid; most of them have thought the matter through and know that only a body will constitute proof. Naturally they will do all they can to prevent the discovery of something that will terminate their chosen profession and thus reduce their own social significance.

If the sasquatch hunt is a small part of their lives, the "professionals" stand to lose little, and producing the proof will have little effect on their lives. Those who are more deeply involved have more at stake, and they more actively oppose any serious hunting. My deepest sympathy extends to anyone who lives only for his/her involvement in making a name in this business. Such a person might thus think that they will have nothing left to live for when the quest is over and the previously skeptical scientists take control.

This is reminiscent of the old March of Dimes organization that put itself out of business by helping to find a cure for polio. Some of the participants may have realized that this might happen and they would lose their jobs, but the work went ahead anyway. Other societies that are working on specific diseases have been accused of seeing the same handwriting on the wall, and thus devising ways to divert funds *away* from the most promising lines of research. The same reasoning applies to all other professions. If crime were significantly reduced, many police officers would lose their jobs; dentists depend on people continuing to have bad teeth; welfare workers owe their existence to social inequity; and if sin disappeared, preachers would have much less to do. Sasquatch hunting is a trivial profession when compared with any of these, but it follows the same pattern.

Some of the sasquatch "professionals" may actually have information that could be useful to the scientific investigation, if and when it begins. If they have gathered specific data on footprints and sightings, with a healthy degree of skepticism, these data might be used to help determine the distribution of the species. Most ecological information, however, would probably not be taken seriously; scientists usually insist on determining all of that for themselves. Any information that was collected before the proof was found will be suspect to some degree. When people collect information on the basis of belief rather than on knowledge, it is only reasonable to suspect that some or all of that information is less than objective.

All of the hard-core hunters, even those who might not be involved in trying to take the definitive specimen, probably have good distributional and behavioral evidence that the scientists will then want. Their motivation for being objective in their studies need not be questioned. The "professionals," on the other hand, will turn out to be quite a diverse group—some with no useful information at all, and others with quite a bit. It will be up to them individually to convince the scientists that they have something of value.

At the present time it is difficult to determine which of the "professionals" actually think that the sasquatch is real, whether in the strict biological sense of a species of primate or in one of the paranormal aspects that are so often advocated. They might think there is nothing to it at all, but are capitalizing on a segment of public belief in real animals, superior humanoids, or UFOnauts depending on which audience they are trying to work on. They might consider the animal species to be real, but think they can find a better social niche by advocating one of the paranormal aspects. Or they might actually believe that they are dealing with some kind of superior beings.

I have been contacted by several rational-sounding people who say they are or have been in telepathic contact with sasquatches. Each of them presents a very different version of what the creatures really are. If one of them is right, the others are totally wrong. Since all but one version must be wrong, there obviously has to be some explanation of how a false impression of telepathy has been experienced by the rest of them. It then becomes a simple step to apply that explanation to the single remaining version. What most likely occurs here is that a person is having a conversation with him/herself, and is silently verbalizing both sides of the discussion. It is a known psychological phenomenon that many such people, at one time or another, fail to note that both sides of the discussion are their own creation, and ascribe one of them to an outside source. In most instances of this phenomenon, that outside source is attributed to an entity very different from the sasquatch, but the principle is still the same. This is classed as a minor mental disorder, but it is fairly common and generally has no serious repercussions.

The association of sasquatch activity with a higher order of intelligence or technology is contradicted by virtually all of the known accounts. The exceptions are so few that inaccurate reporting or fabrication would more easily explain them. To suppose the other way around would require a hundred times more such explanation, and perhaps even more, depending on which paranormal version is presumed to be the true one.

I was recently contacted by a man who, like a few others, was concerned about how sasquatch tracks mysteriously started and ended with no explanation, and by the "inexplicable fact" that no physical remains of them have been found. He thus knows that they are not normal creatures, and he and others are into "channeling" in an attempt to contact their spirits. He was quite bothered by my refusal to have an "open mind" on this interpretation. Needless to say, his two premises are quite wrong, thus he is going to considerable trouble to try to explain phenomena that do not exist. If and when a sasquatch is taken, this person will have no input into further investigations by the scientists.

At the opposite end of the practical scale are the people whom I suspect may be paid by the timber industries in the Pacific Northwest. There is no hard evidence that this is actually occurring, but the behavior of some individuals is otherwise difficult to explain. There are various reasons to take a stand against shooting a sasquatch, and some can be quite legitimate from a personal moral point of view. But when it is claimed that sasquatch is made of titanium, and yet we still must not shoot him, then there is something quite illogical going on. The best way to make sasquatch research look ridiculous is to make outlandish and absurd claims of this kind, with as much publicity as possible, and to try to associate yourself with the scientists and laymen who are doing serious research. By this means the whole subject of the sasquatch becomes tainted by association, thus making the government, most scientists, and much of the public think it is all a fantasy.

There is one other variation of the sasquatch "professional," one who is simply looking for personal publicity of *any* kind. Some individuals report fake sightings just to get the attention of the news media in order to liven up an otherwise dull existence. In itself, this may be a motivating factor with certain people who are well known in the field. Unfortunately this cannot easily be separated from the legitimate fact that any kind of publicity tends to provide contacts that bring in more information. Most of the hard-core hunters do not need this coverage, but it is very useful for the recorders and the "professionals."

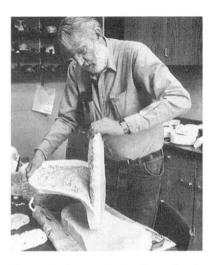

Figure 81. John Green. This recent photo shows Green at his home in Canada holding one of his sasquatch track casts.

Figure 82. Grover Krantz. The author is in his lab pulling the Silastic mold from a sasquatch track cast.

Figure 83. Dmitri Donskoy. In the center is Dr. Donskoy, Chair of Biomechanics at the U.S.S.R. Central Institute of Physical Culture in Moscow. His analysis of the Patterson film is mentioned in Chapter 4. To the left is Dmitri Bayanov. To the right is Igor Bourtsev holding a photograph of a footprint from the Tien Shan Mountain area. In the foreground are two models based on Patterson's film. This photograph was taken in 1976, and kindly supplied by Bayanov.

10

THE SCIENTISTS

Within the academic community there are only a few areas in which the proven existence of the sasquatch would have a significant impact. Foremost among these is physical anthropology, where this mixture of ape and human traits would certainly have an impact on our understanding of human evolution. Also within anthropology we find the study of folklore, where a physical referent for one widespread story could tell us something about what is invented by the story tellers and what is not. Zoologists in general, and primatologists in particular, would have a new species of higher primate to study and classify. Wildlife biologists and ecologists would have a new set of relationships to work out, and a decision to make on its endangered status and what, if anything, should be done about it. (Some philosophers and theologians might also try to get involved where they probably do not belong.)

The majority of scientists in these concerned areas, if asked today, will express their opinion that no such animal exists. If pressed for details, they will also admit that they know next to nothing about the evidence that has been gathered. This reminds me of the scientists who roundly denounce the work of Imanuel Velikovsky, yet proudly point out that they have never read the man's books. Actually Velikovsky was dead wrong on most of what he proposed about astronomy and earth history, but one ought to have at least the common decency to read what he said before passing judgment on it. There are many other examples of this kind of behavior in science where it should not occur, just as in human activities in general where it is expected.

Within the community of potentially concerned scientists, there may be many who are curious about what information might be available on the sasquatch, and some who have investigated it to a small degree. A few of these have learned enough to become convinced that it is a legitimate field of inquiry about an animal that might well be real. Most of those who take a keen interest are also cautious enough to say nothing about it, or at least to keep a low profile. They all know that this interest might damage their scientific reputations. Anything that suggests association with the lunatic fringe, and sasquatch is a classic, can certainly retard one's professional career. Older scientists who have made their names can afford to indulge in the luxury of exploring a subject like this. Some of the younger scientists who have not yet realized how the Scientific Establishment works might also extend themselves along this line until they learn better.

Most scientists know the criteria that are used for granting tenure and making promotions, and they are understandably cautious about being involved in any investigations that are not in the mainstream of acceptance or in recognized specialities. If the existence of sasquatch had somewhat better evidence, or if public and government opinion were more tolerant, many of the cautious scientists would look at it more willingly, and those who have already done so would talk more freely about what they know. Over the last twenty-seven years, during which I have followed the subject closely, there has been a clearly perceptible move in this direction.

Resistance

The Scientific Establishment generally resists new ideas, preferring instead to work out minor details about things that we already know. There is good reason for this attitude, and there are social mechanisms in place to maintain it. Quite simply put, new and innovative ideas in science are almost always wrong. In fact, the only accepted scientific method of dealing with a new idea is to try to prove it wrong. This may sound like a very negative approach, which it is, but it makes sense in the long run. When a theory has passed a number of rigorous tests that are designed to disprove it, only then is it considered likely to be true. Obviously, scientists have limited resources and cannot spend their time systematically testing, and thereby disproving, every strange new idea that someone comes up with. They must exercise their informed judgment as to which ideas might have some chance of passing a test, and which are simply not worth bothering with. It is equally obvious in hindsight that the Establishment has made some mistakes in the past. After rightly debunking a thousand nutty ideas, one tends to get into the habit and might miss the next idea that just *looks* stupid, but isn't.

Science deals with data—verifiable facts. Theories are made to relate these facts to one another, and to the world of human experience in general. Facts are true; what they mean is subject to theory. It is a *fact* that there are many indentations in the ground that look like gigantic, humanoid footprints; it is a *theory* that giant humanoids made them while walking. Roger Patterson's movie is another fact; that it actually represents one of these giant humanoids is a theory. It is a fact that Bob Gimlin says he watched the creature that his friend was filming; it is a theory that he is telling the truth. By gathering together all of these facts, and others like them, scientists can sort through them for consistencies and contradictions. Theories can be proposed and then tested by re-examining some of the data that is already at hand. Theories about sasquatch can be tested against our knowledge of the environment, biomechanics, and human nature—to name just the obvious. But if the scientists do not have the factual material that is relevant to the sasquatch phenomenon, theories will not even be generated, let alone tested.

Science is being constantly deluged with facts—more facts than can possibly be coped with. Every piece of material and every relationship in the universe is a fact; only a tiny fraction, even of those that are accessible, are used to formulate and test theories. Every untoward observation made by any human being is a piece of information. That someone made the claim is a fact, but again only the tiniest fraction of these can ever be examined. To complain that science is ignoring the facts is to state the obvious. That this involves the ignoring of *important* facts is a matter of judgment, and I would think that the scientists themselves are almost always in the best position to make that judgment.

Having defended the Scientific Establishment in general terms, it is now my turn to criticize it in some particulars. The major problem I see is that those who determine the direction of research are usually not those who produce innovations. New theories, especially those that eventually pass the tests, are mostly generated by novices and outsiders. Younger scientists, who have not yet become ingrained with all the "absolute facts," might explore areas that are ruled out-of-bounds by the experts. People who are trained in one field will sometimes see what their colleagues in another field have been carefully trained *not* to look at. This is the normal state of affairs. Again, the new ideas are usually wrong, but this is generally where the few right ones in fact come from.

Research funds and facilities to test new ideas are allocated by the established experts in each field. They receive far more requests for assistance than they have resources to satisfy. These advanced scientists, along with concerned politicians, naturally deny support for research into areas that, in their judgments, are futile, wasteful, or just plain silly. Most of their decisions are sound, but if their discipline is guilty of consistently missing an important factor, they are among the least likely people to see it.

More than this, scientific grants come in large part from the government, and that means from taxpayers. Political input into the disbursement of research money is aimed at avoiding any expenditures from which no tangible rewards can be obtained. Almost any reasonable expenditure in the area of sasquatch research is not likely to produce anything in the way of positive results, and its negative results would be of little value. Large private foundations disburse money in much the same manner, and with similar goals in mind. Most scientists who are working on the sasquatch problem do not even bother to ask for research grants; I learned this long ago.

Some of the resistance to investigating the sasquatch phenomenon can be ascribed to a personal desire on the part of the authorities that such an animal should not exist. This is a practical matter that goes beyond all those discussed up to this point. Individual scientists have a stake in the status quo and their positions within it. There is a fair degree of predictability about how progress occurs in each field, and how this affects the participants (public opinion to the contrary). A major new discovery might upset this status quo, and scientists' reputations and careers can be affected in unpredictable ways. Some people, especially those in lower positions, look forward to such disruptions. Those who are in higher and/or more secure positions, and especially those who are moving along clear professional trajectories, naturally see such events as potentially threatening.

A new discovery can redirect scientific research funding, and any resources that are put into a new area are necessarily taken away from someplace else. Certain skills and training might acquire enhanced value, which means that other skills will become relatively less important. There is even a finite amount of public interest in reading popular books on science; what is increased in one field will be subtracted from others. Established scientists thus risk some relative loss of influence from any major discovery that does not involve their own field, and they are at an even greater risk if it happens to be within their field and they were not part of it.

If nothing else, finding proof of the sasquatch would mean that almost all anthropologists and primatologists would have to admit that they were wrong about something. Those who had not specifically denied the existence of this animal, nevertheless had not included it in their list of living primates. Not to mention a species of this importance is tantamount to saying that it does not exist.

The F.B.I. expert told me that the implications of these tracks were just too incredible for him to believe that they were real. A prominent physical anthropologist told me that a biped cannot walk without a longitudinal arch in its foot. Another anthropologist pronounced flatly that there was no ecological niche in America for this animal to occupy. These statements are just a few illustrations of how much backtracking and rethinking would be required if the sasquatch were ever shown to be real.

By the fervor with which some experts defend their negative position, one might think that the basic integrity of their field was being threatened. If anthropologists could have missed something as big and important as the sasquatch for all this time, what other colossal blunders might they be making? We would do well to remember what happened twenty years ago when continental drift was proven to be real, contrary to the opinion of almost all experts in the field. Geology did not collapse in disarray, but rather it emerged from this reorientation considerably enhanced. I think that anthropology could recover from this event just as easily.

Certainly the discovery of the sasquatch would require some reorientation in our understanding of living primates, but nothing on the scale of what the acceptance of continental drift did to geology. This would help to clarify the relationship between erect posture and such things as brain size, pharynx development, lumbar curve, breast fat, and foot arches. We can find out more about how absolute size affects hominid body design, how nocturnal vision works, maybe a new type of hand, and we will have a whole new set of biochemical relationships to work out. Folklorists will probably want to do some rethinking about the possible biological basis of other animallike stories.

The opening up of recognized sasquatch research would have major repercussions in only a few areas of anthropology and some related fields. Most of the discipline would be no more affected than it was by finding out that the australopithecines were real, or that Piltdown man was not. Yes, a few reputations would be affected, but anthropology has lived through adjustments like this before, and it certainly will do so again.

My Position

It was never my intention to become a leading academic authority on the sasquatch, and I'm not particularly comfortable with the position. Human evolution in its entirety is my field of interest, and the sasquatch is only a relatively small part of that. I would like to think that the quality of my research into the evidence for this animal is the source of my recognition, but it also followed largely from default. Many of my colleagues could have done the same kind of work, and perhaps should have, but they did not. The academic niche was open, at least in America after Sanderson died, and I just fell into it.

Some older and more established scientists were interested in the subject and have been very supportive of my efforts, but they devoted only a small amount of their own efforts in this direction. Rupert Murrill, who chaired my PhD committee at the University of Minnesota, was enthusiastic about the subject and was thoroughly delighted to find out that I had been investigating it too. Carleton Coon and I became good friends is his later years, and unknown hominoids was one of our favorite topics of conversation. I never met John Napier, but we did correspond; he stuck his neck out farther than most primatologists by writing a book about hairy bipeds in which he took the subject quite seriously. Vladimir Markotic has been a close friend for many years now, and I assisted him in editing a book of collected scholarly papers on the sasquatch. None of these men became known as the expert in this field, partly for lack of really putting in the effort, and partly because they would have been competing (and being compared) with Ivan Sanderson. Bernard Heuvelmans, whom I have come to know more recently, is in a class by himself. He is the father of cryptozoology in its entirety. For another scientist to specialize in just one part of the field, that particular "ecological niche" is always open, much to the delight of Heuvelmans himself.

There are many younger scientists who are interested in sasquatch, though most of them are still keeping a low profile for now. Certainly one or more of them will move openly into this field and make notable contributions. For now, one of my functions has been to serve as a role model for them, showing that one can get by with this kind of research. But I also show them the price that must be paid for doing it.

My first serious work in this field was an analysis of the presumed anatomy of Cripple Foot in 1970. I was just as naive as any of the younger scientists today, perhaps more so; the idea that such studies ought *not* to be published never occurred to me. Getting it in print at all was my only concern, and *Northwest Anthropological Research Notes* was my tenth attempt to find a publisher.

Somehow a local newspaperman soon found out about my study and wanted to know if I thought the animals really existed. At this first encounter with the press I tried to take a neutral stance, admitting only that the evidence was very impressive. A few months later when the next newsman contacted me about it, my real opinion of full acceptance came out. This was something of a relief because I had not told the whole truth before, and one of my major character defects is honesty.

I always have been, and continue to be, interested in any unusual phenomena without having any particular belief in any of them. The Bermuda Triangle turned out to be no mystery at all; von Danniken's chariots came out of his imagination rather than from the gods; the UFO problem has too many diverse interpretations for me to cope with; and ESP can have only a minimal reality, if any at all. In sharp contrast, the sasquatch reports cannot be accounted for by any other natural phenomena; they are not one person's invention; they indicate a quite normal animal; and the evidence is large in every sense of the word. To this might be added the fact that the indicated animal would be very pertinent to my own field of human evolution. Given all of the above, there is no way that I could *not* investigate the matter and openly report my findings.

Back in 1970 I had only a rough idea of the trouble that could result from openly working on this subject, but I didn't expect it to last more than a few years. My first shock was to be deferred on tenure for one year, in spite of the fact that I was already more frequently cited for my normal work than most of the other members of the department. Some lame excuses for this deferral filtered back to me, but the media coverage of my sasquatch work was a more likely reason. Much later, when my promotion to full professor was denied, the only reason the dean could come up with was that my work was not favorably received in all quarters. (By this criterion, Charles Darwin and Albert Einstein could not possibly have gotten this promotion at my university.) Though it was quite specifically denied to my face, I have no doubt that my sasquatch work was the major deciding factor against promotion.

Some of my colleagues have pointed out that if I just laid off the sasquatch and kept my "nose clean" for a few years, the promotion would come through and then I could do anything I wanted. My response was that I am doing what I want right now, so the only thing that procedure would accomplish is to cost me a few years' work.

It should be mentioned at this point that my sasquatch research has not infringed on my regular work in any way. I have always taught a full load of classes (with high student reviews), and have produced enough of my regular work to rate a high-profile international reputation. It would appear that, like being black or female in many occupations, the sasquatch is a stigma that demands a more-than-adequate performance to earn the same promotions that others gain with less productivity.

Sasquatch work involves perhaps one-tenth of my active time, at most, and it never detracts from my regular duties or normal anthropological research. In effect, it is done strictly on my own time and money. The taxpayers not only do not finance this research, they get a break by paying me a far lower salary than would otherwise be the case. In the twenty-two years since 1970 about $100,000 has been spent out of my own pocket for sasquatch-related research, and a similar amount of lost salary probably can be attributed to the same cause. This is an acceptable price to pay; I expected it and I cannot complain.

What is more costly in terms of what I value is the diminishing of my professional reputation that has resulted from working on the sasquatch. For every one of my colleagues who admires my courage to do this work, perhaps another five think that I am acting rather like a fool. Few of them ever say this to my face (I'm bigger than almost all of them), but the word filters back quite freely. Of course it doesn't help matters that my regular work is often rather innovative as well. Being the first to accurately sense a relationship in someone else's field of expertise is something that is often praised, but it is just as often resented by the concerned people. At least with sasquatch it cannot be said that this is more properly in some other scientist's area of academic concern.

The news media have been a constant source of both support and annoyance. They are just doing their job, but it can be time-consuming for me. I have maintained a regular practice of talking to any media person who visits or reaches me by telephone, but if they just leave a message I rarely return calls. Also, I have never initiated a news item on this subject, and probably never will unless it is the real thing. Still, there may be some advantage to be gained from this coverage other than just receiving many new reports.

From the outset I decided to talk openly with the hope that someone would come forward with the remains of a sasquatch that had been shot at some earlier time. I would assure any such person that they had broken no law, and that producing some of the remains, even a few scraps of bone, would remove the need for shooting another one to prove their existence. I could also assure such a person that they could receive full credit for what they did, or else absolute anonymity if that was what they preferred. That I kept two footprint traits a complete secret for twenty-two years should be some indication of how well their secret can also be kept. I would also agree that such a person would receive all monetary rewards that may come from such material; my only "price" is full rights to its scientific uses. Needless to say, that hypothetical person has yet to respond.

Radio stations and newspapers are never able to offer money for their interviews and I don't expect it. Television productions sometimes will pay all expenses and a nominal fee for coming to their studios for an interview. Most of these are not worth my time and trouble, as they are just looking for something sensational. If a serious program is being prepared I try to go along with them—the more serious it is the more willing I am to do it without pay.

For talks to larger audiences my attitude is similar. An interested group that might include people with something to offer can get me easily. When a normal social group just wants an interesting speaker, they have to fit into my schedule and pay a lot more than just my expenses.

There has been some erroneous coverage, but surprisingly little considering the hundreds of potential occasions. By far the most outrageous of these was an article about bigfoot hunters in *True* magazine back in 1975, part of which followed from a long telephone interview with me. About one-third of the printed account of what I said was correct, one-third was drawn from other sources and credited to my interview, and one-third was highly erroneous and often directly contradicted what I had said. My guess is that the writer took only a few notes, then constructed a story around some other items of his own, without paying much attention to what I actually had said. The magazine printed a letter stating my disavowal of the article, but refused even to look at a valid article that I offered to write for them.

More recently, in 1985 a writer for *Sports Illustrated* visited me for a story and laid out some money for my expenses and a helicopter ride to test an item of equipment. The ensuing article, however, was highly critical of my efforts and presented the writer's opinions on many things where his own information was very inaccurate. The most irritating item was that he quoted me as saying that when we found the sasquatch, the first thing I would do is take my wife for a vacation to a particular South Pacific island. He did in fact ask if I would do this, and my reply was that it was about the last thing I would consider doing.

Finally, a newspaper man from Seattle, Washington, called me three years ago about my plans to hunt for a natural body from my homemade helicopter with an infrared imager. I did discuss some unlikely other helicopter uses if the imager didn't succeed, like spotting a live one and even wondered aloud if one could be hit by a gun from that craft. The way the story came out, the public thought I had a high-tech helicopter with electronically guided missiles, and my intent was solely to kill. The story hadn't said exactly that, but it was worded in such a way that all of this was implied. It went out on the news wires and the reaction was devastating. Several editorials were written, mostly in Los Angeles, denouncing me for such narrow-minded stupidity. Several classes of grade school children sent me packets of individually written letters begging me not to do this, and informing me of my errors and about my ignorance of the true situation. Many letters and phone calls came to me and to the Anthropology Department with the same message, often adding that it was me who should be shot, not a sasquatch.

The facts in this case were about as opposite as could be imagined. The ultralight helicopter was built from a kit that cost me $2,200; it is the lowest-tech ever designed, and I have not been able to get it to lift off the ground (Fig. 84). Most of my friends have urged me not to use it because I could so easily be killed or injured. The whole idea of the helicopter hunt was to locate a natural death from the winter, and was decomposing in the spring thaw. The $10,000 imager was to sense the heat generated by such a body. What I was actually planning was to risk my own life in an attempt to save the sasquatch *without* killing one. How this story got so twisted is the most incredible piece of newsmanship and public overreaction I have even seen or could possibly imagine.

Most of the media coverage, despite the above examples, has been reasonably accurate and even sometimes useful. One particularly well-written newspaper article was widely circulated in 1981. An interested woman in Denver, Colorado, reacted to seeing it by writing to me with some intelligent questions. We corresponded for a few months, then met, and eventually were married. She has been participating in the sasquatch investigation ever since, but she is the strongest opponent of my using the homemade helicopter.

Other responses to the media coverage have brought to my attention many reports of sightings and tracks. Most of these just mean putting another spot on a map, and maybe a short note in my files. This has also put me in touch with many other investigators in the field, sometimes leading to associations that may yet result in helping to resolve our problem.

Media exposure also draws in many vague reports of no value, as well as contacts from the lunatic fringe that I can do without. I am becoming increasingly impatient with the nut cases. Years ago I listened patiently to a woman who told me about the twenty-foot-tall man she saw with clean-shaven, handsome, Italian features. Later, when a young man told me that sasquatch visited him often and even

Figure 84. Author's homemade helicopter. This machine was intended for overhead searching for sasquatches that had died natural deaths. The plan was to use an infrared scanner from this aerial platform to detect the heat of decomposition during the Spring thaw. To date, the machine has not flown; I suspect its design was faulty.

sat on his bed, I told him he was imagining it. I said the same to the man who assured me that he saw a sasquatch driving a car. I was downright rude to the most recent caller who is experimenting with contacting sasquatch spirits by "channeling." Another whole book could be written about the opinions and antics of the lunatic fringe.

However problematical the publicity may be, it would all be worthwhile if it leads to bringing in the needed specimen. If this doesn't happen, at least I had fun doing what I had to do anyway. And I did meet my wife this way.

Early in my professional career the pressure to ignore the sasquatch was heavy. The publicity it generated almost cost me my job at tenure review. Some powerful individuals in my department and university were adamantly opposed to any study of this subject, especially if it became known. More recently the academic climate has greatly improved. The major objectors have retired or moved away, some of the other faculty are genuinely interested, my chairman is open-minded and supportive, and even the new president of the university finds the subject very interesting. And the State of Washington declared "Harrison Bigfoot" to be the state's centennial mascot for the year of 1989. It would appear that facilities to deal properly with a specimen are assured, if and when one comes in. But none of this has provided me with any research funds, nor any release-time for me to pursue it more diligently.

Scientific Acceptance

Science will not accept the sasquatch as a living species without a type specimen, but it is beginning to accept, or at least tolerate, serious study of the available evidence. In the mid-1960s when my study was just starting, the scientific world was nearly unanimous in never having so much as heard of the sasquatch. With the publicity following the Patterson film it soon became fashionable for scientists to declare that film and any other evidence to be all mistaken or faked. At the same time, most scientists who made this judgment were careful to point out that they had never looked at the evidence in question. Just like the experts who denounced Velikovsky without reading his books, they seemed to be avoiding becoming tainted somehow by direct exposure to heretical material.

Impressive evidence continued to accumulate, and its documentation by laymen steadily improved. There came to be a high level of public awareness, much of it beginning with Patterson's film, and continuing with the Minnesota Ice Man, John Green's first book, media coverage of my work on Cripple Foot, the Blue Mountain tracks with dermal ridges, and much more. The measure of scientific interest can be traced by the following series of events:

1970 Roderick Sprague printed an editorial in *Northwest Anthropological Research Notes* inviting responsible papers on the subject of sasquatch. Several scientists promptly responded with articles. (Reprinted in Appendix C.)

1972 John Napier, a respected primatologist, published a book about sasquatch that included a favorable view of at least some of the evidence.

1974 Boris Porshnev and Bernard Heuvelmans published a major scientific work on this subject from a worldwide perspective. (Written in French, it had little impact on English-speaking North America.)

1978 Professors Marjorie Halpin and Michael Ames organized a scientific conference on "Manlike Monsters" at the University of British Columbia. Many reputable scientists attended and gave papers, including Carleton Coon. UBC Press published some of the papers, and Vladimir Markotic edited a volume with most of the rest of them.

1982 The International Society of Cryptozoology (ISC) was founded at a meeting hosted by the Smithsonian Institution, and publication of Newsletters and a Journal began that year. Thereafter the ISC has held annual meetings, open to members and their guests, where scientific papers are presented that usually focus on a topic appropriate to the host institution.

1989 The ISC's 8th Annual Meeting was held at Washington State University, and the focus of all scheduled papers was the sasquatch. Many lay investigators attended and some reported on their research. Some of the lunatic fringe was also there, but they were prevented from disrupting the proceedings.

A fair number of qualified experts are now willing to analyze data in their fields, and to openly associate their names with the results. This is perhaps the most encouraging sign of all. Many of the police and scientific experts on dermatoglyphics are willing, and in some cases eager, to apply their skills to interpreting dermal ridges on footprints. Two outstanding biochemists have analyzed suspected specimens, and others are willing to do the same. Most of these are newly established authorities in their fields who are still advancing their careers, just the type who would not touch this subject twenty years ago. It is also gratifying to find out that a few of the youngest scientists had their interest stirred when they first heard about my work on the subject when they were teenagers.

More information keeps coming in—some apparently valid, some false or useless, and always much that could be interpreted either way. Without a definitive type specimen the case can never be proved, but with some qualified experts willing to analyze what does come in, we are at least approaching a time when honest inquiry is acceptable. Whether it will ever be encouraged and supported, in the absence of that essential first specimen, is quite another matter.

11

PROSPECTS

Newsmen sometimes ask me when we might expect a sasquatch to be brought in. My response is to ask them to predict when they will be seriously injured in a car crash. The desirability of these two events may be at opposite poles, but our ability to predict them is about the same. The first sasquatch specimen might already have been obtained on the very day that you are reading this; it might not happen in my lifetime or yours.

So far, there is no way to locate a sasquatch on demand. If this could be done, even with only a 10 percent chance of success on each attempt, there would be no need to bring in a specimen to prove its existence. It would still require several years of the occasional sightings by recognized authorities and skeptics before it would be accepted; obtaining the type specimen would then be just a matter of time and patience. At present, you can go to a suitable location and have less than one chance in a million of seeing a sasquatch, and nobody has any method of significantly increasing these odds.

There is nothing mysterious about the difficulty in locating these creatures; there are many perfectly natural reasons for this. Within the Pacific Northwest there are probably only a few thousand sasquatches, with one individual for perhaps every 250 square miles (650 sq km). Allowing for the fact that much of the area is off limits to them from density of human occupation and utilization, there are still more than 100 square miles (260 sq km) for each of them. This is the proverbial needle-in-the-haystack type of hunt.

Added to this scarcity is the nocturnal behavior of the sasquatch and their shy attitude toward humans. They mostly occur as single individuals, so we don't have the advantage of spotting or trailing them by their group activities. They can move very rapidly when they choose to, and often do so whenever they locate us. Sasquatch eyesight is certainly far better than ours by night, and at least equal to ours by day. Their usual forested habitat provides maximum concealment at any time and includes relatively few places that record footprints. It is also possible that they can deliberately avoid leaving footprints. They probably are good swimmers. Most evidence of their passage and feeding can easily be mistaken for that of bears. Thus the proverbial needle is furtively moving about inside that haystack and leaving little indication of its previous locations.

Gaining information on the sasquatches' locations, movements, and other behavior is complicated by the fact that our available reports are not always reliable. These include vague descriptions, uncertain locations, erroneous observations, and some hoaxes—and we generally do not know which of the reports are tainted in these ways. We know rather little about their habits for all of the above reasons. It may be that much more is known, but this knowledge is jealously guarded by the several hard-core hunters who don't want someone else to bring in the first specimen. It is possible that these hunters are spreading some false information as well.

Just finding footprints is almost as difficult as seeing the sasquatch. I know a few hunters who have located tracks on many occasions in certain areas that they are familiar with. If footprints could be observed on demand, again with at least a 10 percent success rate, more interest could possibly be generated, but most skeptics would not bother to look for them, and even then they would not likely accept what they saw as being genuine.

Locating the physical remains of a dead sasquatch, as has already been explained, is the least likely type of evidence to be found, though it would be by far the most desirable and conclusive. Given that there are something like one hundred bears for every one sasquatch in their shared habitat, and the fact that naturally dead bears are rarely found, the chance of finding any sasquatch bones is essentially zero.

The problem is quite simply that the evidence required to prove the existence of this species is extremely difficult to come by. Unless someone shoots a specimen and brings in all or part of the body for study, it is not likely that suitable evidence will ever be obtained.

Not Good Enough

The scientific community will not accept circumstantial evidence to establish a new species. The legal profession regularly convicts and kills people on a tiny fraction of the kind of evidence that we already have for the sasquatch. Eyewitness testimony from one or two people, especially when combined with some physical evidence, is sufficient proof in most legal cases. John Green has recently suggested (1989) that a formal legal inquiry, if it could be arranged, would almost certainly declare that the presently available evidence conclusively demonstrates the existence of sasquatch. What effect such a legal determination would have is interesting to ponder. Science demands more in this case, or else we might have to accept all other phenomena that have been proposed on similar evidence. Such evidence would be not just unacceptable, it would often lead to contradictory conclusions.

In the eyes of science, no animal exists until it is proven beyond any possibility of doubt. It logically follows that if the species is unproven, then every single piece of evidence for its existence might be spurious in some fashion. It is possible for eyewitnesses to be mistaken or lying. Thus all such witnesses are presumed to be one or the other, without exception.

No investigator who has talked to a good sample of eyewitnesses, say ten or fifteen of them, would agree with this "scientific" attitude of caution. It is likely that a few of these reports can be ruled out of serious consideration because the observers are probably in error and/or had such poor sightings as to yield little useful information. Most of the reports can be tentatively set aside on the grounds that it is at least possible that they were in error. There usually remain just a few sightings that simply cannot be challenged on any reasonable grounds, where the view was clear and the integrity of the person is beyond question. The main mass of reports in the middle range had provisionally been set aside on the grounds that the animal did not exist, therefore some other explanation had to be found. But after accepting the few unquestioned reports, and thus determining the animal to be real, this main mass should then be re-examined in the light of two possibilities either of which might be true in each case. Applying this procedure to my 75 direct accounts, I find 7 that simply cannot be doubted, some 33 that might be otherwise explained but almost certainly are real, 10 more that are possible but uncertain, and 25 reports that are very dubious and probably false.

Any interested scientist might have interviewed the same sample that I did, but only a very few of them actually could have done this. After talking to several skeptics, or twice that many neutrals, most witnesses will either change their story or shut up; having one's honesty repeatedly questioned is difficult for most people to put up with for long. Many investigators avoid this problem by finding a lot of their own witnesses to interview, rather than seeking out those who are already on record. My own practice, which also serves to avoid an atmosphere of confrontation, is to make it immediately clear that I think the sasquatch is real, and that I am approaching this particular story with an open mind. The skeptical inquirer should have an impressive list of interviews if he/she is going to pass judgment on the whole phenomenon. But armed with that impressive list, and an opinion in favor of the sasquatch, the researcher simply becomes one more on the short list of convinced scientists, and in the uncomfortable company of the lunatic fringe.

It is often suggested that lie detectors should be used to check on the claims of the sighters. In the first place this is something of an insult to many observers, and others might refuse simply because the procedure is so formidable looking. Next there is the problem of getting the equipment and skilled operators; no one in the field can afford to pay for this, and there is no outside funding. Finally, the results of polygraph tests are not conclusive, and the doubters would have no difficulty in simply dismissing any such data, no matter how convincing it might seem to the supporters. The reader is probably aware of cases where someone has passed a lie detector test and was still not believed.

Footprint evidence presents a similar picture. The circumstances of discovery cannot be reproduced or proven to most people's satisfaction, so the possibility of a mistake or hoax will be insisted on by the skeptics. Those of us who have made field investigations again find some highly dubious cases, some that could have been faked, and some that are legitimate beyond any question. Given the existence of the last category, most of the indeterminates then logically should fall into the legitimate group.

Most scientists are not in a position to run off to look at footprints in the field. Almost none of them have tapped themselves into the information lines so that they could see the footprints before other people obliterated them. My own experience is that most scientists would pass up the opportunity anyway. Those few who have made some direct field investigations have had no impact on the doubters, and we should not expect them to have any.

A second-hand method of studying footprints is through their plaster casts and photographs. Some of the context is no longer demonstrable with this material, but it is much more substantial than eyewitness reports of anything. The same procedure can again be applied for dividing them into fakes, conceivable fakes, and definitely real examples. With full information on their context, most of these would be classifiable without question. (Even a perfect-looking footprint would be labeled as a fake if it appeared in a flower garden in downtown New York City.)

The skeptics must label all footprints as hoaxes even if they cannot be mistaken for human, bear, or some natural feature. It is a simple matter to say that a footprint is fake; it is quite another matter to demonstrate how it was done. At first glance it might seem that the burden of proof is on the doubters to show how the fake was produced; in practice it is not. Most of the doubters have never looked closely at any track casts, and simply assume that there is no problem that requires an explanation. (This is the same attitude that I take toward reports of sixteen-foot-tall sasquatches; there is no need to explain something that I have no reason to think exists.) When these doubters do look closely at the track casts, they simply announce that they were faked by some means, without feeling any obligation to specify just what those means might have been. A few suggestions have been made as to how this might be done, and these were discussed in previous chapters, but none of the critics have successfully demonstrated that their ideas will work by making actual casts. Quite simply, most of the critics feel themselves under no obligation to explain away the tracks. Unless a significant number of ordinary scientists, as well as the public, start to demand such explanations, the present state of affairs will continue indefinitely.

Repeated footprints from the same individual sasquatch, under different immediate circumstances, are the most convincing evidence to experienced animal trackers. I have several sets of tracks like this, and there are no such trackers who are coming to look at them. I could pack up all of them and find some good trackers who are willing to look at them, but that's a lot of work, and few of these people will have a good place to lay out all of this material for serious study. Even if a significant number of such tracking experts were thereby convinced of the sasquatch, and were willing to say so publicly, this still would have almost no impact on the scientific community.

The detailed dermatoglyphics on several tracks were convincing to almost all experts in the field who saw them. Most anthropologists and primatologists dismissed them, along with the expert testimony, as fakes that were "somehow" manufactured. The opinions of many expert animal trackers would carry even less weight than those of fingerprinters.

If we were to get a DNA sequence from some future acquisition of biological material, it is by no means guaranteed that anyone outside of this specialized field would feel compelled to take notice. This discouraging view is based on direct experience. Roger Patterson really thought his film was solid proof and was able to get a few scientists to look at it. Rene Dahinden got some experts to study the film in detail, with generally favorable results. Others have made similar efforts since then. The result is still the same—very few recognized anthropologists or primatologists take it seriously, and do not even feel under any obligation to explain how Patterson was able to make a film that even Disney Studios could not duplicate. I was under the impression that expert testimony regarding the dermal ridges might lead to acceptance of the species, or at least some concerted efforts to find out more about it, without our having to produce a body. I went to great effort and personal expense to gather these opinions, and published them. And the people in high authority paid no attention. Why then should we expect the authorities to accept sequenced DNA as convincing evidence?

If someone shot a sasquatch, disposed of the body, and mounted the skin for a travelling exhibit, unfortunately this would not constitute any evidence at all. It is not likely that William Montagna or any other skin expert would even bother to check it out. And if they did, and if it passed all tests, who else would care? Actually there was a mounted "skin" exhibited a few years ago in California that was advertised to be of a bigfoot. I have various reasons for being quite sure it was a fake, but no dermatologist even bothered to examine it to check its authenticity. It was written off as a fake, by those few scientists who heard about it, simply because they knew that there is no such animal.

Clearly, the only evidence that will ever be accepted is a body, or a large part of one. And the skeleton is the very best part. But even then it may well take some leg-work to impress the Scientific Establishment. I used to think that if this definitive evidence became available, all of the "great men" would promptly come to see it. Judging from their response (or lack of it) to the casts with dermal ridges, this might not be the case. Not a single person with the appropriate expertise came to my university to look at them; it was I who carried the casts across the country and around the world to seek out those experts. Two of them, an anthropologist and a primatologist, actually called the ridge detail fake from looking at photographs, without even seeing the casts.

Patterson got the same reception with his film. No competent authorities went out of their way to look him up in order to view the film. Three investigators, at their own expense, took copies to the experts to get their opinions, and not all of these were even interested in looking at it.

It was Bernard Heuvelmans who told me that if I found clear skeletal evidence of the sasquatch, none of the "great men," least of all the skeptics, would come to look at it. In his opinion I would have to carry the material myself to the various authorities and professional meetings, and pester the experts with it for years before they eventually would accept it. Richard Leakey or Donald Johanson need only announce a new discovery, and many of their colleagues will gladly come to see it. The accepted scientific paradigm of today includes australopithecine fossils that are three million years old; it does not include their gigantic modern equivalent. "I'll see it when I believe it" is literally true in this case. Eugene Dubois faced that problem in the 1890s when he had to carry his *Pithecanthropus* fossils from Java to the doubting professors all over Europe. Raymond Dart got the same reception in the 1920s when he found the first *Australopithecus* in South Africa. Neither of these fossil hominids was part of the scientific paradigm of their day; but thanks to the efforts of their discoverers, they are today.

What To Do

There are several different scenarios about how the first sasquatch proof might come to light. There are also a number of things that can be done in an effort to hasten that day. For most people the only thing to do is just wait until it happens, much like we are waiting for world peace and the cure for cancer. But for those who are active in the field there are many approaches that might help.

Probably the most important general aspect is to generate and maintain an accurate and honest public image. How the media reports on the subject greatly influences not only public opinion, but government attitude as well. Some common misconceptions need to be countered with accurate information at every opportunity:

1. Sasquatch shows every indication of being a perfectly normal species of wild primate, and it is not connected with any paranormal phenomena. It is a legitimate subject of scientific investigation.
2. There is no reason to think that sasquatch has superhuman, human, or even semihuman intelligence. Accordingly, we should treat them with the same consideration that we give to the great apes.
3. We have no indication that sasquatch is an endangered species. Its population probably numbers in the thousands, and maybe tens of thousands. This is far from certain, however, and this idea might have to be revised when we know more.
4. It is not possible to prove that the species exists by continuing to collect sighting reports, footprint casts, and other minor evidence. Proper scientific study and possible protection will occur only when a type specimen is obtained.

Various sects of the lunatic fringe differ with many or all of these basic concepts. If the claims of some of these enthusiasts are true, we might as well give up on all science and any belief in human progress because it has all been superseded by something much more phenomenal. There is little need to specifically address the claims of any particular paranormalists. They hopelessly contradict one another, so any effort that is made to counter a point made by one group may be interpreted as support by another group. It is more effective simply to promote what we do know and to ignore as much as possible, and avoid any association with, those people who are making the investigation appear ridiculous. Cultivating friends among this lunatic fringe might gain some supporters, but it also gains the opposition of the rest of that fringe, as well as a loss of interest by the vast majority of the public, and the contempt of all scientists.

The International Society of Cryptozoology was founded in order that scientists and responsible lay workers could exchange information on their research within this unorthodox area. Until recently, the field had been left pretty much open to nonscientific, even antiscientific opinions because the academic community had almost studiously avoided it. Now there is a clearly perceptible move of scientific interest in this direction, but it has a long way to go. More information can be obtained on the ISC and its publications by writing to P.O. Box 43070, Tucson, AZ 85733. The reader should be cautioned that only a small part, maybe 10 percent, of cryptozoology publications and meetings deal with the sasquatch and similar phenomena. The society is concerned with all reported animals of unusual size or anatomy, or from unexpected times or places. This covers many other cryptids, as they are sometimes called.

The only way to prove that sasquatches exist is to produce a type specimen. Virtually every established scientist will repeat this same demand. That specimen most likely will be brought in by a hunter, hard-core or otherwise. The problem is whether something can be done to increase the chances of this happening. Whenever I speak publicly on this topic, I make the point that a sasquatch legally can be shot. There can be no punishment for shooting an animal that officially does not exist. Whatever may be determined about its status after the fact, at the time the first specimen was brought down, the sasquatch was a mythical beast with no more legal reality than a unicorn. Reminding hunters that there might be a large financial reward for bringing in the first specimen could stir more interest and effort, but this might not be true. The money motive also has unfortunate side effects like withholding data and otherwise obstructing the efforts of other hunters.

All prospective hunters should also be cautioned that it is illegal to shoot people who walk around the forest in fur coats. Even if they are dressed in gorilla suits at the time, which is tantamount to suicide, the charge would be some form of manslaughter. I would make no effort to defend such a shooter, even in the unlikely event that my opinion would make any difference. This kind of hunting should be left strictly in the hands of experienced people who know exactly what they are doing.

If such a hunter someday succeeds in this endeavor, I have some procedural suggestions. Do not leave the body in order to get help to bring it out, because it might not be there when you return. There are several possible reasons for this:

1. The animal might not have been dead, so it recovered enough to go away.
2. It might have been carried away by other sasquatches. This is unlikely, but possible.
3. One or more bears found it and dragged it away to devour.
4. Some other person found and removed it. From my point of view this makes little difference because its existence will become known anyway. However, the actual hunter would lose all claim to it.
5. In the excitement of the event you might be unable to locate the place upon your return.

The best procedure is to cut off the biggest piece you can carry and then go for help to retrieve the remainder. At least you will have proof of its existence, and probably can make a good argument that it was your specimen even if someone else got away with the rest of it. The best part to take is the head; if this is too heavy, leave the skin behind; but at a minimum, cut out the lower jaw and bring that back. If more than the head can be taken, get a foot; if still more, bring a hand; almost anything beyond that is about equally useful.

However you handle the specimen, certain scientific authorities will criticize you for doing something wrong. Ignore them. If necessary, ask them how *they* collected unknown half-ton primates, or how they are on record as telling other people how to deal with such a specimen. Even if this attitude does not satisfy these critics they are in fact in a ridiculous position, and most scientific and public opinion will be solidly on your side. Any piece of the body would be of great scientific value, but it is understandable that something might have to be sacrificed in order to obtain the best parts. The skull is the most important single piece of evidence, and it is to be hoped that it will not be damaged in this action. But if a shot through the head happens to be the only way to be sure of bringing it down, or to terminate a wounded condition, then by all means do it. A smashed skull is far better than none at all, and it can be reconstructed for the most part.

In late 1988 I was offered the opportunity to take a specimen under circumstances that would have involved great difficulties. My plan was to alert Bob Titmus who would get there rapidly to take away the skin, which would have been the first thing to remove. Then I would rapidly dissect the body, putting various organs (or parts thereof) into a dozen or more Mason jars with alcohol. The rest of the flesh was to be rapidly cut away and disposed of, except for a finger that would be left with the finder as proof of his rights to all monetary compensation. I would then pack up the stripped-down skeleton in many layers of plastic bags and depart the scene in a rented car. With any luck the whole operation would have consumed just one day of concerted effort.

The above scenario, if enacted, would have brought down on me the wrath of many zoologists because of all the information that would have been lost. But the circumstances were such that perhaps everything might have been lost if I tried to follow more conventional procedures. Needless to say, the incident did not occur. My informant decided to try to do it all by himself with the result that the specimen (if it ever existed) was not even shot, let alone retrieved.

The easiest way that a sasquatch can be encountered, where a hunter might take it, is while driving along a back road at night. About half of all sightings occur under these circumstances. A car could be fitted with extra lights facing partly to the sides, and a powerful gun kept at hand. One could then drive slowly along such roads from midnight until just after dawn. I have tried this for about seven or eight nights, on three separate occasions; many animals were seen, but no sasquatch. My usual speed was 25 miles (40 km) per hour. After some practice, I was able to stop the car, set the brakes, turn on the extra lights, pick up and load the gun, and be standing "at point" outside of the car—all in just fifteen seconds. At least half of such sightings in the past have lasted this long or longer.

This kind of road hunting should be done only by those who know exactly what they are doing. On one excursion I saw an erect biped walking by the road, with broad shoulders and no constriction at the neck. I knew immediately that it was too small and too narrow to be a sasquatch. It was a man wearing a hooded jacket. Someone else might have shot him. The procedure is not recommended for anyone except experienced hunters, a mistake of this kind cannot be retracted. Still, if many competent people do this, preferably in teams of two to relieve boredom and otherwise improve efficiency, a sasquatch would certainly be taken sooner than by any other method. The presence of a second person also may help to avoid making the mistake of firing at the wrong target.

Far preferable to shooting a sasquatch would be the discovery of skeletal remains of one that was already dead. I find it hard to believe that no one has ever shot and killed one at some time in the recent past. If so, they had their own reasons, probably mistaken, why they did not acknowledge it at the time. We could probably find a few bones from such an event up to ten years ago, and much longer under some circumstances. In most soils, a hundred-year-old burial would still contain a good skeleton.

I have tried for over twenty years to locate an old shooting event of this kind, so far without success. Even though the chance seems quite small, this possibility should continue to be pursued in public talks, documentaries, writings (like this book), and personal contacts. I once ran an ad to this effect in a small-town newspaper with no results; this might be worth repeating on a larger scale, but several researchers should be involved in case there are many responses of other kinds. One advantage to this approach is that even if we had a freshly taken specimen in hand, additional material might continue to be collected in this manner without harming the living population in any way.

It is also possible that a specimen already exists in a museum collection somewhere. If the bones in question are not especially obvious, and if no expert osteologist has seen them, there could be any number of them packed away in storage boxes. Most people would never recognize a sasquatch wrist or ankle bone, and a vertebra might easily be mistaken for that of an elk or bear. Unfortunately, there is no practical way to pursue this possibility. There are few experts who can easily spot the bones in question, they all have full-time employment somewhere, and few of them would be interested in such a project even if pay could be offered. It would take months for one such expert to train a dozen new people to recognize sasquatch bones, and this would have to be paid for somehow. Finally, most museums would be reluctant to have all their boxed materials opened and sorted through for such a singular project, and many of them do not even have the needed table space to work on. All we can do along this line is keep mentioning the possibility that such bones may have been collected, and hope for the best.

An interesting sidelight along this line was the suggestion by Vladimir Markotic that the already known *Hesperopithecus* might be a sasquatch. This is a fossil tooth that was found in Nebraska in 1922 and was initially described as being from a manlike ape. This diagnosis was soon changed to an old form of peccary, or American pig. If it had looked enough like an ape to mislead one expert, maybe the other diagnosis was not secure either. I studied the matter with some care and decided that there was no chance that it could be a sasquatch, and the pig identification was the most likely. Thus even if it had been sasquatch, there would never be general agreement, and it would not be accepted as definitive evidence. But there might be another such tooth specimen, somewhere in a North American museum, that has been labeled peccary and is actually from a sasquatch.

The possibility of finding a natural death is so much preferable to shooting one that I think more effort should be expended in this direction. A useful approach would be to find out more specifics on exactly where bears go to die. Other large animals, if not taken by carnivores, must also go somewhere because their remains are so rarely found. For that matter, what happens to the many farm dogs and cats who simply disappear one day in their advanced age and/or infirmity?

Knowledgeable people tell me that bears seek out low-lying spots, with available water, and where they will be well concealed by vegetation. Obviously none of these people know this for a fact because they have never found dead bears or their bones in such places. Something like this might be deduced from watching which direction a bear goes when it is wounded by gunfire. Farm dog skeletons are occasionally found in obscure corners under buildings, where shade and concealment occur. Most of this impression apparently follows from logical deduction about what an ailing bear could and should do in its own best interests, combined with the fact that their remains would be almost impossible to find in those locations.

What is missing from this picture is more specific information on just exactly which spot the ailing animal would pick. Which is more important, concealment or water? How critical is the quality of ground that it lies down on? How far will they go, if they can, to avoid minimal human structures like plowed fields and dirt roads? If someone could answer these and other questions they should be able to locate the remains of dead bears on a regular basis. There is no guarantee that sasquatches would seek out exactly the same conditions, but with some allowance for their larger size, simple logic would argue that they should try to do something similar. Whoever works out a method of finding natural bear deaths might eventually find a sasquatch in the same way. It is to be hoped that those people with the pertinent knowledge and skills will see the value in trying to do this. Again, if the method works it can continue to be used even after a hunted specimen is brought in.

I have no special knowledge of bear behavior, but I did spend some time looking at the likely areas where bears or sasquatches might go to recover from ailments and sometimes die. What appeared to my inexperienced eye to be acceptable places amounted to as much as 5 percent of the total habitable territory. In the greater Pacific Northwest this might amount to 50,000 square miles (130,000 sq km), within which about 50 new adult sasquatch bodies should be deposited each year. We might assume that bones can be found in such places from deaths up to five years ago, and that a careful search has a 50 percent chance of locating them. A searcher might walk about 2 miles per hour (3 km), seeing almost anything in a two-yard-wide strip (a meter to each side), and work at this for 40 hours per week. At this rate it should take 11,000 weeks of concentrated searching for each set of bones that might be discovered. Working for as much as 8 months out of each year, that would take one person about 126 years, or 126 coordinated people just one such season.

These odds are impressive, and virtually impossible; though some of my estimates could be well off the mark. I might be able to convince ten people to spend as much as one week in this kind of search; any more would certainly require some form of compensation that I cannot afford. That modest effort would have to be multiplied by maybe four hundred times in order to have a fair chance of a single success. There must be an easier way.

A thorough investigation of where all animals go to die should be of general zoological interest. This is not the same as taphonomy—the study of everything that happens to animals' remains following their deaths. What I am proposing is pretaphonomy, or how they relocate themselves from normal life to the actual sites of their deaths. There may be differences between the places that are selected by sight-oriented animals and by those who depend more on smell. Size itself may be a factor that helps to determine the sought-after death site, and this might also be influenced by the animal's diet, its type of locomotion, and who its predators are. Certain animals may have only limited amounts of time in order to select their retreats; injuries and wounds are abrupt and unpredictable, and an ailment might have a rapid onset. With only a short time available, the animal might hole up in a quite different manner than if it had plenty of time. A pursuing hunter in the vicinity is another variable, as is the presence of human activity and constructions.

If enough information could be gained about animal death locations in general, one might be able to predict the most likely places where sasquatch remains would be found. The remains of other kinds of animals should become similarly easier to locate. This could provide zoologists with useful information on ages at death in the wild, as well as its causes, in order to better understand the ecology of many species.

As a possible start for this kind of study I recently contacted Earth Watch with a proposal to enlist large labor resources. The idea was to have crews of supervised volunteers scour the countryside and poke into all patches of vegetation in an effort to locate all possible animal remains. Since the estimated success rate would be less than one specimen of anything per person per day, it was felt that volunteer motivation would not be sufficiently high.

Another approach to pretaphonomy would be to systematically interview rural households in a given area. We would ask for information on all animal remains that any of the people had ever found. As much data would be recorded as the informants could remember. This would include the species, the general location, and all possible particulars about its immediate circumstances. These would be descriptions of only chance encounters, and the people would have selective memories about various animal types. All environments certainly would not be surveyed with equal intensity. This approach would consume a lot of time, perhaps on the part of many investigators, but not nearly so much as having hundreds of volunteers out beating the bushes. I am not actively pursuing this project at present, but I could have been doing it instead of writing this book. Perhaps a retired zoologist might get a group together and give it a try.

In 1984 it occurred to me that almost all adult sasquatch deaths would be in the winter, when old age, disease, tooth loss, or other infirmities would weaken them too much to get through this difficult season. In my geographical area, all such bodies would quickly freeze. During a short period in each spring the bodies of a year's worth of dead sasquatches would thaw and decompose. Such decomposition raises the temperature about 5° C above that of the surrounding area, and it should be possible to read this with an infrared heat sensor. I found just such an instrument, called an I.R. imager, that gives a picture of the variations in heat emissions. It cost me $10,000 out of my own pocket, which represented almost half a year's salary at that time, and left little more where that came from. This imager can sense a heat source even if it is under a light cover of fallen vegetation, but it cannot "see" through much living foliage. My idea was to view the likely areas from above, looking for weak heat sources of an appropriate size, then investigating each of these on the ground to see if it was a bear, an elk, five careless campers, or a sasquatch.

In order to use the heat imager effectively it is necessary to view the likely terrain from directly above; looking diagonally down from a hillside picks up too many atmospheric heat waves. All fixed-wing aircraft move much too fast for me to use this device, so a helicopter was the only possible viewing platform. My resources were then too thin to consider renting helicopter time, and buying one was totally out of the question. Up to then I had received considerable public criticism, including printed and verbal abuse, for suggesting that a sasquatch should be shot. I thought that some of these critics might now come forward with financial help for a search method that would remove the need to kill anything. The new idea got some mention in press coverage and in a small item in the journal *Cryptozoology*. It was also described in detail in the *Sports Illustrated* article that was previously mentioned. No offers of help came to cover the costs of renting or buying a helicopter. I can only conclude that my critics on this point simply wanted something to complain about, and were not at all interested in avoiding killing a sasquatch. With that failure I set about building my own ultralight helicopter from a kit, as already described, and this has not yet flown. It is always possible that some other assistance may yet appear.

There have been many other proposals to use high-tech equipment to locate sasquatches, for whatever purpose. Trip-wired cameras have been tried for years without success. Even if one did produce a good picture, it could never equal the evidence value of Patterson's film, and that failed to convince any of the skeptics. Better lenses, electronic triggers and guiding devices, and video cameras all might produce better images, but they would still be rejected as hoaxes. If the skeptics think it can be faked, it will be assumed to be fake. I don't know of any photographic evidence that can overcome this objection.

Modern aerial photography is so good that it could clearly show a sasquatch on the ground. Many square miles of enlarged pictures of this kind can be searched for such images, but the same amount of manpower could locate them just about as effectively in the field. And when an image is found on a photograph, this simply means that something of that appearance was at that location on some earlier date. If a computer could be programmed to scan the films for sasquatches (who pays for this?) the labor factor might be resolved, but it still is not proof, and it is still a photograph from another time.

Helicopter-borne urine detectors have been used by the military to locate large formations of hidden soldiers. They could hardly distinguish one large mammal among many, and only on special occasions. Given the blade wash, helicopter sensing cannot pinpoint any location closely enough for present purposes.

At least fifteen years ago a couple of enthusiasts flew up from California just to talk to me about their foolproof plan to find sasquatch. It was so important that they couldn't risk talking about it on the phone, so they made an appointment to see me in person. What they wanted to know was the exact body temperature of a sasquatch so that they could spot one with an infrared seeker from an airplane. This approach was abruptly terminated when I told them that nobody knows the body temperature of a sasquatch. If I could have determined that directly, I could have captured the subject myself. Even if we knew the temperature (impossible), and if it was different from other mammals (unlikely), a reading of that exact amount could as easily be from a sick deer. And unknown to these two men, the equipment in question could distinguish one-tenth of a degree variations only within a closed room, and the device does not record this temperature in actual numbers.

Other electronic devices have been suggested, as well as elaborate tricks with conventional equipment. In most cases these cannot distinguish what kind of animal is involved, and will photograph, trap, shoot, or tranquilize bears and/or other animals. And this is only if they work at all. Devices that locate something at a great distance do not offer the operator the opportunity to do anything about it, simply because he/she is too far away. Ground-set motion sensors might be useful in some circumstances, but these can provide information on many other animals; and they require time to set and reset in various locations. And all such items tend to be very expensive.

The starlight scope that enhances natural light thousands of times has some possible uses. With it a sasquatch might be seen at night, assuming you are so skillful or lucky as to be in the right place at the right time. But then what do you do? A night scope can be mounted on a rifle for the obvious use, but having experimented with these devices, I must caution the unwary that it becomes much more difficult to distinguish between a sasquatch and a human. Only the most experienced hunter who is very familiar with this scope should ever hunt with it.

Many investigators are, up to now, not convinced that any electronic device can be used to advantage. Instead, they continue to gather information on sightings and footprints to build an ecological picture of sasquatch behavior, and one that is specific to their area of search. In this way, they hope, enough can be learned in order for them to be able to predict the most likely time and place of an encounter. What they plan to do at such an encounter depends on the particular investigator, and what he/she is trying to accomplish.

Ecological picture building seems to be making only a little progress. Most of the diligent workers are hard-core hunters who won't share their good information. Each of them is working on his own, whereas a combined effort would be much more productive. These hunters have little knowledge of wild primate behavior, are hesitant to contact authorities in this field, and in most cases would be rebuffed even if they tried. New hunters, hard-core and otherwise, are constantly entering the field and mostly starting from scratch. Old hunters are dropping out, through disinterest or death, and in most cases taking their accumulated information with them. No method has been devised to coordinate more than small parts of this diverse activity. Funds are not available, dedicated people have little time to spare, and the competition for the elusive first prize will always stifle communication.

Organized Hunts

People often ask if they can go on my next "expedition" to hunt for sasquatch. I don't go on expeditions, nor do most of the hunters, at least not in the usual sense of the word. All of us make frequent trips, either to a specific goal or just to scout some territory. Rarely do such trips involve an overnight in the bush. Given the presence of sasquatch right on the edge of civilization, and the fair network of roads in much of their territory, there is little reason to go to a lot of trouble to search for them somewhere else. From our point of view sasquatch encounters are virtually at random; there is no known place in the Cascade Mountains where you are more likely to encounter one than in the woods just outside of town. On the other hand, some hunters do make long-term investigtions in remote places where they can observe sasquatch behavior where it is unaffected by humans. An inquisitive companion is about the last thing such a hunter would want to have tagging along.

If a large group of people, with lots of equipment and horses, went into a particular valley to set up their search camp, any sasquatch that might be there would almost certainly be aware of them first. It would simply leave the area, and the people could hunt all they wanted. If just two hunters parked their car at the road end, and then walked farther along old logging roads, they would have a far better chance of encountering that same sasquatch. If the twenty-person expedition were instead divided into groups of two, these could cover ten times as much area, and collectively would have perhaps a hundred times more chance of seeing that sasquatch.

Theoretically, an organized hunt might work if the concept is run to the limit. Armed men could be lined up for 60 miles (100 km) across the base of the Olympic Peninsula in western Washington, spaced about 10 feet apart (3 m). They could then move north, sweeping the entire peninsula for 60 miles up to the sea. No large animal would likely be missed by this line, and offshore boats could watch for any animals who were trying to escape to the adjacent islands. One problem with this plan is that it would require at least 30,000 people, or three divisions of the U.S. Army, and a substantial part of the U.S. Navy would be needed to cover all the sea approaches. Another weak spot in the plan is how the line would be held overnight. Ground-motion sensors could be installed that trigger bright lights at the indicated spot, and night sentries could direct their fire accordingly. This involves a lot of equipment, especially the lights, in addition to all the human support supplies for two or three weeks.

A few sasquatches might be able to slip unnoticed through such a line of men, by day or night, though most of them probably would be contained. But just imagine the pandemonium if a sasquatch suddenly stood up a few yards ahead of the line and charged it. No matter how well trained these soldiers may be, it is not likely that the four closest of them would keep their composure enough to shoot accurately. They would just as likely shoot each other in the panic. And no, this encounter would not be treated as proof of the animal; it would just be four more excited witnesses to add to the two thousand we already have on record. The skeptics would say that it was a bear, elk, or hermit that crashed the line, even if it happened fifty times during the operation. Anyway, there is no prospect that the army would be interested in a training exercise of this kind, and no one could collect and organize thirty thousand hunters to do the job.

It is still possible that funding might appear to support the more conventional approaches. With enough money an information base could be established. This would probably begin by acquiring copies of John Green's files and looking for all other files of a similar nature. Several salaried workers would also search out new reports and dig into old newspapers and biographies. All of the information would be put on computers so that any particular kinds of data can be retrieved, independently of the remainder. Primate experts can be consulted (and maybe paid) to get their input on what the animals' behavior patterns might be, and this tested against the reports. And the reports themselves must all be ranked in terms of probability of truth. The paid workers must also sign absolute commitments that they will not use any of this information to hunt the animal on their own initiative. Or if they do, all proceeds will revert to the organization anyway.

The above procedure could be specified in much more detail, but I think the general point has been made. Such an organization eventually might be in a position to put hunters into the field with a good chance of obtaining the quarry. The cost of setting up and maintaining this organization would be far greater than anything that could be gained from the sale or exploitation of that first specimen. It would require a philanthropic grant probably amounting to millions of dollars.

Only two types of agencies would be willing to invest large sums of money in the kind of research that might upset the scientific status quo. The news media would love it, but it is doubtful that they could come up with this much money, and anyway they would demand the kind of immediate results that cannot be provided. Private foundations are the other source, but such a venture might generate a lot of bad publicity because of the most likely manner in which the hunt would end. Another factor is that almost all private funders would insist on a high degree of personal input into how the organization proceeds, and this is likely to cause serious disagreements and defections. Nevertheless, these are the only possible people to approach with such a proposal. An organization of this kind was set up by Tom Slick, though on a much smaller scale than is described here. His workers scoured parts of northern California from 1959 to 1962 and gathered a large amount of information. All of this was effectively lost when Slick's death terminated the operation.

Gregory May has initiated a program in the same direction, officially known as Northwest Hominoid Research, and based here in Pullman, Washington. He is the Director of the tax-exempt organization and I am its nominal President. There is little hope that we can tap into the necessary resources in order to start operating on a grand scale, but at least it's a try. Some very rich person just might choose this route to historical notoriety instead of supporting one of the more usual causes.

There is an arrangement in place with the Washington State University Foundation whereby research contributions to my university can be earmarked specifically for sasquatch investigation. This was set up back in 1986, and no donations of any kind have been received for this work. Exactly what would be done with such funds would depend on the amount, and on what stipulations the contributor might make. I don't seriously expect any funds to materialize, but this machinery is in place just in case.

Wealthy people donate money only to causes that they are aware of, and I have no special means of locating any potential doners. But an opportunity of this kind presented itself several years ago when an art exhibit, titled "The Right Foot," was to be installed at the San Francisco Airport. Some artist friends suggested that I show some footprint casts there, just for the sake of publicity. With their help I did just that, using the casts of Cripple Foot (Fig. 25). Probably thousands of international travelers passed by this exhibit, but not one contacted me as a direct result of seeing it.

With enough money, say about half a million dollars, a sasquatch could almost certainly be obtained by expert hunters. There are two basic approaches to this, the first and simplest being to advertise a reward of this amount to the first hunter who brings one in. Most of the serious hard-core hunters already seem to think that they can turn the specimen into this much money on their own, so it might not be any added incentive for them. But if this were to be on top of anything else they can earn by themselves, it might help somewhat. The prospect of offering such a reward is a bit discomforting because it might tempt many incompetent hunters into the field where they would shoot up the countryside and each other. I would be reluctant to have a hand in a venture as potentially chaotic and dangerous as this.

The same amount of money could be directed to four or five carefully chosen hunters of known competence who might be motivated to work full time on the hunt. They could be paid $20,000 or $25,000 per year to compensate for their time that otherwise would be needed to earn a living. Each hunter would work an area that he is already familiar with, and would be free to enlist any aid and follow any procedures he chooses. The only goal is to deliver the first sasquatch. Casting footprints, collecting hair and feces, or gathering any other data should be at the discretion of the hunters. There would be no requirement to take notes or photographs, mark things on maps, have regular meetings with me, or in any way account for their time.

If and when the specimen is taken, the hunt would be over and the species would presumably be protected. All remaining salary money would be divided up equally among all these hunters, and they would also share equally in all publicity money that the activity generates, with one exception. Personal accounts of their activities would be marketed on an individual basis; thus the story of the hunter who actually got the sasquatch would be the most in demand. The hunters would be motivated to conclude the search as soon as possible, in order to minimize the time that is expended to earn a fixed amount of money. It would also be in their best interests to get together occasionally to exchange information that might help one of the others to succeed in the quest.

Given a successful outcome of this kind of hunt, the scientists will then want to know as much as possible about the activities and habits of the species. Our hunters should have a great deal of valuable information along this line, especially if they gathered all possible evidence and kept detailed notes. Other hunters' field notes and knowledge might also be of some value, but the hired hunters would have the most valuable information because there would be no question as to their competence and their motivation in gathering it.

With half a million dollars to spend, the hunt could be financed for five years. I would rather set it up for ten years just to be on the safe side, but five years is probably enough time for it to succeed. The weakest part of this plan is that the required money is not available, and any much smaller amount would not be worth using in this manner. The next problem is selecting the hunters; I have only two in mind, but they could well lead me to others. Finally there is the ever-present problem of the adverse publicity that such a hunt would surely generate. There would be the usual outcry of "don't kill a sasquatch" (let it go extinct instead), "use a tranquilizer" (kill and maim a dozen of them), and "it might be human" (but let us never find out). The lunatic fringe would be out in force, making efforts to help or hinder as they individually see fit, and generally trying to make a circus out of the whole operation. Somebody else may have thought this all through and the hunt may currently be underway with absolute secrecy.

Interested individuals and groups are constantly forming organizations to investigate the sasquatch. Most of these have no clear concept of what they are actually trying to accomplish or how this might best be done. Perhaps some such group will have a better plan than any of those described here. If so, I would like to know about it—there might be some way for me to help, and I certainly want to be in on the scientific prize if it succeeds. On the other hand, I will not be a party to any sasquatch hunt that has some other primary goal in mind, like making money even without the quarry, for the purpose of proving (or disproving) evolution, in order to glorify Jesus, or to get rich enough to build the best bomb shelter in the world. Exactly these motives have already been expressed to me by various individuals, and there are no doubt others. I recognize only scientific progress and simple greed as legitimate motivations.

Just as a parting shot to any efforts that do not involve me directly, here are some recommendations. If you succeed, and not before, get coverage from the news media to protect your rights and to insure that the Scientific Establishment will have to take notice. Get the body, or whatever parts you retrieved, to the Biology, Veterinary, or Anthropology Department at a good university—don't let some private group exploit it or you might end up getting nothing for your trouble. And I wish you all the luck in the world!

12

KEEPING IT IN PERSPECTIVE

Sasquatch is not the most important subject in the world. Proving their existence just might be critical to the survival of that species, and our continuing ignorance of them is a continuing loss. But there are hundreds of other kinds of animals whose existence has been noted by local people, and which science has so far failed to recognize. This one may well be the most important of all such unproven animals because it is probably our closest living relative. Still, it is not human, and there are millions of real people in this world who need help far more desperately than the sasquatch does.

Some enthusiasts act as though all pertinent scientists should be studying the sasquatch today. This would require that these scientists must stop some of their present work. Do these enthusiasts have any idea what these scientists are presently doing and how important it might be? And do they have a list of research topics that they propose should be set aside? I think not. Even those scientists who are interested in sasquatch research, and who are doing it on their own time and money, still have to earn a living and maintain a reputation for competent work. Given the attitude of the Scientific Establishment, this is no easy task.

Not to study sasquatch does not in itself constitute a denial of its existence. Most scientists are doing nothing to find a cure for cancer, it does not follow that they see no need for this research. Only a few scientists are engaged in agricultural research, the rest of them certainly are not in favor of starvation. Within anthropology, the existence of the sasquatch would not in any way affect the work of the vast majority of the professionals. Most of them are concerned with the total array of human cultural behavior; the sasquatch is not human, and its existence touches only a tiny fraction of humanity. Biologists have over two million species to be concerned with; the sasquatch is only one of them.

If and when the sasquatch is proven to be real, a few dozen specialists will probably get funding to go into the field to gather more data. Those of us who study human evolution and/or living primates will have to down-play a few other things in order to concentrate some attention on this one. All the rest of the scientists, just like the general public, will have a new topic of conversation for a while, but that's about all it will amount to.

The proof will trigger a flurry of activity among a few government officials who will have to make a determination of its endangered status. There might well be a major fuss about whether lumbering and certain other economic activities should stop while the subject is being investigated. Some nuts will almost certainly come forward to charge the successful hunter with murder. The religious faith of a few creationists will be shaken, but only those who were already wavering; others will claim that evolution has now been disproved. The news media will have a hey-day and will badger every participant so much that they will wish (at least for the moment) that it had never happened. There will be profound statements from many politicians, philosophers, theologians, and from all of the lunatic fringe.

Eventually the whole subject will die down and mostly be forgotten, just like every other attention-getting event throughout history. A handful of scientists and naturalists will continue to work directly with the sasquatch, while others will make a few changes in their lecture notes and in the next textbook they write. Public interest will soon drop back to about the same level that it currently devotes to the panda, and the news media will follow suit. All of the sasquatch hunters will eventually stop bragging about it and inventing stories about the part that they played in the discovery, and go back to their normal lives. The science of cryptozoology will have received a boost in prestige that it may never recover from, but that will be mainly in the form of a slightly increased interest in the the possibility that other unverified animals might be real. My own prestige in the scientific world will rise a couple of notches, but it's not likely that the authorities will allow me to participate significantly in the ongoing investigation.

Life will go on, almost as if nothing had happened.

APPENDIX A

Reprinted from *Cryptozoology*, Vol. 6, pp. 24-39. 1987.

A RECONSTRUCTION OF THE SKULL OF GIGANTOPITHECUS BLACKI AND ITS COMPARISON WITH A LIVING FORM

Grover Krantz

Abstract: A skull of *Gigantopithecus blacki* has been constructed by the author based on the adult male jaw from China. This presumes erect, bipedal locomotion for the original, and an ape-sized brain scaled to the appropriate body size. The final product is far larger than a male gorilla, and compares favorably with reports of the unverified North American Sasquatch (Bigfoot).

Introduction

The largest known primate, *Gigantopithecus blacki*, lived in southern China somewhere between a half and one million years ago. It is known from the tooth-bearing parts of three lower jaws and over a thousand loose teeth. Dental traits clearly show it to be hominoid (in the superfamily of apes and humans), but authoritative opinion is divided as to whether or not it should be classified within the human family, Hominidae.

Upright, bipedal locomotion is the ultimate criterion for inclusion in the human family, as opposed to that of the great apes, Pongidae. Weidenreich (1946) and Eckhardt (1972) classed *Gigantopithecus* as a hominid, and proposed it as an actual human ancestor, but were vague on the point of bipedalism. Wu (1962) and Robinson (1972: 6) made the species hominid and bipedal, but on a separate line from ourselves, and presumably extinct.

As far back as the early 1950's, Heuvelmans (1952) suggested, on the basis of the few teeth then known, that *Gigantopithecus* might be the direct ancestor of the reported Himalayan Yeti. Later, Sanderson (1961) and Coon (1962: 207) also speculated on its possible relationship to the Yeti.

In 1968, Green made the connection with the North American Sasquatch, or Bigfoot. More recently, I formally proposed to equate the two species under *G. blacki*, but expressed the hope that *G. canadensis* would become the accepted name if the Sasquatch proved to be a separate species (Krantz 1986). I also suggested using the name *Gigantanthropus canadensis* if it should prove to be generically distinct, or *Australopithecus canadensis* if future discoveries should point in that direction. However, such proposals carry no legal weight under the established rules of zoological nomenclature.

All of these ideas presently suffer from the fact that there is no direct overlapping of evidence between the known fossils and the reported living species. We have no footprints or eyewitness accounts of the Chinese fossil animals; we have no skeletal remains of the North American Sasquatch, or of any other unverified hominoid.

Pilbeam et al. (1980) allowed about 100 kg body weight for the possibly related fossil jaw from India. Simons and Ettel (1970) assumed all gigantopithecines were knuckle-walkers. Helmut Hemmer (personal communication, 1985) questioned our ability to make any predictions of body size or locomotion from dentition. If all or any of these opinions are correct, we have little reason to seriously equate *Gigantop-ithcus* with the Sasquatch, or with any other of the reported unknown hominoids.

Contrary to the common view, I think a great deal can be determined about body size and locomotion from dentition alone. This depends on correctly identifying the type of teeth and how they were used. But with *Gigantopithecus* we also have much of the jaw itself, thus greatly improving our predictive ability from that based on teeth alone.

With some tooth-to-jaw ratios in hand, it should not be difficult to reconstruct the entire mandible. Extant upper teeth can be fitted, with supporting bone, to restore much of the upper jaw directly. The necessary muscle crests and other supporting structures follow almost automatically. Given the great divergence of the jaw, as well as the reduced sectorial complex in the teeth, an erect posture may be deduced (Krantz 1981). This tells us how to orient the muscle crests at the base of the skull. The overlap of *Gigantopithecus* with early *Homo* allows us to eliminate the former from consideration for cultural behavior, and thus predict apelike cognitive abilities. Scaling up from the chimpanzee at 400 cc of braincase volume to the gorilla at 500 cc, one can reasonably assign 600 cc to this fossil form. A full reconstruction of the skull thus should offer no serious problem. Such a reconstruction would give strong indications of the total body size and general appearance of these animals in life. And this, in turn, might allow for some more direct and perhaps meaningful comparisons with the reported living form.

The Reconstruction

Having made the above observations many times. I have been urged repeatedly to put my hands where my mouth is, and actually produce this reconstruction. During the autumn of 1985 I made the mandible, and in the spring of 1986 the rest of the skull was completed. What follows is a description of the more detailed reasoning and procedures that were employed in this work. I began by moving the right third molar laterally from its obviously disturbed position to line up the tooth row like the undistorted left side. The right second molar and the two medial incisors were added, and a few surface irregularities were filled in. None of this required any serious judgment, much less reconstructive imagination.

The first step was to establish the most likely breadth of the ascending ramus of the mandible. Simply stated, this means extending a line along the lower tooth row beyond the last molar to where it meets the upright, rear edge of the jaw. I measured the actual breadth of this ascending ramus, at the level of the tooth row, in my available sample of hominid and pongid jaws. This measurement was then laid out along the length of the tooth row in each specimen, from the back of the last molar, to see how far forward it went.

The most common result was that the ramus breadth equaled the distance from the end of the tooth row to the middle of the anterior premolar. This was true for such specimens as the Upper Cave Zhoukoudian male, the La Ferrassie Nean-derthal, one robust australopithecine, a male gorilla, and a male orang-utan. The Heidelberg jaw had a greater ramus breadth, equal to a line running just onto its canine. Other jaws had slightly narrower rami, such as Cro-Magnon, Skhul V, male "Sinanthropus," three robust australopithecines, and a female orang-utan.

Since the existing part of the *Gigantopithecus* jaw shows excessive height and thickness relative to its teeth, I assumed that its length (ramus breadth) might lean in this same direction. Accordingly, I chose the slightly above-average measurement basis of midanterior premolar to last molar. This was 88 mm, well above the largest of my comparative sample (75 mm in a male gorilla), and twice the average for spec-imens within the genus *Homo*.

Fig. 1. Side view of reconstructed jaw, with flat surface to camera. The 88-mm breadth of the ascending ramus (rear, rising part) is based on the length along the tooth row shown in dotted line. The 199 mm height of the ascending ramus, from resting surface, is twice the height at the third molar, shown as a another dotted line.

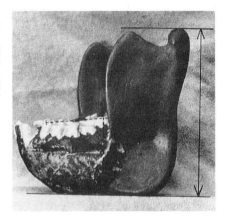

Figure 2. Bottom view of reconstructed jaw. The basal portion is outlined, and the general trend of divergence is drawn in as straight lines. These spread at 76°, while an earlier reconstruction by the author put this at 84° by concentrating more on the lowermost edge. The posterior parts follow this trend but are inflected slightly at the corners.

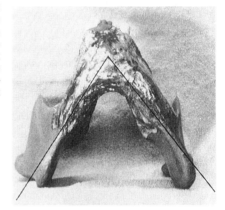

The front edge of the ascending ramus, the coronoid process, is preserved in its lowest part on each side. Since this edge runs almost straight up (perpendicular to the occlusal plane of the teeth), it provided the anterior edge of the 88 mm wide ramus (Fig. 1).

The two rami are set far apart and continue to diverge strongly toward the back. This divergence follows the approximate trend of the molar-premolar row, and also the direction of the lower edge of the mandibular body. It is normal in most primates—and in all specimens in my hominoid sample—for the jaw to continue this divergence in a nearly straight line along each side (Fig. 2).

Reconstructing the height of the ascending ramus followed a similar procedure. The total ramus heights to the condyles were measured perpendicular to the surface on which the sample jaws rested. The heights from the crowns of the third molars to the same resting surface were then measured. (I measured from the center of the molar crown to neutralize most wear differences.) Seven *Homo* specimens clustered tightly around the mean of ramus height being 1.64 times M3 + body height. Four robust australopithecines clustered tightly around 2.0 times taller. Three apes ranged widely around 2.08 times taller.

I made the *Gigantopithecus* ramus exactly 1.96 times taller (199 mm); I was aiming for 2.0 times, but the clay slumped slightly. This height also followed from trying to visualize the condyle's vertical position in order to give the jaw the motions that would produce the observed tooth wear. Here, the cuspal interlocking is worn away by an anterior migration of the lower jaw. This requires a highly placed condyle, well above the occlusal plane, so that the jaw moved forward as well as upward as the tooth crowns eroded in life (see Fig. 1).

After settling on the breadth and height of the ascending ramus, I was able to model the details with typical hominid contours. There were some guides in the extant fossil jaw. The divergence of the body of the mandible was continued to the rear corners (gonia), then thickened with a slight outward flare as in normal hominoid jaws. This gave an excessive breadth, but any attempt to narrow it would have produced an unusual shape with no justification.

The leading edge of the ascending ramus (coronoid process) is preserved enough to show it also has a strong outward flare. This obliged me to reconstruct a considerable concavity in the lateral surface of the ramus. This implies a very powerful masseter muscle, and, in turn, very strong zygomatic arches (cheek bones) above, where the masseter originates.

The size of the condyle is proportional to the jaw. Its shape, and the entire outline of the ramus as well, follows a generalized hominid/hominoid design. Relative thickness of the reconstructed bone is greater than is usual in primates. This is an allometric effect, as relative thickness increases with absolute size in extant forms, so this is simply extrapolated a considerable step beyond the gorilla.

In all this, as well as other parts of the skull, I first made numerous drawings and partial restorations showing the new parts both larger and smaller than what was ultimately decided on. Each of these extremes was then studied in order to determine if the implied anatomical relationships were unworkable, inefficient, or wasteful of biological material. After bracketing with too large, too small, too wide, too narrow, too tall, too short, etc., I was able to close in on what appeared to be the most likely size and/or shape. This involved placing all muscles, locating all levers, judging all moving masses, and so on, for all normal as well as abnormal movements of these parts.

I would not be so bold as to suggest this procedure was perfect and yielded exact results, but it is not likely that any serious error could have been introduced. Of course, only the finding of an actual *Gigantopithecus* skull will serve to check its accuracy.

This mandible might now be compared with the earlier reconstruction by Wu Rukang (1962). Our differences are only of degree. Wu made the ramus somewhat less tall, but prolonged it backward much more than I did. He seems to have tried to turn the sides inward slightly to avoid some of the indicated divergence, and thereby give it a more "normal" appearance. By giving it such length, however, his jaw is actually wider at the back than mine is. Overall, Wu's reconstruction is somewhat the larger and more apelike. A more serious comparison of actual measurements is saved for later in this paper, but it is fair to say at this point that a 500-kg body size is quite possible.

The upper dentition is based on Wu's description of the recovered teeth. These fall into two size categories, the larger of which correspond to those in the mandible and are presumed to be of males. Average measurements of these larger teeth were laid out in an arch that would normally occlude with those in the lower jaw. This involves having the upper teeth overlap outside the lowers around most of the arch, but close in to meet just about crown-to-crown at the third molars. The observed wear pattern and its slopes follow from this occlusion, which is also true for almost all primates.

In constructing this upper dental arcade, I was unable to fit in teeth of average male size, but had to reduce them slightly. This implies that this individual was somewhat below average size, at least in its dentition.

The alveolar (tooth-supporting) part of the upper jaw was made relatively thick, corresponding to its thickness in the lower jaw. The hard palate was placed at a medium height, typical of early hominids. This may not be correct, but minor variations in this have little repercussion on any other traits. (The reader might note that the restorations are based on hominoids when apes and humans are the same, and on hominids when there is a difference.)

Recovered upper canines have long roots (45 mm). This would place their supporting alveolar bone well above the lower edge of the nasal aperture. The distance between the upper canines thus strongly influences the breadth of the nasal aperture (Coon with Hunt 1965: 250). The spacing between these canines can be determined from the sizes of the four incisors that form an arc between them, and by the positions of the lower canines which the uppers should partially overlap. These two methods agree in placing the canine roots' medial edges about 30 mm apart at the gum line, and spreading to at least 50 mm at their tips. This allows a lower breadth of nasal aperture also of about 50 mm and higher up it can have little or no greater breadth (Fig. 3).

The height of the entire nasal chamber can be roughly deduced from its breadth and from the total body size. The volume of inspired air must be proportional to the body's needs. With a nasal chamber breadth somewhat more than that of a male gorilla, and an all-over body at least twice as great, the same level of activity can be maintained with a chamber half-again taller. This kind of nasal height (115 mm vs. 88 mm in the gorilla) was introduced into the reconstruction and was found to fit nicely with the high placement of the mandibular condyles. This internal cross-checking was gratifying (see Fig. 3).

The braincase was built from a core of plaster—a cast of an australopithecine skull of 510 cc—which was thickened somewhat to approximate a 600-cc capacity

Figure 3. Front view of reconstructed cranium. The 50-mm nasal breadth lines up with the spacing between the canine tips. The 115-mm height of the nasal chamber is slightly arbitrary at the top, but corresponds well with the great height of the mandible. Orbit diameters of 65 mm are also indicated.

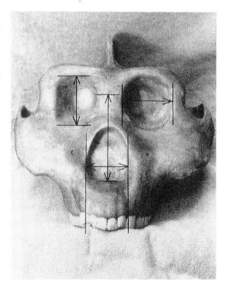

with a presumed vault thickness of 6 to 7 mm. This was placed between the mandibular condyles, about balanced in front and behind them, and elevated so that about one-tenth of its height was below the condyles' tops. This is the standard brain location in hominoids in relation to the condyles, with almost no variation.

From the sides of the braincase I built up typical mandibular sockets (glenoid fossae) that reached out and capped the condyles. From the lower front part I added material to join with the palate and growing nasal chamber that had already been constructed. This formed a basic frame upon which I could then add all other superstructures.

At the base of the braincase, from one jaw socket around the back to the other socket, I built a horizontal crest standing out about 30 mm (Fig. 4), and typically 15 mm thick (Fig. 6). This constitutes the supramastoid crest in each ear region, and the occipital crest across the back. The size of this crest was carefully calculated for leverage for the muscles of the neck that would have inserted below it in an erect body. The size and shape of this structure was further refined as the rest of the reconstruction progressed. If this errs, I think it is on the conservative side; it could have been made more prominent.

Orbit size was extrapolated up from the gorilla, much as was done with brain volume. I made cones of plaster, gradually enlarging them until they looked about right—inside diameters at rims of 65 mm in both directions, and with depths also correspondingly greater than in the gorilla (Fig. 3). Their thickness, including brow ridges, was again scaled up from the gorilla as would appear to have been necessary to avoid breakage from rough handling in life. Considering the inertial mass that emerges, such bony strength would have to be very great. Again, I may have underestimated the strength of the structures involved.

The orbits had to be placed well forward of the cheeks in order for them to clear the coronoid processes of the mandible. The evidently vertical emplacement of the upper incisors and canines argued for a nearly vertical upper face, also putting the

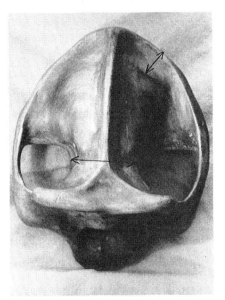

Figure 4. Top view of reconstructed cranium. The 30-mm flange of the occipital crest is indicated near the top of the picture. The notable narrowing, or postorbital constriction, is indicated near the center, beyond which are the great spaces available for the temporal muscles on each side.

Figure 5. Side view of reconstructed cranium. The 50-mm extension of the sagittal crest is indicated near the top of the picture. Vertical thickening of the zygomatic arch is shown nearer the center.

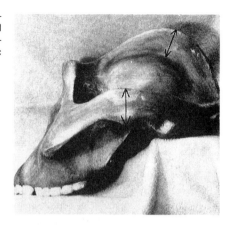

orbits well forward. Vertical placement of the orbits was roughly dictated by the nasal cavity that had already been built. At this level, the optic foramina would enter the braincase at the anatomically correct place. Again, there is internal cross-checking of the design.

Having built and placed the orbits in relation to other facial parts, I then found they were extraordinarily far forward from the braincase (Figs. 4 and 5). Likewise, the back of the upper jaw was also well ahead of the braincase, in addition to being placed far below it. In effect, the apparent joining of facial to cranial parts was reduced to remarkably slender connections. I therefore felt obliged to arbitrarily add extra thickening to much of this connecting area, and to introduce something of a diagonal brace from the lower front of the braincase to the back of the upper jaw. The position of this brace was determined for maximum strength and minimum interference with muscular actions in this area.

Still, the depression left between face and braincase remained impressive (see especially Fig. 4). The more modest development of this same depression in other skulls is known as the temporal fossa. It contains the anterior portion of the temporal, one of the major chewing muscles. It does not automatically follow that the fossa was entirely filled with temporal muscle; however, given the power needed to move a jaw of this size, such a large temporal muscle may well be expected.

The temporal muscles, in all mammals, originate on the sides of the braincase, pass forward and downward under the zygomatic arches, and insert in the coronoid processes of the mandible. In this case, as with the larger apes, the muscle is so large relative to the brain that it covers the braincase entirely and originates from a sagittal crest. This crest extends above and behind the braincase in the midline. Its prominence appears mainly to provide for length of action of this muscle rather than for area of attachment.

As a given type of animal is increased in size, jaw muscles increase in proportion to the total body, while the braincase increases only slightly. Smaller apes lack sagittal crests, the relatively large braincase providing sufficient attachment for the temporal muscles. Male orang-utans and female gorillas often have slight crests, while the male gorilla regularly shows a prominent one. The absolute size of both sexes of Gigantopithecus evidently exceeds the male gorilla, and would be expected to have correspondingly larger sagittal crests. In the reconstructed male specimen here, a crest standing 50 mm tall, twice that of the gorilla, is thus a reasonable expectation (Fig. 5).

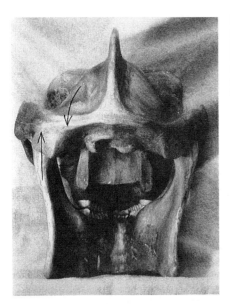

Figure 6. Rear view of reconstructed skull. The 15-mm thickness of the projecting occipital crest is indicated on the right between the short arrows. On the left are shown the opposing forces of jaw pressure and cranial-wall resistance which conspicuously mismatch.

In gorillas, the major projection of the crest is toward the rear of the braincase; in *Australopithecus*, when it occurs at all, it is more at the top of the skull. Given the hominid design of the skull being reconstructed, the upper emphasis might be expected (Tim White, personal communication). On the other hand, the recently discovered earliest example of A. *boisei* has a more posterior emphasis to the crest (Walker *et al.* 1986). I designed the *Gigantopithecus* crest, on the basis of an indefinable "feel," to have this same posterior emphasis. The accuracy of this detail remains uncertain.

Gross restoration of the zygomatic arches was simple. They arose above the first molar, as in most hominids, swung around well clear of the coronoid process, and joined the base of the skull above the condyles and ears to merge into the occipital crest. Their thickness and height, at least anteriorly, posed no problem, though a somewhat greater size and lateral flare might have been added (Alan Smith, personal communication). The masseter muscles, running from the underside of this part of the arch down to the angle of the mandible, were evidently powerfully developed. This means that the arch itself must be strongly built to resist their downward pull.

Reconstructing the rear part of the zygomatic arch posed an unexpected problem when it was observed that the jaw sockets were much more widely spaced than the sides of the braincase. In chewing, a considerable force is exerted upward through the condyle and into its socket, and which must then be dissipated into the skull. In the human skull, the side wall of the braincase passes down just to the outside of this socket, and thus braces the socket against upward displacement. In the gorilla skull, the side wall of the braincase passes down just to the inside of this socket, and thus likewise braces the socket against upward strain. In the *Gigantopithecus* skull, the side wall of the ape-sized braincase passes down some distance medial to the inside edge of the wide-set condyle, thus affording almost no direct resistance against upward strain (Fig. 6). The occipital crest of the gorilla, passing upward and backward from the socket, adds considerably to its bracing. But in *Gigantopithecus*, the horizontal occipital crest offers almost no such bracing.

Some structural support for the jaw socket was achieved by thickening the lower braincase wall, and making it spread out widely just above the socket. This mass would presumably be lightened by pneumatizing the bone—a network of air cells within a mesh of internal boney struts. This supramastoid inflation could go up only a short distance without interfering with the line of action of part of the overlying temporal muscle. A similar thickening on the underside, behind the socket, amounted to a very large mastoid process; but its stabilizing ability was limited. Perhaps mastoids should be even larger, as White (personal communication) has suggested he would have made them.

Seeing that more strength was probably required, I introduced considerable vertical thickening of the rear part of the zygomatic arch (Fig. 5). This allows upward force at the socket to be braced from above, and thus transmitted through the entire arch, and to the rear of the skull as well. This design was modeled on that of the horse skull, which I found has the same discrepancy between the locations of the condyles and braincase walls, as well as a chewing mechanism that closely parallels hominids.

A few other cranial details had to be included for the sake of completeness, but these are of no great significance to evolution or taxonomy. The shape of the brow ridges and the scrap of horizontal forehead just behind them were copied much along gorilla lines. The major muscle insertions on the base of the occipital (neck attachment) were just roughed in according to the hominid pattern. The occipital condyles were located up high against the base of the skull for lack of any reason to draw them down, and also to afford the head the most stable positioning. Petrous bones, basioccipital, and pterygoid wings were all primitive hominid and only roughly indicated.

My construction technique differed between jaw and skull. The jaw was built up in five steps by modeling the parts in Sculpy, which was baked hard after each step. The original plaster jaw was oiled repeatedly to preserve it through these bakings, and it barely survived intact.

In building the skull, I made the jaw sockets of sculpy, baked them, then glued them to the plaster braincase that was used as a core. The maxilla was made from a half-depth copy of the lower jaw, greatly thickened with more plaster, then carved down. Orbits were made by thickly coating plaster on the outside of a small plastic funnel, which was then removed. The rest of the skull construction involved a slow process of mixing small amounts of hydrocal plaster and adding it on, often incorporating suitably shaped plaster scraps. The final product was scraped and sandpapered until it approached perfection, or until I tired of it.

The skull and jaw were then molded in Silastic (silicone rubber), in two pieces each. Good plaster copies are now being made and distributed.

Discussion

I have taken all possible measurements of the finished reconstruction and compared these with the cast of a large male gorilla. Needless to say, *Gigantopithecus* far exceeds the gorilla in every measurement. In three heights and three breadths, the gorilla clustered tightly around 70 percent of this new reconstruction; in three lengths, the discrepancy was less, with the gorilla averaging just over 80 percent.

Wu (1962) gives some measurements of his jaw reconstruction based on the same male specimen. He adds an admittedly speculative total facial height, and I have calculated the mandible length from his photographs. With this information, we may compare the length, breadth, and height of these two reconstructions with the gorilla.

Measurement	Gorilla (mm)	Krantz (mm)	X-Gor.	Wu (mm)	X-Gor.
Mandibular length	184	208	1.130°	253	1.375°
Bigonial breadth	134	189	1.410°	200	1.493°
Condyle height	124	199	1.524	183	1.476
Facial height	178	255	1.432	320	1.798
Mean of two heights	—	—	1.478°	—	1.637°

Since there are two height measurements from quite different parts of the skull, these are here averaged so their total will be weighted equally with length and breadth. These total ratios, averaging length, breadth, and height (indicated by asterisks) make my reconstruction 1.339 times larger than the male gorilla, and Wu's 1.502 times larger. Whether these figures can be translated into statures or any other gross body dimensions is a matter of speculation.

The volumetric comparisons are found by multiplying the three lineal dimensions together. By this reasoning, my version of *Gigantopithecus* should have weighed 2.3546 times as much as the male gorilla; Wu's version should be 3.3145 times heavier. If the gorilla weighed 180 kg (396 lbs.), then my figures put *Gigantopithecus* at 424 kg (933 lbs.), while Wu's figures give it 597 kg (1,313 lbs.).

These weights need not be taken as definitive estimates because *Gigantopithecus* and gorilla body builds are not necessarily the same. However, if one chooses to use a significantly different weight estimate, then some justification ought to be given for doing so. My own inclination is to use the 424 kg from my reconstruction as the probable male body weight. A relatively more elongated body would be expected in an erect biped as opposed to a knuckle-walker, thus lowering the estimate. On the other hand, the individual used here may be smaller than average, and some of my reconstructions may also be incorrectly small.

And what if Wu's reconstructed size is more accurate?

Most people who have viewed my reconstruction are in no position to compare it with the supposedly living Sasquatch in any knowledgeable way. Those who possess the technical expertise to appreciate the structure of a primate skull have not seen the living animal, and those who claim to have seen a living Sasquatch cannot well interpret their observations in terms of cranial anatomy.

One notable exception is Robert Titmus, a hunter and taxidermist of long experience who claims to have seen several Sasquatches, one of them in full face and close-up. His opinion, after long study, is that my reconstruction has about the size and general form that he would expect to find in the skulls of the animals he saw. Titmus had one reservation—that the eyes of the animal he claims to have seen were considerably farther apart than my reconstruction would allow. My positioning was based on an expanded gorilla, and certainly could be in error. At the same time, Titmus' observation is from many years ago, and his recollection might not be accurate. There could also be a difference between *Gigantopithecus* and Sasquatch in this part of the anatomy.

Summary

The skull reconstructed here is not likely to be far from the actual condition of *Gigantopithecus blacki*. The jaws and teeth are firmly based on actual fossils, and indicate a hominoid primate with affinities more hominid than pongid. Erect posture and a 600-cc brain size are strongly indicated, and these dictate most of the remaining cranial morphology. The total size of the resulting skull would call for a body more than twice as big as that of a male gorilla. That a bipedal hominoid of gigantic size lived in China half a million years ago seems to be well established. Whether an animal of this description is alive today is obviously a different matter, but at least the possibility should be considered open.

References Cited

Coon, Carleton S.
   1962 *The Origin of Races.* New York: Knopf.
Coon, Carleton S., with Edward E. Hunt
   1965 *The Living Races of Man.* New York: Knopf.
Eckhardt, Robert
   1972 Population Genetics and Human Origins. *Scientific American*, Vol. 226: 94-103.
Green, John
   1968 *On the Track of the Sasquatch.* Agassiz, B.C.: Cheam Publishing.
Heuvelmans, Bernard
   1952 L'Homme des Cavernes a-t-il connu des Geants mesurant 3 a 4 Metres? *Sciences et Avenir* (May).
Krantz, Grover S.
   1981 *The Process of Human Evolution.* Cambridge, MA: Schenkman.
   1986 A Species Named from Footprints. *Northwest Anthropological Research Notes*, Vol. 19: 93-99.

APPENDIX B

Reprinted from *Northwest Anthropological Research Notes* 19(1):93-99. This paper was originally given in a slightly modified form at the 3rd International Congress of Systematic and Evolutionary Biology in July, 1985 at Brighton, England.

A SPECIES NAMED FROM FOOTPRINTS
Grover Krantz

Abstract: A reconstruction is presented of the living appearance of the fossil species *Gigantopithecus blacki*; this is then compared with evidence for a reported wild animal in North America. These two forms are provisionally equated, thus giving a formal name to the living animal known as sasquatch, or bigfoot. Alternative taxonomic designations are also suggested in view of the possibility that future discoveries might show this equation to be incorrect.

Gigantopithecus blacki was named by von Koenigswald in 1935 from a giant primate tooth he found in a Chinese drugstore. Weidenreich (1945) described several teeth in detail, and he decided they showed hominid (human) rather than pongid (ape) affinities. They were attributed to "Middle Pleistocene" deposits from southern China on the basis of adhering matrix. A date of about a half a million years ago was suggested at that time.

Subsequent discoveries now include the tooth-bearing parts of three mandibles and perhaps a thousand additional loose teeth (Woo 1962). Another similar mandible was recovered in India that has been named *G. bilaspurensis* (Simons and Ettel 1970). Most opinions would now give the Chinese fossils an antiquity of at least a million years, and the Indian specimen several times that.

Anatomically, *G. blacki* is a higher primate of the hominoid superfamily of man and apes. Its dentition is substantially more humanlike than that found in any living ape. The incisors are greatly reduced and vertically implanted; the canines are somewhat reduced and tend to grind down with use. The lower anterior premolars are basically bicuspid, though the labial cusp is much the larger and spreads considerably toward the base; it is slightly rotated and can accurately be called semisectorial. The molars are high-crowned, have thick enamel, and their cusp and fissure pattern is distinctly hominid. In total, the dentition is intermediate, but leans a bit more to the human than to the ape side—much as that of the recently discovered *Australopithecus afarensis*, but not in exactly the same ways. It is clearly more hominid-looking than the briefly famous "Ramapithecus."

All living hominoids are giant brachiators, or at least have the adaptations for this arm-swinging type of locomotion. It is a reasonable presumption, though not a demonstrated fact, that *G. blacki* also has these same adaptations. Important among these are conspicuously wide shoulders, with long arms oriented laterally rather than ventrally. This also includes a broader-than-deep chest, with the rib cage closely approximating the pelvis. The external tail is missing as well, its base being tucked under to help support the viscera. *Gigantopithecus* is large, as the name implies. The mandible of the adult male specimen from China is half again larger than a male gorilla in most lineal dimensions, and over twice as thick. If one mentally completes this mandible, fills in a corresponding maxilla, and adds the necessary muscle-supporting structures for chewing, then a head of phenomenal size results. A normal body weight twice that of the male gorilla would be required just to support this head in a reasonable manner. About 350 kg would be the probable body weight. The smaller female jaw from China suggests a body of something like 250 kg, as it also exceeds the male gorilla in all measurements.

Ratios of jaw size to body size vary somewhat among living and fossil primates but with those of a given morphological design the ratio is more regular. *Gigantopithecus* does not show the extreme molarized design of the australopithecines, so its jaw would not be as relatively oversized. In fact, a reconstruction of its head and neck, at 40 kg, involves as much mass as the entire body of some australopithecines.

Gigantopithecus jaws are exceptionally broad in the back; the horizontal rami diverge toward the rear to a degree unmatched by any other primate. The dentition diverges to the rear in a corresponding manner, in part resulting from the much reduced incisors. But the jaw spread is the major causative factor here, the divergence of the molar rows being much less impressive than that of the body of the jaw itself. This posterior breadth would mean that the mandibular condyles were also widely spaced on the base of the skull. This spacing would alter the direction of swing of the jaw in each one-sided chewing action, and in turn would render the sectorial complex ineffective. The semisectorial character of the premolar is thus consistent with the jaw design.

The most obvious reason why the jaw should spread in this manner is because the neck must have been situated somewhat between, rather than behind, the ascending rami. Thus we may conclude that the head was habitually placed atop a vertical neck rather than being hung forward from a sloping neck. This in turn implies that the entire body was normally held in an erect position, and they were necessarily bipedal. They would have stood and walked in an essentially human manner.

That the jaw diverges even more than in humans is the allometric result of relatively more massive neck musculature in this absolutely larger body. The high weight-to-strength ratio would also call for a very heavyset body build in general. Given a weight of 350 kg and a strongly lateral body build, a stature of about 2.5 m can be predicted.

No tools or habitation sites are known for *G. blacki*. They existed within the time range of *Homo erectus*, which was a tool-using, hunting, early form of hominid. It is not likely that two culture-bearing species could have coexisted, so we may safely presume that *G. blacki* was not human in any intellectual sense of the word.

The lack of hunting would also mean they would not have reduced their body hair as part of the human sweat-cooling adaptation; they would be hair covered just like other primates. Their brains would be a little larger than in living apes, perhaps 600 cc. Allometry would suggest this added 100 cc over the gorilla because of their body size. Combining this with much larger facial bones and jaw musculature would give them apelike faces with tall sagittal crests in both sexes. The small incisors would somewhat reduce their prognathism. The face would project far down, and the shoulders should rise higher than the level of the mouth. No visible constriction at the neck should be expected.

Dentition and ecological logic both point to an omnivorous diet, predominantly vegetarian. They may have been opportunistic carnivores, but no special abilities in this direction are indicated. They would not have had exceptional speed or endurance, nor would they have the fangs or claws of the usual carnivores.

The picture of an adult male *Gigantopithecus* may be summarized from these data and deductions. It was an erect, bipedal primate with the wide shoulders and strong arms of an ex-brachiator. Its body would be ape/human-like in its broad chest, short waist, and lack of external tail. It would weigh about 350 kg (800 lbs.) and stand perhaps 2.5 m (8 ft.) tall, on legs and feet of roughly human proportions and stout design. It would be covered with normal primate hair and have a gorilla-like face. Its intelligence should be in the general area of the living apes, with no cultural capacity or language. The female would be smaller, at 250 kg and 2 m, but otherwise the same.

An animal exactly fitting this description is often reported as seen in North America. (Similar reports from other continents are not dealt with here.) Considerable evidence has been collected to support the existence of this sasquatch, but none of it has been definitive in the eyes of most zoologists and anthropologists. Footprints have been observed, photographed, and cast by the hundreds. Eyewitness accounts on record number a thousand or more; and most sightings are probably not reported. At least one film has survived the usual debunking claims in good order. Hair samples and feces have been collected, and sometimes analyzed, with uncertain results. Native American legends and folklore often include creatures that seem similar (Green 1978).

This impressive array of evidence is badly weakened by the fact that much of it has been shown to be in error, faked, or at least highly suspect. Some eyewitnesses saw standing bears, men at a distance, or oddly shaped tree trunks; other have invented their accounts for personal publicity. Many footprints were faked with carved wooden feet. At least some of the claimed films of sasquatches are demonstrable fakes. Most of the hair and fecal samples were from known animal species, and the rest remain simply unidentified. Indian legends also include many other creatures that are no more real than angels or unicorns.

That the sasquatch could be real, is not sufficient argument to say that it is real. Definitive evidence must be used to support it that is not subject to hoaxing or misinterpretation. Such evidence is currently available in the form of three footprint casts that show dermal ridges and sweat pores on large areas on the sole of the foot and toes. Silicon rubber molds have been made of these, and exact copies can be produced for further study. The original casts are in my possession.

Expert opinion on these track casts is sharply divided. Most anthropologists and zoologists have summarily dismissed them as fakes. They all agree that real primate skin is represented, but claim that this was somehow transferred from known animals to these out-sized footprints. Most dermatoglyphic experts have declared them to be genuine, and incapable of being faked by any means (Krantz 1983; Berry and Haylock 1985).

The biologists were all on record as denying the existence of this supposed animal—if not explicitly, at least implicitly by failure to include it in their lists of living primates. The policemen have made no such pronouncements; the animal's possible existence was of no professional interest to them. If anything, they were more concerned about the possibility of someone having discovered a technique that could be used for faking fingerprints.

The formal description of new species requires a type specimen. Such a specimen may consist of several parts of the same individual, such as various bones of one skeleton. In this case, the type specimen may consist of three foot impressions of one individual. The circumstances of discovery preclude the possibility that more than one individual is involved.

We need not be concerned that footprints are not the actual remains of the animal itself. Natural casts of bones and shells are routinely used in describing fossil species. In such cases no remains of the animal are directly involved. Rather, we record the physical impact that a part of the animal once made on its environment.

Nonskeletal impressions of hair, scales, and feathers are also found in fossil form; impressions of dermal ridges should be equally valid.

The main logical distinction in the case at hand would appear to be the recency of the impressions. Fossil feather impressions, or even dinosaur tracks, normally have an antiquity measured in tens of millions of years or more. In this instance the footprints were about two hours old at the time of their permanent documentation. I fail to see a good reason why this should make any difference in their acceptability. Obviously it would be desirable to have actual remains of the body, but this desire applies equally to many fossil species as well. Whether the species is recent or ancient, we name it from the best material evidence that is available.

Such a type specimen of the North American sasquatch, or bigfoot, would consist of the three footprints of one individual that were cast on 16 June 1982. These footprints were found by U.S. Forest Service employee Paul Freeman within the Umatilla National Forest, in the Blue Mountains of southeastern Washington state, at a locality known as Elk Wallow. The circumstances of their discovery were recounted in the Newsletter of the International Society of Cryptozoology (1982a, 1982b). A description of the track casts themselves was subsequently published (Krantz 1983). The authenticity of these tracks has also been questioned (Dahinden 1984) and answered (Krantz 1984).

The sasquatch tracks indicate a foot of hominid design, the first toe is not opposed. It is probably too long (38 cm) and definitely too wide (17 cm) to be of *Homo sapiens* origin. The partial pattern of dermal ridges was of a generalized higher primate design. No recognized living species fits this description. *Gigantopithecus blacki*, as described above, would necessarily have left footprints of just this kind; while the maker of Elk Wallow tracks must have had a gigantic, bipedal, primate body. That these modern track makers have reportedly been seen and described allows us to assign some additional traits to them.

The reconstructed appearance of *G. blacki* and the description of the sasquatch are identical in all respects where they deal with the same features. This is true even if we limit our sasquatch data to the "type" footprints. These features are both numerous and distinctive enough that the possibility of two gigantic, bipedal, higher primate species can be considered very unlikely. In spite of this close correspondence, the normal procedure for naming the sasquatch would be to assign it new generic and trivial names. And the normal sequence of events would then be to sink these names as it becomes evident that the sasquatch is indeed *G. blacki*.

Rather than follow this time-honored procedure, I wish to reverse the sequence of taxonomic events here. Its equation with the known fossil form is proposed, then suggestions are made to upgrade its level of taxonomic distinction if and when new data should warrant this. It is realized that such upgradings as given here cannot be taken as official names, but it is hoped that they will be considered if and when the time comes.

The three footprints discussed above are hereby referred to the known species *Gigantopithecus blacki*, thus making it pointless to label them as the "type" specimen. Any and all other data relating to the animal commonly known as the North American sasquatch or bigfoot is similarly referred to this species. This genus is also treated as belonging to the family Hominidae on the basis of erect bipedal locomotion. This last point is in agreement with Weidenreich (1945), Woo (1962), Robinson (1972), Eckhart (1972), and Frayer (1974). It should also be noted that the identification of sasquatch with *Gigantopithecus* was suggested by John Green in 1968.

Future events may alter this identification. A temporal separation of about a million years, and a geographic separation of a few thousand kilometers could well mean there is a species-worth of difference between these two animals. The tropical location of the fossils, as contrast with the temperate forest habitat of the living form, should have led to considerable differences in diet and climatic adaptation. As soon as there emerges a consensus that these contrasts merit a specific distinction, the sasquatch should be designated *Gigantopithecus canadensis*. This trivial name reflects the Nearctic distribution of most of the currently available reports of likely validity, as well as the location of the "type" footprints used here.

The future recovery of osteological remains of the sasquatch might also affect even its generic assignment. For example, gnathic parts might include much reduced canines and fully bicuspid lower anterior premolars. This would almost certainly refer the sasquatch to the other known fossil hominid genus, *Australopithecus*. Given at least the same temporal and geographic distinction as from *Gigantopithecus*, and especially with an additional size contrast, a new species certainly would be warranted. In this eventuality it should be known as *Australopithecus* canadensis.

The future discovery of postcranial remains of the Asian *G. blacki* might show that our presumption of erect bipedalism for the fossil form was incorrect. It is at least remotely possible that *G. blacki* may someday prove to have been a terrestrial quadruped, maybe a knuckle walker like the recent African apes. Such a locomotor contrast with the known bipedalism of sasquatch would require a generic distinction. Assuming in this scenario no reason to link sasquatch with *Australopithecus*, we would then have to create a new genus for it. For this eventuality I propose *Gigantanthropus*, with the same trivial name of *canadensis*. The "anthropus" would fit well with its continued inclusion in Hominidae. The "pithecus" ending of *Gigantopithecus* would become more appropriate, as these fossils would then have to be moved into the Pongidae. (The generic name of "*Gigantanthropus*" was proposed by Weidenreich in 1945 as being more accurately descriptive of the fossil form, but priority ruled out this usage, and the name is still available.)

The desirability of recovering more physical remains of this species is self-evident, both for the fossil and the living forms. Better evidence is needed for all cryptozoological species, by definition, otherwise they would not have been classed as "hidden" animals. Any and all efforts in this direction should be encouraged. However, I think it is equally important that serious scientific investigation be made of the existing evidence for the sasquatch. The fact that much of this evidence has been fabricated and/or misinterpreted should not rule out such studies. False leads have often hampered science, and they continually plague criminal investigations as well. We have well-established procedures for separating fact from fiction; they need only be applied in an open-minded manner to the subject at hand.

We cannot rule out the possibility, however remote it may be, that our "type" specimen of the sasquatch was somehow fabricated. By exercising the same degree of caution we might also be reluctant to accept many fossil species that have been described from no better evidence. I think it is more prudent to proceed on the assumption that the existence of the sasquatch is at least a reasonable possibility and to give it a formal scientific name. This should serve to structure further inquiry into this matter along sober lines, and to discredit some of the unfounded speculation.

References Cited

Berry, John and S. Haylock
    1985 The Sasquatch Foot Casts. *Fingerprint Whorld*, 10(39):59-63.
Dahinden, Rene
    1984 Whose Dermal Ridges? *Cryptozoology*, 3:128-131.
Eckhardt, R. B.
    1972 Population Genetics and Human Origins. *Scientific American* 226(1):94-103.

Frayer, W. D.
   1974 A Reappraisal of *Ramapithecus*. *Yearbook of Physical Anthropology*, 18:19-30.
Green, John
   1968 *On the Track of the Sasquatch*. Agassiz, B.C.: Cheam.
   1978 *Sasquatch, The Apes Among Us*. Seattle: Hancock House.
International Society of Cryptozoology
   1982a Sasquatch in Washington State. *Newsletter*, 1(2):7-9.
   1982b, Walla Walla Casts Show Dermal Ridges. *Newsletter*, 1(3):1-4.
Koenigswald, G. H. R. von
   1935 Eine fossile Saurgetier—fauna mit Simia aus Sudchina. *Proceedings, Koeniglich Akademie van wetenschappen* 38:872-879. Amsterdam.
Krantz, Grover S.
   1981 The *Process of Human Evolution*. Cambridge, MA: Schenkman.
   1983 Anatomy and Dermatoglyphics of Three Sasquatch Footprints. *Cryptozoology*, 2:53-81.
   1984 Et Tu Rene? *Cryptozoology*, 3:131-134.
Robinson. J. T.
   1982 *Early Hominid Posture and Locomotion*. Chicago: University of Chicago Press.
Simons, Elwyn and P.C. Ettel
   1970 *Gigantopithecus*. Scientific American, 222(1):76-85.
Weidenreich, Franz
   1945 Giant Early Man from Java and South China. *Anthropological Papers of the American Museum of Natural History*, 40:1-134. New York.
Woo Ju-kang (Wu Rukang)
   1962 The Mandibles and Dentition of *Gigantopithecus*. *Paleontologia Sinica*, Whole Number 146, New Series D, No. 11. Beijing.

APPENDIX C

(Originally published in *Northwest Anthropological Research Notes* 4(2):127-128. 1970.)

EDITORIAL
Roderick Sprague

In 1968, John Green of Agassiz, British Columbia, published a booklet entitled *On the Track of the Sasquatch*. While not following the multiple working hypothesis, Green did present an unemotional discussion of the evidence for an indigenous non-human primate form in North America. The response to this work was so great, especially with reports by individuals long remaining quiet for fear of ridicule, that in 1970 Green published a second work entitled *Year of the sasquatch*. Green reviews literally hundreds, if not thousands, of recorded footprints of some unknown creature in situations where they could not have been made by pranksters, machinery, or known animals. His amusing approach to logic runs this way: Is there an unknown species of animal that is very heavy, has humanlike feet and walks erect? The very idea is ridiculous. Is there, then, a person or organization that has been using specialized equipment to make giant footprints over an area of hundreds of thousands of square miles, for the best part of a century, without being detected? That too is ridiculous. The only comfortable explanation is that the tracks don't really occur at all, but the plain fact is that they do.

Green takes the anthropologists to task for several reasons, the first of which and the most obvious is the fact that no one has yet gathered together the many legends concerning sasquatches or related phenomena. Green goes even further and indicates that the anthropologist is making the mistake of viewing these as mythological or legendary creatures and fails to realize that the informants are speaking in strictly zoological terms. To put it in our terms, because of our ethnocentrism we fail to recognize that the Indian informants are talking about real animals, not mythological creatures.

Whether we are willing to acknowledge that there may indeed be such a living thing as a sasquatch, the fact remains that as anthropologists we have an obligation to study the sociological and anthropological implications of the belief systems which contain or encourage the continuation of such beliefs. For several years I have been trying to interest a graduate student in the thesis topic that Green has already suggested, namely the comparative analysis of ethnographic data on the sasquatch phenomenon. Anyone familiar with the ethnographic literature of the Plateau and Northwest Coast must be impressed with the quantity of references to evil smelling, hairy, giants and water monsters (the literature assembled by Green frequently mentions the affinity of the sasquatch for water). There are any number of descriptive studies awaiting the imaginative student in such areas as the comparative analysis of plastic and graphic artistic representation of the sasquatch, analysis of the dance and music forms associated with the sasquatch, and the comparative study of the linguistic terms used to describe the various hairy giants. Likewise I am sure every archaeologist in the Pacific Northwest has run across one or more amateurs who have described in intimate detail the eight or nine foot skeleton that their grandfather (cousin, hunting partner, barber, etc.) saw at some time in the past. A number of these have even been reported in area newspapers with surprising frequency. To the best of my knowledge no one has suggested in print that perhaps the carved stone anthropoid ape heads of James Terry and later workers from the John Day region on the Columbia River could well be associated with the sasquatch phenomenon. If indeed the sasquatch is found in the next few years, as many of the devotees are claiming it will, then the possibilities of research by the social anthropologist, archaeologist, linguist, and physical anthropologist (primatologist) are incredible to contemplate. This editorial was prompted by Green throwing down the gauntlet on page 35 of his second publication where he quotes the editors of the journal, *Soviet Ethnography*, in a preface to a scholarly work by a Russian on the question of subhominid forms in Asia. The quote reads: Research and views of B.F. Porshnev on the problem of hominid relics basically differ from those of the majority of specialists in this field. The editor of the journal *Soviet Ethnography* feels that it is important to publish Porshnev's work on this subject in order to introduce the readers of the journal to one system of approaching the problem. Green twists the knife when he states in the next paragraph, "One could wish that there were scientific publications in North America with editors who took a similar attitude." After an informal survey of the majority of the Associate Editors of NARN at various meetings during the past year, it is now obvious that the editors favor a similar policy for NARN. It gives me pleasure to announce to the anthropologists, zoologists, and other interested researchers of the Northwest that the editors of *Northwest Anthropological Research Notes* will welcome and view favorably for early publication any reasonably scientific paper dealing with the sasquatch phenomenon. This might include models for study; comparative studies in ethnology, mythology, or linguistics; or bibliographic works. We are not suggesting the acceptance or rejection of belief in the sasquatch but rather the unfettered anthropological study of such beliefs either positive or negative.

BIBLIOGRAPHY

Baird, Donald. 1989. Sasquatch footprints: a proposed method of fabrication. *Cryptozoology* 8:43-46.

Bord, Janet and Colin. 1982. *The Bigfoot Casebook.* Harrisburg, PA: Stackpole Books.

Byrne, Peter. 1975. *The Search for Bigfoot: Monster, Myth or Man.* Washington, D.C.: Acropolis Books.

Cachel, Susan. 1985. Sole pads and dermatoglyphics of the Elk Wallow footprints. *Cryptozoology* 4:45-54.

Ciochon, Russel, John Olsen, and Jamie James. 1990. *Other Origins: The Search for the Giant Ape in Human Prehistory.* New York: Bantam Books.

Coon, Carleton S. 1962. *The Origin of Races.* New York: Knopf.

Dahinden, Rene. 1984. Whose dermal ridges? *Cryptozoology* 3:128-131.

Green, John. 1968. *On The Track of the Sasquatch.* Agassiz, BC: Cheam Publishing. (Reprinted by Ballantine Books, New York, in 1973.)

Green, John. 1970. *The Year of the Sasquatch.* Agassiz, BC: Cheam Publishing.

Green, John. 1973. *The Sasquatch File.* Agassiz, BC: Cheam Publishing.

Green, John. 1978. *Sasquatch: The Apes Among Us.* Saanichton, BC: Cheam Publishing and Hancock House Publishers.

Green, John. 1989. The case for a legal inquiry into sasquatch evidence. *Cryptozoology* 8:37-42.

Groves, Collin P. 1986. The Yahoo, the Yowie, and reports of Australian hairy bipeds. *Cryptozoology* 5:47-54.

Grumley, Michael. 1974. *There are Giants in the Earth.* Garden City, NY: Doubleday.

Guenette, Robert and Frances. 1975. *Bigfoot: The Mysterious Monster.* Los Angeles: Sun Classic Pictures, Inc.

Halpin, M. and M. Ames, editors. 1980. *Manlike Monsters on Trial: Early records and Modern Evidence.* Vancouver: University of British Columbia Press.

Heuvelmans, Bernard. 1952. L'Homme des Cavernes A-T-il connu des Geants Mesurant 3 a 4 Metres? *Sciences et Avenir* (May).

Heuvelmans, Bernard. 1959. *On the Track of Unknown Animals.* New York: Hill and Wang.

Heuvelmans, Bernard and Boris Porchnev. 1974. *L'Homme De Neanderthal Est Toujours Vivant.* Paris: Libraire Plon.

Hunter, Don and R. Dahinden. 1973. *Sasquatch.* Toronto: McClelland and Stewart.

Johnson, Rodney L. 1982. Documentation of investigation into sighting of "bigfoot" tracks in the Mill Creek Watershed. U.S.D.A. Forest Service Memo to Roger E. Baker. Umatilla National Forest, Pendleton, OR.

Joyner, Graham C. 1977. *The Hairy Man of South Eastern Australia.* Canberra: National Library of Australia.

Joyner, Graham C. 1984. The orang-utan in England: an explanation for the use of Yahoo as a name for the Australian hairy man. *Cryptozoology* 3:55-57.

Krantz, Grover S. 1971. Sasquatch hand prints. *Northwest Anthropological Research Notes* 5(2):145-151. (Reprinted in *The Scientist Looks at the Sasquatch.*)

Krantz, Grover S. 1972a. Anatomy of the sasquatch foot. *Northwest Anthropological Research Notes* 6(1):91-104. (Reprinted in *The Scientist Looks at the Sasquatch.*)

Krantz, Grover S. 1972b. Additional notes on sasquatch foot anatomy. *Northwest Anthropological Research Notes* 6(2):230-241. (Reprinted in *The Scientist Looks at the Sasquatch.*)

Krantz, Grover S. 1975. An explanation for the diastema of Javan *erectus* skull IV. In *Paleoanthropology, Morphology and Paleoecology*, ed. by R.H. Tuttle, pp. 361-372. The Hague: Mouton.

Krantz, Grover S. 1981. *The Process of Human Evolution.* Cambridge, MA: Schenkman.

Krantz, Grover S. 1983. Anatomy and dermatoglyphics of three sasquatch footprints. *Cryptozoology* 2:53-81.

Krantz, Grover S. 1984. Et tu Rene? *Cryptozoology* 3:131-134.

Krantz, Grover S. 1986a Some friction over sole pads. *Cryptozoology* 5:132-134.

Krantz, Grover S. 1986b. A species named from footprints. *Northwest Anthropological Research Notes* 19:93-99.

Krantz, Grover S. 1987. A reconstruction of the skull of *Gigantopithecus* and its comparison with a living form. *Cryptozoology* 6:24-39.

Krantz, Grover S. 1990. Enlarging on some footprint details. *Cryptozoology* 9:119-120.

Markotic, Vladimir (ed.) and Grover S. Krantz (assoc. ed.) 1984. *The Sasquatch and Other Unknown Hominoids.* Calgary, Alberta: Western Publishers.

Napier, John. 1972. *Bigfoot: The Yeti and Sasquatch in Myth and Reality.* London: Jonathan Cape.

Patterson, Roger. 1966. *Do Abominable Snowmen of America Really Exist?* Yakima, WA: Franklin Press, Inc.

Perez, Danny. 1988. *Big Footnotes: A Comprehensive Bibliography Concerning Bigfoot, the Abominable Snowmen and Related Beings.* Norwalk, CA: D. Perez Publishing, Inc.

Sanderson, Ivan T. 1961. *Abominable Snowmen: Legend Come to Life.* Philadelphia & New York: Chilton Co.

Schultz, Adolph H. 1968. The recent hominoid primates. In *Perspectives on Human Evolution, 1*, ed. by S.L. Washburn and P.C. Jay, pp. 122-195. New York: Holt, Rinehart and Winston.

Shackley, Myra. 1983. *Still Living?: Yeti, Sasquatch and the Neanderthal Enigma.* New York: Thames and Hudson.

Sheldon, William H. 1954. *Atlas of Men.* New York: Harper and Brothers.

Sprague, Roderick and Grover S. Krantz, editors. 1979. *The Scientist Looks at the Sasquatch (II).* Moscow, ID: University of Idaho Press.

Strassenburgh, Gordon. 1984. The crested *Australopithecus robustus* and the Patterson Gimlin film. In *The Sasquatch and Other Unknown Hominoids*, ed. by V. Markotic and G. Krantz, pp. 236-248. Calgary, Alberta: Western Publishers.

Tchernine, Odette. 1970. *In Pursuit of the Abominable Snowman.* New York: Taplinger Publishing Co.

Weidenreich, Franz. 1945. Giant early man from Java and south China. *Anthropological Papers of the American Museum of Natural History* XL, No. 1.

Wylie, Kenneth. 1980. *Bigfoot: A Personal Inquiry into a Phenomenon.* New York: Viking Press.

INDEX